THE
QUAKERS
of
IOWA

Louis Thomas Jones

HERITAGE BOOKS
2020

HERITAGE BOOKS
AN IMPRINT OF HERITAGE BOOKS, INC.

Books, CDs, and more—Worldwide

For our listing of thousands of titles see our website
at
www.HeritageBooks.com

A Facsimile Reprint
Published 2020 by
HERITAGE BOOKS, INC.
Publishing Division
5810 Ruatan Street
Berwyn Heights, Md. 20740

Originally published
The State Historical Society of Iowa
Iowa City, Iowa
1914

International Standard Book Number
Paperbound: 978-0-7884-1283-7

EDITOR'S INTRODUCTION

THIS volume on *The Quakers of Iowa* was written by Dr. Jones at the request of The State Historical Society of Iowa. For the task the author was peculiarly fitted both by temperament and by training. Moreover, his membership in the Society of Friends gave him ready access to much material which an outsider could not have hoped to obtain.

Although the Quakers have not been numerous in Iowa, the influence of their attitude toward life has been considerable in the history of the Commonwealth.

BENJ. F. SHAMBAUGH

OFFICE OF THE SUPERINTENDENT AND EDITOR
THE STATE HISTORICAL SOCIETY OF IOWA
IOWA CITY IOWA

AUTHOR'S PREFACE

In the present work the author has endeavored to present the essential features of the history of the people called the Quakers, from the time of their first appearance in Iowa down to the present time. To accomplish this within the limits of a single volume the writer has been compelled to omit many matters of local interest. Space permitted only the briefest mention of those who have been the leaders in many of the fields of church activity; while as regards the Friends' communities, many Iowa Quaker meetings, particularly in the western part of the State, are not even so much as mentioned. To explain this omission the writer desires to state that it has been his purpose to trace in detail the rise of only those settlements which formed the basis of Iowa Quakerism before the founding of the Iowa Yearly Meeting of Friends in 1863. After that time the subject has been dealt with as a whole. Much of local and personal interest has thus been sacrificed in these pages.

Much of the initial work on this volume was done during the three years when the writer was connected with Penn College at Oskaloosa, Iowa, where he had access to the rich collection of manuscript records stored in the college vault. During the last fifteen months of his researches the writer lived at Iowa City and was connected with The State Historical Society of Iowa, thus having the advantage of its valuable library. Most of the materials used, however, were secured from outside sources which are indicated in the notes and references. The writer's acquaintance with almost the entire Iowa field, together with his personal correspondence with the principal members of the various sects, made possible a familiarity with the present conditions in the various branches of the Society in Iowa which proved to be of great value.

The writer desires to take this opportunity to express his gratitude to the large number of persons, both in Iowa and elsewhere, who have coöperated in bringing together the materials used in this work. To Dr. David M. Edwards and Dr. Stephen M. Hadley, both of Oskaloosa, Iowa, the writer is greatly indebted for valued assistance. Thanks are also due to Miss Florence Franzen and to Mr. Jacob Van der Zee of Iowa City, Iowa, for their help in verifying the manuscript. Much credit for whatever merit the work may possess is due to Dr. Dan E. Clark, Assistant Editor of The State Historical Society of

Iowa, for his many suggestions, corrections on the manuscript, and for the index. And finally, only through the continued interest, assistance, and advice of Dr. Benjamin F. Shambaugh, Superintendent of The State Historical Society of Iowa, has the publication of the volume in its present form been made possible.

LOUIS T. JONES

THE STATE HISTORICAL SOCIETY OF IOWA
IOWA CITY

CONTENTS

PART III

THE MINORITY BODIES OF FRIENDS IN IOWA

PART IV

BENEVOLENT AND EDUCATIONAL ENTERPRISES

PART V

RELIGIOUS AND SOCIAL LIFE OF THE QUAKERS

PART I
HISTORICAL NARRATIVE

I

THE RISE AND SPREAD OF QUAKERISM

It was during the reign of the Stuarts in England that Quakerism first appeared. The absolutism of Charles I was at that time in sharp conflict with the chartered rights of Englishmen; and the great and influential Church of England was doing all in its power to crush the new-born Puritan advance. Royal tyranny had come face to face with the rising spirit of popular liberty, and religious intolerance was being met on every hand by an insistent demand for freedom of worship. There were Roundheads and Cavaliers, High-churchmen and Non-conformists, Puritans and Separatists, Presbyterians and Independents; and in addition to this turmoil of conflicting and contending factions in religion, England was plunged into all the horrors of a civil war. In this period of political, social, and religious upheaval Quakerism was born.

The real message of Quakerism contained little that was new: from a religious point of view it was little more than a revival of primitive Christianity.[1] With all the vitality of a new movement it grappled with the great religious, social, and political problems of the day; and, partly because of the resistless power of its simple message, many of the forces which have oppressed humanity have since disappeared. Against Roman Catholic and Puritan intolerance alike, against the wrongs of human slavery, and against the ravages and the barbarity of war, the Quakers have consistently raised their protest. Time after time they have suffered persecution for the sake of their testimonies; but what has cost them dear has been the world's gain.[2] Small as has always been the Religious Society of Friends, in the work of reform and in the uplift of humanity it has borne a share out of all proportion to its numbers.[3] And now at a time when internal decay and the larger religious movements of the day threaten the existence of this peculiar sect, the world is just beginning to awaken to an adequate appreciation of the work which the Quakers have done.[4]

For the origin of the message, the testimonies, and the fundamental principles of the Society of Friends, one instinctively turns to the life and the work of its founder, George Fox. From him came the cardinal teachings of Quakerism and its form of organization — at once so simple and so efficient that, notwithstanding the altered circumstances of the Society and the changing times, both remain to-day, in all parts of the world where Quakers are found, essentially as they were within forty years after the rise of the order.

George Fox was born "in the month called July, in the year 1624, at Drayton in the Clay, in Leicestershire." His father, Christopher Fox, was a weaver by profession, and because of his upright character was often spoken of as "Righteous Christer".[5] His mother possessed a deeply religious temperament, and was tenderly devoted to her family. In his youth, George was of a retiring disposition, being "religious, inward, still, solid, and observing, beyond his years".[6] As he grew into a larger consciousness of life he became troubled in spirit over what he believed to be the inherent sin within him. Amidst the intensity of his inward struggles, at the age of nineteen years, on "the ninth of the seventh month, 1643", he left home, "broke off all familiarity or fellowship with young or old", and began to wander from place to place in search for rest of soul. He sought the counsel and comfort of many priests and religious people of England, but he "found no comfort from them." A certain priest at Mansetter in Warwickshire at one time bade him "take tobacco and sing psalms"[7] to quiet the agony of his troubled heart. Often he walked in lonely places, and out under the stars at night. So heavily weighed the sense of the world's lost condition upon him that he said his blood seemed "dried up with sorrows, grief, and troubles", and he almost wished that he had never been born.

As Fox longed for spiritual rest, so he continued to search. For over a year he wandered through Derbyshire, Leicestershire, and Nottinghamshire, during which time he relates: "I fasted much, walked abroad in solitary places many days, and often took my bible, and sate in hollow trees and lonesome places till night came on; and frequently in the night walked mournfully about by myself: for I was a man of sorrows in the time of the first workings of the Lord in me."[8] When he had come to the point where his confidence in the priests and his faith in men generally were gone, so that he had nothing outwardly to help him, "then, O then," he says, "I heard a voice which said, 'There is one, even Christ Jesus, that can speak to thy condition.' When I heard it, my heart did leap for joy."[9]

From this time on Fox had a realization of God such as few men in any times have experienced. Indeed, from the intense inward struggles of this one man have emanated influences which have profoundly affected the world's thought. Consciousness of inherent sin, futility of all earthly agencies to redeem, personal and direct divine revelation, and a universal and inherent ability to perceive God — these constitute the message which George Fox brought to the world. He preached these ideas with all of their power and freshness to a people already torn with many dissensions, and they were like oil thrown upon flames. The very term "Quaker"[10] tells the story. With astounding rapidity the teachings of George Fox spread in England, and for a time it seemed as though the faith of the whole nation would be shaken.

England was well prepared to receive the message of the Quakers. The English Reformation had done its work. About the middle of the seventeenth century great gatherings for the discussion of religious questions were common in the fields, at the fairs, in the market-places, and at the churches. In his *Journal*, Fox makes frequent reference to his attendance at such meetings even before he began to preach. There was also a widespread knowledge and interest in the scriptures among the masses of the people. The half-century before the time of George Fox has been described as a period when ''England became the people of a book, and that book was the Bible. It was as yet the one English book which was familiar to every Englishman; it was read at churches and read at home, and everywhere its words, as they fell on ears which custom had not deadened to their force and beauty, kindled a startling enthusiasm.'' Moreover, the ''whole moral effect which is produced now-a-days by the religious newspaper, the tract, the essay, the lecture, the missionary report, the sermon, was then produced by the Bible alone.''[11]

Fox early took advantage of these two agencies. The general religious gatherings offered an excellent opportunity to propagate religious ideas; and his extensive knowledge of the scriptures made it possible for him to appeal strongly to the masses of the people. At first he seems merely to have attended these meetings, occasionally taking part in the open discussions, but by 1647 he was actively engaged in preaching. Throwing his influence boldly against ecclesiasticism, he soon became one of the most powerful preachers of the day.

William Penn, who knew Fox personally, said of him:

He was a man that God endowed with a clear and
wonderful depth, a discerner of others' spirits, and very
much a master of his own. . . . And his ministry and
writings show they are from one that was not taught of
man, nor had learned what he said by study. . . . He
had an extraordinary gift in opening the scriptures. He
would go to the marrow of things, and shew the mind,
harmony, and fulfilling of them with much plainness, and
to great comfort and edification. . . . But above all he
excelled in prayer. The inwardness and weight of his spirit,
the reverence and solemnity of his address and behaviour,
and the fewness and fullness of his words, have often struck
even strangers with admiration, as they used to reach others
with consolation. The most awful, living, reverent frame I
ever felt or beheld, I must say, was his in prayer.[12]

Such was the man and such was his message. He
began his work in the northern counties of England,
and with marvelous rapidity his doctrines spread in
all directions. In an epistle written to a friend in
1676 he says:

The truth sprang up first to us, so as to be a people to the
Lord, in Leicestershire [his home county] in 1644, in
Warwickshire [the county adjoining on the south] in 1645,
in Nottinghamshire in 1646, in Derbyshire in 1647 [both
counties adjoining on the north], and in the adjacent
counties in 1648, 1649, and 1650; in Yorkshire in 1651, in
Lancashire and Westmoreland in 1652, in Cumberland,
Durham, and Northumberland in 1653, in London and most
of the other parts of England, Scotland, and Ireland, in
1654.

In 1655 many went beyond sea, where truth also sprang
up, and in 1656 it broke forth in America and many other
places.[13]

Thus, within a period of about ten years the new movement had taken root in Great Britain and Ireland, and then spread to the colonies. Naturally enough, persecution pursued the Quakers; but persecution served only to fan the flames and spread the sparks. Fox imbued his followers with his own spirit and enthusiasm. In the year 1654 he records that there were about sixty ministers whom "the Lord raised up, and did now send abroad out of the north country."

One distinguishing feature marks this period of Quaker history, namely, its all-absorbing missionary spirit. To the Quakers there was no sacrifice too great to be made, and no suffering too keen to be endured for the sake of the spread of "truth". A second order of Jesuits seemed to have appeared. They were persecuted, it is true, but they wore out persecution by their passive resistance. To the confiscation of their estates they patiently submitted. They were thrown into loathsome prisons, but even there they preached the message. Nothing could crush them. Driven by the spirit within them and by the severe laws, they migrated to other lands. France, Germany, Holland, Norway, Italy, Turkey, and Palestine were visited. The Czar of Russia was supplied with literature which explained the new message, and an attempt was made to convert the Pope at Rome.[14] Then the movement swept westward, and Barbadoes, Bermuda, and Jamaica were overrun by the Quakers.[15]

On the eleventh day of July, 1656, a day full of

import to the red men of America, to the white men who were to supplant them, and to the negroes here to be enslaved, the first Quakers landed on the shores of New England — a landing long to be remembered in the annals of that Puritan realm.

II

THE QUAKERS IN THE AMERICAN COLONIES

THE first Quakers known to have set foot on American soil were two women, Ann Austin and Mary Fisher, who appeared in Boston harbor on July 11, 1656, having come from the island of Barbadoes for the express purpose of bearing testimony against the religious deadness and formality of the Puritans.

Long had the Puritans of New England heard of the turmoil raised in the home-land by the troublesome Quakers; and now they had them at their very doors. Why should they come hither to disturb the peace and quiet of the wilderness? These were Puritan shores. The Puritans, as "Pilgrims" in a strange land, had come to New England in order that they might live according to their own ideals and worship God in their own way. They had their own institutions and their own customs, which to them were dear and sacred. At infinite cost they had built up a commonwealth in the wilderness, based on the laws, statutes, and ordinances of God. They had convictions as strong as were the convictions of the Quakers. Why should they give way to these newcomers? The very purpose of this transient visit of members of the despised sect was to scatter their books and pamphlets — firebrands of disruption and discord — and overturn the very foundations on which the Puritan community rested. The Puritans were determined that they would not allow themselves thus to be disturbed; while the Quakers were just as determined to bear their testimonies.

The scenes which followed the first arrival of Quakers in America were indeed dramatic. An irresistible force seemed to have met an immovable object. The two women were at once taken into custody by the authorities of Boston, their books and tracts were publicly burned in the market-place as heretical, and being "stripped stark naked" and searched for marks of witchcraft, they were confined in prison without light, writing materials, or the privilege of speaking to anyone on the outside. They were then ruthlessly thrust out of the colony; while Simon Kempthorne, master of the ship which brought them thither, was strictly charged with speedily taking them back whence he got them, at his own expense and under heavy penalty if he refused.[16]

Two days after the departure of Mary Fisher and Ann Austin from the port of Boston, another vessel came into the harbor bearing eight Quakers — four men and four women. These, likewise, were seized and thrown into prison, where they remained for about eleven weeks. They, too, were finally driven out of the colony and transported back to England, whence they had come. The first law, bearing date of October 14, 1656, was then passed against the intruders.[17]

Entrance from the sea being barred, the commonwealth was soon invaded from another quarter. By 1658 Rhode Island, the earliest home of religious toleration in America, had been visited by the Quakers, and there the new ideas had spread rapidly. Through this ''back door'' the Quakers again began to appear in Massachusetts in defiance of the stringent laws which that colony had passed.[18] Time after time they were flogged, tied to the cart's tail, threatened, and banished from the jurisdiction, but all to no avail. Finally, on October 19, 1658, this beset, defied, and outraged Puritan colony passed the fatal act, carrying with it a death penalty.

Laws thus framed and intent upon blood were not long in finding their victims. Mary Dyer, a Quaker from Rhode Island, had been banished from Massachusetts as an Antinomian; Marmaduke Stephenson had also been banished for making a disturbance in Boston; William Robinson had been whipped and banished for abusing the court; and William Leddra had been several times whipped, imprisoned, and banished. Their devotion to the cause of truth was, however, greater than their regard for man, so they fearlessly returned. On October 22, 1659, Marmaduke Stephenson and William Robinson paid the penalty on the scaffold, and thus sealed their testimony in Boston with their blood. In the spring of the following year, Mary Dyer swung from the same scaffold in obedience to

what she believed to be the will of God, and on March
14, 1661, William Leddra offered up his life in the
same way. All four of these persons, we are told,
were of unsullied character. Constant, heroic, fear-
less, they faced death for the sake of religious
toleration. Upon hearing of these atrocious crimes,
Charles II at once ordered his Puritan subjects to
forbear, and the flow of innocent blood ceased. Thus
Quaker fortitude had met Puritan intolerance in
Massachusetts, and, with the tongue as its only
weapon of defense, the former had prevailed,[19] there
to build up the first Yearly Meeting of Friends in
America.[20]

With the arrival of George Fox in Maryland in
1672[21] the movement in America was given a new
impetus. He and his devoted followers traveled in
all directions, bearing their message. Day after
day Fox plunged through pathless forests and over
dangerous bogs from New England to the Carolinas,
planting here and there in the scattered settlements
the germs of the new faith which soon sprang up
into prosperous Quaker communities. Many times
the missionaries lay down to rest beside their camp
fires in the lonely woods, and "sometimes in the
Indians' wigwams or houses", there taking the
opportunity of speaking the word of life to these
savage "kings".[22] In New England, in the middle
colonies, and in the sea-board colonies of the South
the work went forward, strongly tincturing the commonwealths of the Jerseys, Maryland, Virginia, and
North Carolina with Quaker doctrine.[23]

Persecuted by the established church in the mother country, suppressed by the Puritans in New England, and maltreated by the Roman Catholics of Maryland and the cavaliers of the more southern colonies, the Quakers longed for a home which they could call their own. The keen mind of George Fox early perceived the advantages which the uninhabited woods of America offered as a place of refuge from the storms of persecution which beat so fiercely upon the "Friends of Truth". In 1660 steps were taken to secure by purchase a tract of land from the Susquehanna Indians, but due to a war then raging among the tribes the attempt failed.[24] It was not long, however, until a new avenue was opened; for when Lord Berkeley offered for sale one-half of New Jersey in 1674 it was at once purchased by two Quakers, John Fenwick and Edward Billinge. Thus a new opening was made in America for the growth of Quakerism.[25]

The importance of this incident does not lie so much in the purchase of the New Jersey land by two Quakers, as in the fact that the transaction brought into play the vital interest of William Penn — a man whose name became almost a synonym for Quakerism in America. Fortunate, indeed, was it for the Quakers that he allied himself with the new faith. Rich, scholarly, and powerful, Penn threw his whole influence and fortune into the cause.

From Admiral Penn, his father, William had inherited a large estate, together with a claim of some 16,000 pounds against the British crown.

Knowing that a demand for cash payment would be all but useless he besought the King, Charles II, to grant to him in payment of the debt extensive lands to the north of Maryland, ''to be bounded on the east by the Delaware River . . . . to be limited on the west as Maryland was, and . . . . to extend northward as far as it was plantable.''[26]   It should here be said, much to Penn's credit, that the ''holy experiment'' which he here proposed to make was not solely for the benefit of himself and his religious order; but his colony was to be a place where all who chose might be ''as free and happy as the nature of their existence could possibly bear in their civil capacity, and, in their religious state, to restore them to those lost rights and privileges with which God and nature had originally blessed the human race.''[27]

In view of the broad and liberal terms which Penn outlined for both the settlement and the government of his colony, it is no marvel that many who were oppressed in other parts of the world should come to this haven of religious toleration. Pennsylvania rapidly rose to a commanding place among the colonies on the Atlantic seaboard; and when the forces began to shape themselves toward the formation of an independent nation, the Commonwealth which bore its founder's name was in the forefront of the struggle. Moreover, Pennsylvania — so long the bulwark of religious freedom in the new world — has always remained the stronghold of Quakerism in America.

III

WESTWARD MIGRATION

A GLANCE at the history of the Quakers in America reveals the fact that in this country they have been pioneers — a fact which is of immense importance in interpreting their annals. Whether this is due to the mystical nature of their religion or to the spirit of the new world — a spirit which has always been characterized by a craving for greater and greater expansion — is difficult to determine. Both influences have no doubt been at work, and as a result the one hundred thousand Quakers in America are scattered from the Atlantic to the Pacific coast, and from the Gulf of Mexico to Canada.

Before following the westward movement of the Friends it may be well to note the fact that an important change had taken place within the Society before the opening of the nineteenth century. During the early period, when the Friends were face to face with persecution both in England and America, they displayed a most remarkable vitality. They produced powerful ministers in great numbers, who, fired with an intense missionary zeal, traveled far and wide proclaiming their message, and literally tens of thousands were thus brought into the Quaker fold. But within ten years after the death of George

Fox, which occurred on the 13th day of November, 1690, there was an apparent decline in the vitality of the Society. In America the aggressive spirit of propagandism seems largely to have expended itself on the eastern seaboard. As the fires of missionary zeal burned low, a new movement set in — a movement destined to mould and fashion more than any other force the history of the Quakers on this continent — namely, westward migration.

The first striking evidence of this migratory tendency made its appearance in the southern colonies. ''As the meetings in eastern Virginia are the oldest under consideration,'' says one writer, ''so they are the first to decline. Quakers seem to have disappeared from Norfolk County before 1700. They had no doubt 'gone West.' ''[28] The same stirring was to be noticed among the North Carolina Friends as they began to shift towards the West and South. Then came a larger movement which has been called ''The Replanting of Southern Quakerism''. Large numbers of Quakers from Nantucket, New Jersey, and Pennsylvania now poured into the Southland, settling in Maryland and Virginia, or pressing on into North Carolina, South Carolina, and Georgia. This migration, which threatened to change the very complexion of the southern colonies, stopped, it has been said, ''almost as suddenly as it began''; and the cause assigned was the shifting of the War of the Revolution to the South.[29]

After this first impetuous migration of the Quakers into the South they turned their faces westward. It is generally asserted that the westward movement was along the lines of the parallels of latitude, but in the case of the Quakers the lines of migration crossed and recrossed each other, some of the emigrants from the northern colonies finding homes in the Southland, while others wended their way from the Southland into the Old Northwest.

It was early in May, 1769, that Daniel Boone threw his long gun across his shoulder and left ''his peaceable habitation on the Yadkin river, in quest of the country of Kentucky''.[30] Reared and trained in a Quaker home, the influences of the simple faith of the Friends deeply marked this man of the wilderness.[31] Typical pathfinder and Indian fighter that he was, Boone blazed the path along which a motley mass of humanity was soon to follow in the building of the great Commonwealths of Kentucky and Tennessee. As early as 1768 the general movement from North Carolina had begun; and among those who early took part in the new work of State-building were those who could easily be distinguished as Quakers.

In 1787, the very year in which the famous Ordinance was drafted for the government of the Northwest Territory, a request came to the New Garden Monthly Meeting in North Carolina for the establishment of a Friends meeting west of the mountains at Lost Creek near the Holston River. Although this request came from former members of the New Garden community the petition was refused and complaint was entered by the Monthly

3

Meeting against the petitioners that they "had settled on lands the title to which was still in dispute with the Indians."[32]   Time after time the home meeting tried to check the westward movement of its members, but all to no avail. Unable to get the recognition they desired, and imbued with the free spirit of the western wilds, one Quaker settlement after another organized its own meetings without reference to the parent community. By the close of the century there had grown up the monthly meetings of Lost Creek and New Hope; and of the Quaker families which there helped to lay the foundations of the State of Tennessee one reads names which now sound familiar in Iowa — names such as Marshall, Hodgins, Maxwell, Pearce, Stanfield, Phillips, Thornburgh, Macy, Bernard, Mendenhall, Beales, Hayworth, Reece, and Beard.[33]

The next region into which the Quakers migrated was the Northwest Territory. Hard upon the close of the American Revolution the vast stretch of country acquired by the young nation to the west of the Allegheny Mountains was turned over to the Federal government by the various States. With the rapid settlement of the region to the south of the Great Lakes intense pressure was brought to bear upon Congress for the establishment of some form of local government, and the result was that monumental document of July 13, 1787: "An Ordinance for the Government of the Territory of the United States, north-west of the river Ohio."[34] It was with the adoption of this Ordinance and the provision which the final article contained, that the interest of southern Quakers in the region really begins.

The migration of the Quakers into this new land of promise began even before 1787. Stragglers from Virginia and western Pennsylvania early moved across the Ohio and began the formation of the Quaker settlements in the present counties of Columbiana, Jefferson, and Belmont in the eastern part of the State of Ohio. Over the Kanawha, the Kentucky, and the Magadee-Richmond roads the Quakers came in from the South and all but took complete possession of the present counties of Highland, Clinton, and Warren in southwestern Ohio, where they built up numerous and prosperous communities such as Center and Miami. Later they entered into the fertile Whitewater Valley in eastern Indiana, there laying the foundations of the Indiana Yearly Meeting of Friends. To this latter region it is said that no less than six thousand Quakers came from the four States of Virginia, North Carolina, South Carolina, and Georgia, between the years 1800 and 1860.[35] It may be asked: Why did the Quakers migrate from the South in such numbers? The answer to this question has a direct bearing upon the history of the Quakers in Iowa.

For many years there had been forces at work within the Society of Friends which had made the holding of slaves not only incompatible with membership in the order, but had also rendered the institution of slavery extremely repugnant to the Quaker mind.[36] As the slave power seized with a firmer grasp the economic control of the South, the Quakers there, most of whom were agriculturists with small holdings, were thrown into unbearable competition with cheap slave labor, and at the same time were held in contempt, because of their objection to the holding of "property in man", by those in authority. Numerous Quaker ministers, among them the well-known John Woolman, had traveled throughout the South, pointing out to their brethren the danger of their position. The whole situation came to a climax in 1803 and in the following manner.

Zachariah Dicks, a prominent minister in the Society of Friends and supposed to have the gift of prophecy, appeared at the Bush River Meeting in South Carolina and began to warn the Friends of a terrible "internecine war", which was to come upon America because of slavery "within the lives of children then living." He there raised his voice in prophetic utterance and said: "Oh, Bush River! Bush River! how hath thy beauty faded away and gloomy darkness eclipsed thy day!"[37] He continued southward with his words of warning, going as far as Wrightsborough, Georgia. Everywhere, the Friends took alarm and began their "hegira". In 1800 the Quakers in South Carolina and Georgia could have been counted by the thousands; in 1809 they were nearly all gone. They "sold their lands, worth from ten to twenty dollars per acre, for from three to six dollars, and departed, never to return." They poured into western Ohio, and on into the

Whitewater Valley in Indiana. They sought a land where, by the Ordinance of 1787, there was to be "neither slavery nor involuntary servitude . . . . otherwise than in the punishment of crimes".

Thus were the two sides of the Ohio Valley peopled with those who in derision were early called Quakers, and who were now to struggle with the social, economic, and political problems peculiar to the two regions.[38] Moreover, when the sons and daughters of these same pioneers once again loaded their heavy wagons and moved off to the westward they came directly to Iowa. Here upon the soil of the first free State west of the Mississippi River the lines from the North and the South converged; the varied habits of life, traits of character, manners, customs, and beliefs were to be moulded and fashioned together; and out of the combination was to come that which to-day is characterized as "Western Quakerism".

IV

THE PLANTING OF QUAKERISM IN IOWA

HARDLY had the wigwams of the Indians disappeared[39] from the Black Hawk Purchase on the west bank of the Mississippi River before the first Quaker appeared. In the summer of 1835 a heavy wagon, covered with white canvas and laden with all of the necessities for a long journey, might have been seen wending its way out from the lonely pine-clad hills of South Carolina. The ox-goad held in the hand of the driver, Isaac Pidgeon, was pointed towards the distant home of his sister who had earlier married and moved to Rushville, Schuyler County, Illinois. From her he had received many letters telling of the great inrush of settlers into the land across the Mississippi, and, like many others who had risked their fortunes before him, he decided to try life in the western wilds. It was with this in view, therefore, that he sold his small plantation for some four hundred dollars, hitched his oxen to the wagon, and with his family of a wife and seven children left forever the scenes of slavery and embarked for the West.[40]

Fifty-two long days the faithful oxen trudged onward with their heavy load, arriving at their first destination in the midsummer of 1835. Leaving his

wife and children with his sister at Rushville, Isaac
Pidgeon crossed the Mississippi, pushed his way
about thirty miles into the ''back country'' of the
new purchase, and there put up sufficient prairie hay
for the cattle which he intended to bring from the
Illinois side. This done he returned to Rushville,
and late in the same fall recrossed the Mississippi to
Iowa with his family and all his possessions. Proceeding inland to the place where he had put up his
winter's supply of hay, he located a claim on what
is now Little Cedar Creek, about a mile and a half to
the south of the present town of Salem in Henry
County.

In 1841 the following account appeared in John
B. Newhall's *Sketches of Iowa:*

About six years ago, two plainly dressed travellers might
have been seen on horseback, slowly wending their way
westward from the Fort Madison ferryboat towards the
wide and pathless prairies of the ''Black Hawk purchase.''
The country was then new and uninhabited: they travelled
onward from grove to grove, and from prairie to prairie,
until the shades of night were closing in upon the long
summer's day. . . .

When morn at length arrived, while one of our travellers
prepared the breakfast, the other perambulated the surrounding country to spy out the beauties of the land. . . .
Having, at last, arrived at a beautiful elevation of the
prairie, and surveyed on every hand nature clad in her
most attractive attire, the bright sun chasing away the
vapory mist of the morning, causing the flowers to display
their variegated hues, and the dew-drops to glisten like
diamonds on the grass, ... *Aaron Street* returned to

his companion, and said, "Now have mine eyes beheld a country teeming with every good thing. . . . Hither will I come with my flocks and my herds, with my children and my children's children, and our city shall be called Salem, for thus was the city of our fathers, even near unto the seacoast.''[41]

In view of the accepted history of the community, and the records in the possession of the Pidgeon family, it would seem that Isaac Pidgeon was not the unnamed companion of Aaron Street on the visit above described, but that he had come alone and was the first to appear. From evidence extant it appears that these two men first met while Aaron Street and his daughter Polly Pugh were casting about in that locality for a place of settlement — though it is possible that this was the expedition an account of which was subsequently related to Mr. Newhall. Thus thrown together in this far western country, both of them Friends from different sections of the East, the two men conceived the idea of founding a Quaker community in the Iowa country; and in order to carry their plan into execution, it was decided that Polly Pugh and her four children were to remain with the Pidgeon family while Aaron Street returned to Indiana to bring hither his family and effects. During his friend's absence, Isaac Pidgeon raised a log cabin on the banks of the Little Cedar Creek and prepared for the approaching winter; and this, so far as is now known, was the first Quaker home to be founded on Iowa soil.[42]

Upon the return of Aaron Street with his family,

he and Isaac Pidgeon, together with Peter Boyer, a Quaker who had recently arrived, proceeded to carry out their plan for a Quaker settlement by the laying off of a town-site on land staked out as claims by Aaron Street and Peter Boyer. Being poorly prepared for the duties of a surveyor they used a long grape-vine for a measuring rod, it is said, cutting notches in it for the desired widths of the streets and alleys. The streets were laid off at right angles to each other, and in the center of the town there was left a space of about two acres for a public square. The town was named Salem, the fourth by that name founded by the family of Streets.[43]

The new-born town of Salem was not long in attracting other settlers to its site and its fertile and healthful environs. In the fall of 1836 there came a number of Friends on horseback from Randolph County, Indiana. Upon hearing of the founding of Salem they visited the locality, were much pleased with it, and recrossed the prairies of Illinois with the glad news to those who anxiously awaited their return.

As soon as the springy prairie sod would bear the weight of their heavy wagons, on the 10th day of May, 1837, a caravan of nine families — all but one members of the Cherry Grove Monthly Meeting — moved out from the neighborhood of Williamsburg, in the northern part of Wayne County, Indiana, bound for the Black Hawk Purchase. In a little sketch written when his life's toils were well-nigh ended, Henry W. Joy, a member of the party, states that the caravan was made up of Reuben, Henry, and Abram P. Joy, Dr. Gideon, Stephen and Thomas Frazier, Lydia Frazier, Thomas Cook, Levi Commack, and their families. All that can be learned from the account written by the unsteady hand of this aged pioneer is that they had "considerable of stock" to drive, that it was "a long and tedious journey", and that they "landed in the neighborhood of Salem the 17th of 6th" month, 1837.[44]

It would be interesting to know the rest of the story: how the wagons creaked beneath their heavy loads, and how the oxen toiled across the plains; how the families grouped themselves about the cheerful camp-fires in the evening; how the children were lulled to sleep at night in their tired mothers' arms, sheltered only by the white canopy of the pioneers' wagons; how the sharp bark of the dogs made answer to the desolate howl of the wolves upon the lonely prairie, while the stars kept their silent watch; how the golden-petaled helianthus faced them all the way, how nature's guide, the compass plant, stretched its arms to the north and to the south; and how the fern-like rattlesnake-master warned them of the dangers lurking in the greensward. These and a thousand other details we would like to hear, but time has removed every member of that caravan who might have told the tale.

Since this first memorable arrival but four weeks had passed until a second caravan might have been seen coming slowly over hill and dale and approaching Salem from the eastward. Who were these strangers? The broad brimmed hats of the men and the plain bonnets of the women were sufficient insignia to insure the travelers a hearty welcome in the new community, where they were received with open arms. It was soon known throughout the village that Stephen Hockett, Stephen Hockett, Jr., John Hockett, and Harrison Hoggatt, all with their families and all but one members of the Society of Friends, had arrived. Eager questions no doubt were asked on every hand, and good cheer ran free as these newcomers were cared for in the humble dwellings at Salem. As soon as possible they selected desirable lands, and from the native timber erected log cabins. When food ran short, it is said, some one or more would go "75 or 80 miles to Ill. for provisions" without a murmur.

During the memorable fall of 1837 other Quakers arrived at Salem. The Fraziers and Joys, the Hocketts and Hammers, together with the Beards, Hoskinses, Johnsons, Osborns, Thomases, Teases, Canadas, Lewellings, Wilsons, Jessops, Hiatts, Emerys, Hinshaws, Mendenhalls, Cooks, Pidgeons, Stantons, and Commons, all found their way to the new settlement beyond the Mississippi.[45] By the middle of August, in the second year of its history, so strong had grown the communal interest at Salem and so keen was the desire for a place where the settlers might regularly come together for worship that the way was made open, and in the hospitable home of Henry W. Joy, every week for over a year these sturdy pioneers came together for worship.

On account of the continued influx of settlers it
soon became apparent that steps must be taken not
only for the establishment of a regularly recognized
meeting but also for the erection of a meeting-house
of adequate capacity. A petition was accordingly
sent to the Vermillion Monthly Meeting in eastern
Illinois for the setting up of a Preparative Meeting
at Salem; but before the request could be granted it
was amended with an appeal for the establishment
of a Monthly Meeting. The committeemen sent out
to investigate the petitions of this remote settlement
were well satisfied with what they saw in the
"Wisconsin Territory", and through their report,
borne to the Western Quarterly Meeting at Bloom-
field, Indiana, the request was granted.

In the month of October, 1838, Abraham Holaday,
Thomas Ruebottom, Jeremiah H. Siler, Henry
Pickard, and Achsah Newlin appeared at Salem as
members of the committee directed to set up the new
meeting, and by their authority and in their presence
the meeting was opened under the following minute:
"Salem Monthly Meeting of Friends, first opened
and held in Salem, Henry County, Iowa Territory,
on the 8th day of the 10th Month 1838". Then the
meeting proceeded to conduct the first regular
business of the Society of Friends west of the
Mississippi.[46]

Interestingly intermingled are matters of spiritual and temporal concern in the records of this
pioneer Quaker settlement beyond the Mississippi.
At one moment the Monthly Meeting would direct a

committee to deal with a member ''for getting in a passion and useing unbecomeing language'',[47] and then proceed to hear the report of a member who had taken up a collection of $17.18¾[48] for the purchase of a stove ''by direction of friends of this neighborhood . . . . before this meeting was established''.[49]   Although religion and the business of the church were the Quaker's chief concern, it was found, at least on one occasion, absolutely necessary to adjourn the Monthly Meeting owing to the absence of ''so many of its members who are in attendance of the land sales at Burling[ton]'',[50] where they had gone to bid in at public auction the lands which they had staked out as claims.

As has been seen, one of the most pressing needs of the new community was for a proper place for worship. On the very day that the Monthly Meeting was established a committee composed of Henderson Lewelling, Aaron Street, John Hockett, and Enos Mendenhall was entrusted with this matter, and on November 24th they were able to report that ''they have attended to the appointment and have rented a house [valued at $350.00], at 7 per cent of the cost of said house.''[51]   The renting of this property was, however, but a temporary arrangement, for in May, 1839, a lot of five acres was purchased for $25.00, and arrangements were made for the erection of a ''hewed log meeting house with two rooms 22 feet square each, a roof fixed with rafters and laths and covered with three feet boards. The house to be finished off on as cheap a plan as can be, to be made tolerably comfortable".[52]   It was of the congregation in this house, erected at a cost of "about $340.00", that John B. Newhall wrote in 1841:

> Spending the Sabbath, "first day," there last summer, I attended meeting in company with my venerable friend [Aaron Street]; there were more than 300 in attendance, and it was estimated rather *less* than over the usual number. We had an excellent discourse, an "old-fashioned Quaker sermon." There, too, were the venerable and devout old patriarchs, ranged along the "high seats," some whose whitened locks told of threescore years; and there, too, were the motherly-looking matrons, with plain caps and drab bonnets, sitting in solemn silence, and devoutly waiting upon *Him,* whom they profess to worship in spirit and in truth.[53]

When the aged folk of this interesting community assembled for their first "Old Settlers Meeting" in 1883, and lived over the events of almost fifty years — years full of both joys and hardships — a few facts seemed to stand out conspicuously. William K. Pidgeon had the distinction of being the oldest living settler, having come to Salem with his father, Isaac, in the fall of 1835. Isaac M. Hoggatt was greeted as the first child born in the village. Peter Boyer, it was remembered, kept the first hotel. Aaron Street "was the first to handle Uncle Sam's mail". R. Spurrier was praised as being Salem's pioneer merchant; while Thomas Frazier was reverenced as the first minister in their midst.[54]   Thus through the drowsy summer days and the long winter evenings the easy-going people of this quaint old Quaker town recount the events of the past, seeming never to tire of the story of the early days; while the outer world all but forgets that there is a Salem or that such were the beginnings not only of Iowa Quakerism, but of the Commonwealth of Iowa as well.

V

THE QUAKERS IN THE BACK COUNTIES

In 1836 the population of Iowa numbered 10,531; while in 1840, only four years later, it had more than quadrupled and stood at 43,112.[55]   For a time the eastern counties, like dykes along the Mississippi, received and held this westward-moving mass of humanity, but soon the stream of immigrants broke all barriers and spread rapidly to the westward, building villages and towns as if by magic, and changing the very face of the prairies.   Close upon the heels of the surveyor — indeed, more often running before him — went the squatter; while repeatedly the legislature of the new Territory of Iowa was called upon for the creation of new counties and the establishment of county boundaries.[56]

In this rapid work of settlement, the Quakers bore a prominent part.   Somewhat clannish in nature, wherever they located they usually monopolized the land of the region.   Owing to the harmony which generally prevailed among the Friends "claim associations", so common in the West, were unnecessary in Quaker communities and law-suits over land disputes were almost unknown.[57]   On an equal footing with other settlers they attended the government land sales, and there bid in their claims at the customary $1.25 per acre.

Keokuk and Fort Madison were the natural gateways to Iowa for those of the Quakers who came from the East and the South by the river route (i. e., down the Ohio and up the Mississippi); while Burlington was more accessible to those who crossed the prairies of Illinois by the overland route from Indiana. It will be seen at a glance that the lines from these three points converging at Salem brought the Quakers directly into the fertile lands between the Des Moines and the Skunk rivers — a region of great fertility which extended almost without a break to the northwest for nearly a hundred and fifty miles into the very heart of the State. With that keenness for good agricultural lands which has always characterized the Quakers, those of the order who came here settled in this promising country, building up community after community which they christened with such appropriate names as New Garden, Pleasant Plain, and Richland.

The first of these new Quaker settlements to spring into being was that of the Lower Settlement on Cedar Creek, about four miles to the northwest of Salem. In the minutes of the Salem Monthly Meeting for March 30, 1839, one finds the first mention of this community in the following statement: "Friends of the lower settlement request the privilege of holding an Indulged Meeting". A committee was appointed to visit these "friends making the request Judge of the propriety of grant-

ing it, and report to next meeting.'' In the following
month the committee reported to the Monthly
Meeting that they had ''attended to the appointment
to midling good satisfaction though way did not
oppen to grant their request''. So close were these
Friends to Salem, and so easy of access was that
meeting that the request was not granted until
January, 1841, when a new Preparative Meeting
was directed to be set up — a meeting which has
been maintained to this day.[58]

The second new community of Friends in Iowa
chronicled in the records of the Salem Monthly
Meeting was that of Pleasant Prairie (or Pleasant
Plain as it was soon called), a settlement located
about twenty-five miles northwest of Salem. At the
October session of the Salem Monthly Meeting a
committee composed of Gideon Frazier, Enoch
Beard, Eli Cook, Henry Joy, and William Hockett
was directed to visit the Friends composing the new
settlement ''for their help and incouragement'', and
''if way should open mak[e] choice of a friend in
that settlement to be appointed to the station of
overseer''. In making a report of their visit to the
Monthly Meeting in November the committee stated
that ''a part of them attended to the appointment to
good satisfaction'', and in consequence an Indulged
Meeting was directed to be officially opened at
Pleasant Prairie on February 3, 1841.[59]

While Cedar Creek and Pleasant Plain were thus
forming to the north of Salem there were at least
three new Quaker communities collecting to the south

and east. The first of these to receive mention was New Garden, located about midway between Fort Madison and Salem. For a time New Garden received a remarkable influx of settlers and so grew rapidly; but before long the tide moved on to the northwest, leaving this once prosperous settlement to struggle against destructive forces, and finally to decline and disappear, only a lonely graveyard and desolate grave stones remaining to keep watch over the now forgotten dead. East Grove, about five miles southeast, and Chestnut Hill about the same distance directly south of Salem were also important settlements which flourished during the first generation about this early Quaker center in Iowa; but of these Chestnut Hill alone remains, a mere remnant of its early strength.

It is but natural that inquiry should be made as to the cause of so marked a disappearance of the Quakers from a land so thoroughly adapted to their needs. Therein lies a unique and interesting story. When the Friends came to Iowa it was primarily for economic reasons. At the same time they clung to their anti-slavery sentiments. In coming west they had deliberately chosen the free soil of Iowa; but to their dismay they soon found themselves annoyed by slave-catchers from the Missouri border. The second factor entering into the abandonment of the early settlements was their close proximity to the Mormons.[60] In the face of these undesirable conditions the Quakers of southeastern Iowa did as their ancestors had always done under such circum-

stances — they moved into the back counties.[61] And
so, out upon the prairies of Jefferson County the
second Quaker stronghold in Iowa grew into being.
In this fair and fertile land the onward-moving
Quakers once again bade their oxen ''Whoa''; and
upon a prairie now called ''Pleasant Plain'' they
planted homes, and erected church and school.[62] To
this new settlement many Quakers moved, peopling
the land with their industrious and happy families.

Rapid, indeed, must have been the growth of the
settlement which in less than a single year raised
Pleasant Plain from the stage of a Preparative to
that of a Monthly Meeting. On the 28th day of
December, 1842, the members of the new community
assembled, together with a committee composed of
Zedediah Bond, Sarah Ann Pickering, and Rachel
Reader, properly directed and authorized, to solemnly establish a meeting in accordance with the ancient
order of the Society.[63] From the very first, certificates of membership[64] began to pour into this new
Monthly Meeting from all parts of the East and
South. During the nine years from 1842 to 1850
one hundred and fifty members came from various
Quaker centers in Ohio, Indiana, North Carolina,
and Tennessee.

Again the movement pressed onward, finding its
way into Keokuk County, where P. C. Woodward,
with the Bray, Williams, Haworth, Moorman, Hadley, and other Quaker families quickly built up the
thriving communities of Richland and Rocky Run.[65]
Thence others migrated into Mahaska County,

where, by February of 1844, Joseph D. Hoag of Salem was to be found at Spring Creek, preaching the Quaker message from the rough-hewn doorstep of Thomas Stafford's log cabin, by "the light of a pile of burning logs . . . . the house being filled with women, and the yard with men and boys."[66]

To the eastward of this advanced Quaker outpost, Spring Creek — a name soon to be known throughout the Quaker world — a new gateway into Iowa was soon found by this peculiar sect at the growing river town of Muscatine. To the westward, within the brief space of half a decade, in the beautiful region of the "Three Rivers" in Warren County, members of this same sect were chopping and hewing the logs which were to be used in the erection of peaceful Quaker homes.[67] And again, to the northward, as the nineteenth century came half way to its close, the migration which was so soon to dot the counties of Jasper, Marshall, Story, and Hardin with Quaker settlements began with the appearance in that region of a family by the name of Hammer.

On account of the continuous pressing of the Quakers across the frontier line in Iowa, and the unparalleled increase of their numbers in this western country, the position of Salem had become relatively more and more important as time went on. On coming to Iowa the immigrant Quakers usually passed through and made acquaintances at Salem, and as they occasionally returned from the interior to the river towns for supplies they again partook of the hospitality of its people. With the rise of new settlements in the back counties and the consequent increase of church business to be transacted the need of a Quarterly Meeting to supervise the whole new field became apparent. With this end in view the two Monthly Meetings of Salem and Pleasant Plain united in a joint request in 1844 to the Western Quarterly Meeting in Indiana that such a meeting be established.[68] Due to the remoteness of the field and the scattered condition of the communities, action was deferred, and it was not until its gathering in October, 1847, that the Indiana Yearly Meeting, held at Whitewater, authorized the granting of the request.[69]

In the meantime the Friends at Salem had outgrown their little hewed-log meeting-house, so that steps were early taken for the erection of a new place of worship, for which by 1846 the sum of $1,149.00 had been subscribed.[70] Here, from far and near, on May 20, 1848, a large and enthusiastic company assembled to attend the opening of this the first Quarterly Meeting beyond the Mississippi. As was customary, an official committee of both men and women Friends from the Indiana Yearly Meeting was in attendance to render such assistance as might be necessary, and on that day the new meeting was properly established. Concerning this event a member of the attending committee wrote:

They had built a substantial brick house for the accommodation of the Quarterly Meeting, which, when completed, will perhaps be, if not the best, among the best, belonging

to Indiana Yearly Meeting. . . . The meetings for
worship are Salem, Cedar Creek, Pleasant Plain, Richland,
New Garden, East Grove, and Spring River. There are,
besides, two or three other places where Friends have
settled, who are taking measures to have meetings established. There was some enumeration two years ago, when
they numbered about 300 families. There has been a large
emigration to that country since, and it will probably be
safe now to set them down at four to five hundred families,
emigrated from almost all places where there are any
Friends.[71]

Having thus far briefly sketched the beginnings
of Quakerism in Iowa, and having traced the rising
Quaker settlements in the back counties, it is now
possible to follow with interest the travels of two
prominent English ministers, Robert Lindsey and
Benjamin Seebohm, who viewed at first hand and
with wondering eyes in 1850 the building of a great
Commonwealth and the planting of one of the fore-
most Yearly Meetings of their faith.

VI

THE IOWA FIELD IN 1850

Robert Lindsey and his companion, having at various times visited together nearly every Quaker community in America (including the Yearly Meetings of North Carolina, Baltimore, Philadelphia, Ohio, Indiana, and the settlements in Canada),[72] in the opening of the year 1850 turned their faces toward distant Iowa.

From some unnamed point in the State of Michigan (probably near Adrian), these two travelers in the ministry journeyed across the frozen prairies of Illinois in a two-horse carriage. They were on their way to the far-famed Quaker town of Salem. On the 19th day of January, 1850, Robert Lindsey records in his journal: "we reached the Mississippi River this morning about 11 o'clock [opposite Burlington], and on enquiry it appeared as if it might be safe to cross over on the ice." Fearing, however, that they might break through, the two men crossed on foot, while a practiced ferryman drove their team and carriage to the Iowa side.

After dining at the "busy and thriving" town of Burlington, they pressed on westward. As the shades of evening settled down upon the prairie the weary and travel-worn Friends approached the little

Quaker settlement of East Grove, which was within
five miles of Salem. Looking wistfully across the
undulating plain at each rise and fall they could now
and then catch a glimpse of the flickering candles
through cabin windows in the distance.[73] With that
impatience which one feels as a long journey comes
to its close they urged their horses on. Thirteen
long and weary days they had steadily pushed westward, covering a distance of nearly four hundred
miles. In all this distance, says Lindsey, "we had
not fallen in with a single member of our Society, or
any in profession with us".

Then came the joy of the end as the heavy carriage pulled up to the door of their friend Joseph D.
Hoag.[74] Tired and weary, they were pleased with
the hospitable welcome which they received under his
roof. Here they stayed for four days, resting and
preparing for the onward journey — spending much
of the time in "writing, reading, walking out for
exercise, and in social conversation". They made
but one brief trip to Salem to attend the First-day
(Sunday) morning meeting.

On the morning of the 23rd, the weather being
"very pleasant", the visitors together with their
host, Joseph D. Hoag, as guide and Amos Hoag as
driver, left East Grove on their way to the new and
rapidly growing Quaker settlement of Oakley in
Cedar County, which was located some eighty miles
to the northward. About noon they reached Mt.
Pleasant where they dined. Leaving there soon
after dinner they "entered upon a prairie, nearly 20

miles over without a single house or inhabitant upon it.'' About sunset they came to an impassable stream, and ''were under the necessity of going back to the last house we had passed, which was at least 10 miles distant'', and which was reached about eight o'clock in the evening.

In the early days it was the unwritten law of the plains that stranded strangers should at least be sheltered for the night, but here the customary hospitality of the West failed. Refused at the first house, they were compelled to push on to the second, some ''2 or 3 miles further'', where they were again refused. On a third attempt, however, they ''succeeded in getting a shelter'', where Lindsey and Seebohm ''were privileged with a bed'' while their two companions ''had to lie on the floor covered with their buffalo robes.'' For this entertainment they paid the sum of one ''dollar & a half'' and departed early in the morning without breakfast.

Having picked their toilsome way over the hills and dales and intervening plains of Henry and Washington counties and the southern part of Johnson County, the group of Quaker travelers crossed the Iowa River on the morning of the 25th and entered Iowa City, the capital of Iowa. Passing almost directly to the eastward, in the afternoon as they were ''within 5 miles of the end'' of their journey they suffered the misfortune of a broken axletree of the carriage and ''had to leave it in the midst of the prairie''. Thus discomfited, the two English Quakers were given ''Joseph D. Hoag's

1 horse buggy'', while he and Amos mounted their friends' horses and so came on to the home of Laurie Tatum. There they were ''cordially received & kindly welcomed into their humble dwelling by him & his wife, an agreeable & interesting young woman, who has recently ventured out into this new country to share in the toils of her husband in providing a home on these western prairies.''

Two very pleasant and profitable days were spent in the Oakley settlement visiting with the Friends. Of Sunday the 27th Lindsey records:

A fine bright winter's morning. The thermometer at 10° above zero. At 10 o'clock attended the usual first day morning meeting at Oakley held at the house of Laurie Tatum. Nearly all their members, & some of their neighbors were present, & it was a satisfactory meeting. At 6 in the evening we had an appointed meeting[75] in a schoolhouse 3 miles from here, which was very crowded, & the forepart of it in consequence thereof a good deal unsettled; but thro' patient waiting a precious calm was mercifully vouchsafed, & dear Benjamin was strengthened to labor among them in right authority, & the meeting concluded to good satisfaction.

Feeling that their work in this community was finished the visitors again turned to the westward on the 28th. Driving to Iowa City they had their carriage repaired, and while waiting, observed something of the town concerning which they wrote: ''It has a handsome State House, several places of worship, some good stores, & probably about 1000 inhabitants.''

From Iowa City they pursued in a general direction the route now taken by the Chicago, Rock Island and Pacific Railway, passing through Marengo, then "containing 8 houses & a log Court House"—"a poor place", they thought, for there they "could not get even a feed of corn" for their horses. Steadily they moved onward across the rolling prairie, now through "scattered timber", and now where "neither tree nor shrub [was] to be seen as far as the eye could reach"; and at the close of the third day out of Oakley they "reached the Hammer's Settlement [near Newton in Jasper County], where 5 or 6 families of Friends are located who removed up here from East Tennessee 2 or 3 years ago." "We took up our quarters", says Lindsey, "at the widow Hammer's, whose husband was a minister in our Society, and deceased since they came out here." That night a strong "northwester" blew across the plains, and the house "being far from tight, the wind had free access through many openings, both in the walls & roof", so that the strangers found it difficult to keep warm.

Having held a religious meeting in the Hammer home for the members of the settlement, on the following day, February 1st, with the thermometer registering "10° below zero", the four faithful friends again took up their journey, bound for the settlements of "Friends on the Three Rivers". By way of Parker's Mill on the Des Moines River and the village of Dudley they reached their destination on the morning of the following day. With that deep satisfaction which comes to one who has achieved the object of his hopes, Lindsey was able to write that he had now reached the "most distant & most westerly meeting of Friends on this Continent, being more than 1500 miles west from New York. We understand it is not more than 4 years since this part of the country was occupied by tribes of Indians. . . . [which] have now been located beyond the Missouri. We may indeed be said to be almost arrived at the bound of civilized life". Here, too, the wind blew cold and the thermometer recorded "20° below zero".

In spite of the hostility of nature, from the Middle River settlement the persevering group drove eight miles to Lower River, where they held a meeting in a schoolhouse; and to those accustomed to the balmy climate of England it was hard indeed to "sit the meeting". That night, February 3rd, they lodged with Joseph Carey, a late arrival from Indiana. In the new log cabin, which consisted of a single room, Lindsey says, "12 individuals were accommodated; our company, consisting of 4 men, were privileged to occupy the 2 beds: & the family consisting of the friend, his wife & 5 children, & a young man who was also there, were arranged on the floor, & on a trundle bedstead which was drawn out from beneath one of the other beds." Of such accommodations Lindsey remarks: "we were more warm & comfortable than we had been for several nights past: & I may say that under this humble roof we were treated with genuine hospitality".

Having now reached the western limit of their journey and finished their labors there, the guide, Joseph D. Hoag, turned to the homeward course. On the 5th of February they passed through Pella, where they observed marks of the "industry & management" of the Dutch in their new American home;[76] and, without mishap, they finally reached the hospitable home of Thomas Stafford at Spring Creek. Here on the following day they attended the Spring Creek Preparative Meeting, where, much to their "inconvenience", the men and women were compelled to transact their business "in the same appartment", due to the absence of the usual partition between them.

From Spring Creek the little company again pressed on to Richland, and then to Pleasant Plain, attending the Monthly Meeting at the latter place on February 9th. In speaking of this meeting Lindsey observes: "The business was conducted in a solid & weighty manner, there appearing to be amongst them a number of well concerned Friends who are endeavoring in faithfulness & in simplicity to uphold our religious testimonies in this far western land." From Pleasant Plain they returned to Richland for the Sunday morning meeting, which was "filled to overflowing"; and after taking dinner with Stephen Woodward they pushed on some four miles for an evening meeting at the new Quaker settlement of Rocky Run.

With that devotion which marked the old-time Quaker ministry, Robert Lindsey and Benjamin

Seebohm had sacrificed the joys of home, traveled thousands of miles, and endured the hardships of this western country, as they would have said, for the sake of "truth" and the encouragement of their brethren. Once arrived at Salem, they were welcomed to "comfortable quarters" in the home of Peter Collins, where they found letters from their dear ones in the homeland. It is not a matter for surprise, therefore, that Lindsey recorded in his journal for February 12th that they "much enjoyed the quiet & convenience of a small bedroom with a fire in it which we were privileged to occupy to ourselves: which we felt to be quite a treat after the rough fare & scanty accommodations we have had for the last 3 weeks."

On the second day after their arrival at Salem the Monthly Meeting convened. This, the second Monthly Meeting which they had attended in Iowa, "was long & interesting, not concluding until ½ past 4 o'clock." Of this session Lindsey remarks:

There was a great variety of business before the meeting, & it was entered upon, & disposed of in a weighty manner. Certificates of removal were read & accepted for 4 individuals, amongst which was one for Walter Crew & his wife and 14 children from Cedar Creek in Virginia, whence they removed a few months ago, having travelled the whole distance of 1500 miles in 2 waggons, & been upwards of 2 months on the road.

On the following day, February 14th, came the East Grove Monthly Meeting which was likewise attended by the visitors. Here again they found that the men and women were compelled to hold their business meetings in a meeting-house of a single room "with only a waggon cover hung up between them . . . . neverth[e]less it was an interesting and satisfactory time".

On the 15th, 16th, and 17th of February came the sessions of the Salem Quarterly Meeting to which all of the subordinate meetings of Friends in Iowa reported. Here again the English visitors were brought into contact with a typical pioneer Quaker gathering. For long distances the Friends came in their heavy wagons, braving the severities of winter, and bringing their families to the quarterly religious and social gathering which played so large a part in the life of the Quakers in the earlier days. The business session being over, at the Sunday meeting for worship the crowd "was very large, the house being filled to overflowing". Though there is no specific record, it is reasonable to suppose that on this occasion, Benjamin Seebohm, the chief spokesman of the traveling pair, preached from the rich store of his religious experience that spiritual admonition and testimony for which he was so widely known.

Having touched the settlement at East Grove upon their arrival in Iowa, there still remained three communities of Friends in the vicinity of Salem for the travelers to visit before the tour of the meetings in Iowa could be said to be complete. The first of these, Cedar Creek, to the north of Salem, they visited on the 18th of February, where they had "an appointed meeting" that proved a "relieving opportunity". Here they found that the settlers had "lately built themselves a good frame meeting house". "Most of the seats", so Lindsey said, "are nothing more than rough boards supported at each end by blocks of wood. Indeed this is the way in which all of the meeting houses in this State that we have yet seen, are fitted up".

On the following day, February 19th, they visited the Chestnut Hill community where they held another appointed meeting and found an "interesting company of Friends, most of them young & middle aged". On the 20th they completed their mission with an appointed meeting at New Garden. Here the house "which was small, was very much crowded, some being unable to get in at all"— a fitting close to so extensive a visit.

At the break of dawn on February 21st, the home of Joseph D. Hoag was all astir. Lonely indeed had been these English Friends far out in this western country; but now their thoughts were on the homeward journey. Then came the "solid parting" and the long remembered "farewell"[77] between those who through days of toil and hardship had learned to know and love each other. Long, it is said, were moistened eyes turned towards the eastward from the little cabin window, as the quaint old carriage moved across the prairie.

Lodged in the quiet of the evening in a little tavern some five miles to the east of the Mississippi, Lindsey turned to his journal and wrote: "Now that

5

we have left Iowa, I may say that we have felt much
& deeply interested about the dear Friends who
are settled there, to many of whom we have felt
nearly united in bonds of Christian fellowship.'' As
they turned to the eastward the nearest meeting, for
which they were bound, was some three hundred
miles away on the border of Illinois.[78]

Such was the Iowa field at the beginning of the
last half of the nineteenth century. Undeveloped
and abounding in possibilities, the great West lay
open to such religious forces as might come in and
possess the land. Herein was a golden opportunity
— an opportunity such as seldom comes to any people of any sect. Here in a new and all but unfettered
environment, touched and jostled on every hand by
men and creeds from every clime, Quakerism as a
religious force was to have a final testing as to its
inherent power of future growth and its ability to
assimilate that not of its own fold. The ''holy experiment'', not in government, but rather in practical religion, has indeed been on trial in the West.
For the Society of Friends nowhere are the lessons
so clear and the results so definite as in the history
of this State where Quakerism first took root in the
land beyond the Mississippi.

VII

A DECADE OF EXPANSION 1850 TO 1860

F ᴇ w movements better illustrate the restless energy of American life than the rapid settlement of the vast region west of the Mississippi River. Under the French and Spanish régimes this land had lain almost untouched by white men — a land of quiet, disturbed only now and then by the passing war cry of the red men of the plains, or the mighty stampede of the bison herds. Then came the Anglo-Saxons — restless, eager, thrifty — looking here and there for homes. As if by magic all was changed within the span of a single century and the great West is now the home of over 28,000,000 souls.[79]

By the middle of the nineteenth century, the settlement of Iowa was well advanced. By this time also the Quakers were rapidly making a place for themselves in the young Commonwealth. Until about 1850 the busy town of Salem had served as the chief point of entry for the stream of Quakers which poured into the southeastern part of the State and settled in the fertile valleys between the Des Moines and Skunk rivers. While settlements were thus rising one after another in quick succession, a new gateway was opened to the northeast, and at Bloomington (now Muscatine) the ferrymen became familiar with the Quaker salutations, "thee" and "thou".

The first Friend known to have entered at this new gateway was Brinton Darlington,[80] who bought a farm near Muscatine in 1843. Then came Laurie Tatum, who pressed on about thirty miles to the northwest and settled in Cedar County in 1844. Close upon his coming followed J. H. Painter and family in 1845. Thus as at Salem, hardly had the waving prairie grass been touched by the first Quaker until it was pressed by the foot of the second. The track then made was soon to become a beaten path across the prairie, then a well defined road, and finally a veritable highway for immigrants.

As has been seen in connection with the visit of Robert Lindsey and Benjamin Seebohm to the Cedar County settlement (then known as Oakley) in the winter of 1850, the Friends in that locality were rapidly building up a prosperous community. A year later in the month of August, William Evans, a Philadelphia Friend, on a religious visit to the meetings in Iowa,[81] came into the Oakley settlement, of which he wrote the following description:

The residences of the settlers in this place, scattered over prairie land, are chiefly log buildings; the settlement being several miles in extent. In the summer season, while the grass is green, the country, with the cabins and little surrounding improvements dotted over it, has a picturesque appearance; yet to a stranger, it gives a sensation of lonesomeness.[82]

The first collective religious meetings to be held

among this new group of Friends began in the ''fore part of 1849'', and were held as the occasion suited at the homes of Laurie Tatum or J. H. Painter. By the year 1852, however, the community had increased in numbers to such an extent that it became necessary to erect a building for ''meeting'' purposes; and to that end a concrete house with a flat roof was built. On April 9, 1853, in this the second house erected in Cedar County for religious purposes,[83] was established the Red Cedar Monthly Meeting, later to be known far and wide as Springdale, with Brinton Darlington as its clerk.[84]

The composite nature of this new center of Quakerism in Iowa and the rapidity with which it grew are well shown by the records of the Monthly Meeting for the first eight months of its existence. At the time of its organization in April the committees appointed show that there were no less than thirty-four men members of the meeting. By the close of the year there had been received by the Red Cedar Monthly Meeting sixty-six certificates of membership, representing 322 men, women, and children. These certificates show that the new arrivals came from Maine, Vermont, New York, Pennsylvania, Ohio, Indiana, and Canada. For the next four or five years the movement continued strong. In the year 1854 alone eighty-four certificates of membership were received, likewise from very divergent sources. The Red Cedar meeting was over-crowded, and then the immigrants moved on to the northwest, settling the region to such an extent that for many years the fertile divide between the Iowa and Cedar rivers to the northwest of Springdale for some miles was known as "Quaker Ridge".

That the population of Iowa should jump from 192,214 in 1850 to 674,913 in 1860,[85] and that the Friends should be ready for the founding of a Yearly Meeting in this State by that time is not surprising when one reads as follows from the pen of an eye witness: "The immigration into Iowa the present season [1854] is astonishing and unprecedented. For miles and miles, day after day, the prairies of Illinois are lined with cattle and wagons, pushing on towards this prosperous State. At a point beyond Peoria, during a single month, seventeen hundred and forty-three wagons had passed, and all for Iowa."[86] What with the advertisement of Iowa lands by great land companies, the frequent descriptions of the country which appeared in both secular and religious newspapers, and the multitude of personal letters to friends in the East from those who had already settled beyond the Mississippi, the fame of this new State[87] was spread in a manner that kept the inflow of settlers steady and strong for many years.

Moving on to the north between the Iowa and Cedar rivers the Quakers invaded Linn[88] and Jones counties,[89] and then pushed on to the northern border of the State as far as Winneshiek County. From this point on the 3rd of March, 1855, a Friend wrote:

The general face of the county is handsomely rolling or
undulating, and along the streams approaching to what may
be called broken. The prairies of this county are generally
of moderate extent, and unsurpassed in beauty and fertility,
by any that I have ever seen.

.   .   .   .

The first family of Friends that located in this county,
arrived here in the 9th month 1853. There are now about
twenty families, and some others have purchased land, and
are expecting to move here this spring. . . . Friends
here are situated in two settlements, about nine miles apart.
We get no established meetings, but hold one for worship in
each settlement regularly twice a week. The upper or
northern settlement, is near the northern line of the county.
The meeting there, is held at the house of Tristram Allen,
an approved minister, from the State of Michigan. Our
meeting in this settlement, is held at the house of Ansel
Rogers, also an approved minister from Michigan.[90]

It was from this far northern settlement that a
letter came to the Red Cedar Monthly Meeting on
February 7, 1855, requesting the establishment of
two Preparative Meetings, to be named Winneshiek
and Springwater, and the two to compose a new
Monthly Meeting to be called Winneshiek. The
letter was urgent in its appeal and bore the signa-
tures of forty-seven Friends.[91] ''After a time of
deliberation'' on the part of the Red Cedar Friends,
a committee of eight[92] was appointed to ''consider
the subject'', and to ''visit them if way should
open''. A short time after their appointment, all
arrangements having been made for the proposed
visit to their brethren, six members of the committee

set off in two carriages.[93]   Snow-clad and wind-
swept plains stretched away one hundred and fifty
miles before them.   Of the hardships of this long
winter journey but little is known.   The only report
which has been preserved reads as follows: "A part
of their number [the committee] had visited them &
were united with them in their request".[94]   Thus
was Winneshiek added to the roll of Quaker centers
of settlement and influence in the West.

While the Quaker settlements of Red Cedar and
Winneshiek were rising into prominence, the movement along the older channel had continued strong,
so that community after community had been formed
in the heart of the State with a rapidity which far
outstripped the earlier settlements of this sect either
in Ohio or in Indiana.   On his second visit to Iowa in
1858,[95] Robert Lindsey, who was this time accompanied by his wife, Sarah, had the unusual experience of being present at the opening of two new
Quarterly Meetings within the brief space of a single
month.   One of these was the former little settlement
of Oakley, now Red Cedar; and the other, bearing
the appropriate name of Western Plain, was at a
place where not a single Quaker was to be found on
Lindsey's former visit in 1850.

Much had transpired in Iowa in eight years.
Under the hand of the pioneer the barren prairie
had been transformed into prosperous farms; where
before had been cross-road taverns and nameless
trading posts there were now growing villages and
towns; and along with all this transformation and

growth the Quakers in Iowa were rapidly coming to the point where their increased numbers demanded the establishment of a Yearly Meeting west of the Mississippi River.

VIII

THE FORMATION OF THE IOWA YEARLY
MEETING OF FRIENDS

The full import of what had actually come to pass in western Quakerism during the decade between 1850 and 1860 can not be fully appreciated without a view of the field as it appeared at the end of that period: a survey of the new meetings which had been established, and the strong tendencies towards more effective organization in the order.

When the year 1850 came to its close there were thirteen Quaker settlements in the State of Iowa, varying in size from a few persons to many families. Ten years later, in 1860, there were no less than forty-five such meetings of Friends, scattered through eighteen different counties.[96] As these settlements increased in numbers and in strength, it was natural that each should pass through the various stages of Quaker church organization for the handling of the community interests, namely: the Preparative, the Monthly, the Quarterly, and the Yearly Meetings. The Preparative Meeting[97] dealt with a single local community; the Monthly Meeting usually cared for a more extended field of one or more settlements; the Quarterly Meeting had supervision over a number of Monthly Meetings in a given district; and finally, the Yearly Meeting exercised final control in religious matters over all those composing its membership.[98] It was through these various steps, therefore, that the Quakers passed as they continued to plant their homes, their churches, and their schools in Iowa.

It will be remembered that with the growth of Salem the first Quarterly Meeting of Friends west of the Mississippi River was organized at that place on May 20, 1848. This meeting having become unwieldy by the rapid rise of the communities of Friends to the west, Pleasant Plain was set off as a new Quarterly Meeting under that name in 1852,[99] with the more western settlements under its care. Then came the Friends of Cedar County, who, in their newly built frame meeting-house with floors of rough and unplaned boards, were granted the privileges of a Quarterly Meeting on the 8th day of May, 1858.[100] The fourth group of settlements thus to organize was Western Plain, now called Bangor. Starting with a little settlement in Marshall County in 1853,[101] the Quakers settled in such numbers upon the fertile lands along the upper courses of the Iowa River that within five years they were prepared for a Quarterly Meeting, which was duly established among them on the 5th day of June, 1858.[102]

The Quakers in Iowa, having developed into four strong and well organized Quarterly Meetings, were now ready for the formation of a Yearly Meeting. It seems that the initial move towards such an organization was made by the Red Cedar Quarterly

Meeting, the matter being considered on the 13th day of November, 1858. In the records of that meeting may be found the following statement:

This meeting was introduced into a deep exercise on the very important subject of the establishment of a Yearly Meeting in Iowa. After a time of serious deliberation during which a very general expression was made the meeting believing the time had come, for action thereon, and being fully united, it was concluded to appoint a joint committee of men and women friends, to meet and confer with similar committees from the other quarterly meetings, and take the whole subject in all its bearings into serious consideration. The place of meeting of these committees to be at Spring Creek, meeting house, on the second seventh day in 12th mo. next at 10 o'clk A. M.[103]

The proposed plan was heartily espoused by the Friends of Pleasant Plain and of Western Plain; and when December 11, 1858, arrived, representatives from all four of the Iowa Quarterly Meetings were present at the appointed place. Having convened, the "conference was introduced into a lively exercise on the important subject", and after a "free expression of sentiment" it was clear to all that the Friends in Iowa were ready for a Yearly Meeting separate and distinct from that of Indiana. Various locations were suggested for the annual gatherings, which, after being "freely discussed in much harmony and condescension", the conference united in recommending to their home meetings that the gatherings be held "in the vicinity of Oskaloosa, in Mahaska County"— an indefinite recommendation which was fraught with many difficulties.[104]

Having confederated their interests, the four Iowa Quarters now pressed their claims for independence upon the Indiana Yearly Meeting at its annual gathering in 1859; and at its session held on October 1st, after "serious consideration, and, under a feeling sense of the responsibility and importance of the proposed movement", the meeting appointed a committee of nineteen Friends "to visit the Quarterly meetings in Iowa, with the liberty of visiting any of their subordinate meetings, if they should think it right to do so, and to report . . . . their judgment as to the propriety of granting the request".[105]

During the summer days of 1860, twelve members of this official committee passed from community to community in Iowa, observing and noting the conditions here existing. In its report to the Indiana Yearly Meeting on October 6th the committee said:

Our Friends in Iowa received us with much kindness, and assisted us in traveling from place to place, as was laid out to suit our convenience. We found large and respectable bodies of Friends at Red Cedar, Bangor, South River, Pleasant Plain, and Salem Quarterly meetings, and entered into much sympathy with them in their situation, and also in regard to their proposition, concerning which we found a united sentiment at each meeting.

In recommending that the request of the Iowa Friends be granted the committee suggested that "the time of opening the new Yearly Meeting be fixed not earlier than 1863, nor later than 1865 . . . . in order to give ample time for suitable preparation and arrangements". Adopting the recommendations of their committee, the Indiana Friends now authorized the opening of the new Yearly Meeting "to be held in the vicinity of Oskaloosa, in Mahaska County, Iowa, on Fifth-day preceding the second First-day in the Ninth month, 1863." It was in accordance with this direction that the Iowa Yearly Meeting of Friends came into being at the Spring Creek meeting-house on the 10th day of September, 1863.[106]

This project for a Yearly Meeting had apparently moved along smoothly, and peace and concord seemed to prevail. But unexpectedly an almost insuperable difficulty arose. In the early part of January, 1861, representatives from the five Iowa Quarterly Meetings reconvened at Oskaloosa to lay plans and make arrangements for the opening of the Yearly Meeting two years hence. They early agreed upon the erection of a permanent building for the Yearly Meeting, at an estimated cost of $16,000; but when they came to consider just where this building was to be placed, grave and embarrassing differences of opinion appeared.[107] That it was to be "in the vicinity of Oskaloosa" had been made clear both by the former conference at Spring Creek in 1858 and by the direction of the Indiana Friends in 1860. But how to satisfy the demands of the Friends of the Spring Creek settlement about two and one-half miles to the east of Oskaloosa, the demands of the Friends of the Center Grove settlement about two miles to the north of Oskaloosa, and the demands of the Friends in the town of Oskaloosa — all contending for the erection of the proposed building in their midst — was a puzzle.

Unable to come to any mutual agreement the conference of January adjourned until April. Upon reviewing the whole situation, a dead-lock again appeared at the adjourned meeting, and the joint committee was compelled to report back to the home meetings that "we cannot agree upon any location".[108]   The Bangor Quarterly Meeting now proposed to submit the contention to an impartial body of Friends outside of Iowa,[109] but Pleasant Plain refused to concur in this suggestion.[110]   Then Red Cedar appealed to the Indiana "Meeting for Sufferings"[111] to interfere, and asked that the opening of the new Yearly Meeting be indefinitely postponed.[112] The Indiana Yearly Meeting was now compelled to act; and in a statement made on October 2, 1862, it informed its Iowa offspring with true Quaker firmness "that it would [not] be proper for it to make any change in the conclusion heretofore had".[113] Thus left to make the best of the situation, the western Quakers for the time being laid aside their differences and made haste to prepare for the long to be remembered birthday of the first Yearly Meeting beyond the Mississippi.

IX

THE FIRST YEARLY MEETING IN IOWA

The place chosen for the holding of the first Yearly Meeting of the Friends in Iowa was indeed a beautiful spot. Situated in a rich agricultural region of rolling hills and valleys, dotted here and there with peaceful Quaker homes, the Spring Creek settlement presented a pleasing aspect. Crowning a knoll which overlooked all that region, the long, low, frame structure of the Spring Creek meeting-house nestled in among the foliage of a native grove; while near by stood a two-story school building.

Being pressed for time in the making of their arrangements, the joint committee of the Quarterly Meetings seized upon the offer of the Spring Creek Friends granting the use of their comfortable quarters. Then, in the spring of 1863, the committee let a contract ''for the erection of a temporary building adjoining Spring Creek meeting-house at an estimated cost of Five hundred dollars''.[114] A temporary building it indeed must have been, for in an account written in 1909, Charles Coffin, the only surviving member of the Indiana delegation,[115] declares that a ''shed of rough posts placed in the ground covered and enclosed with unplaned boards, was erected adjoining the Quarterly [Spring Creek]

Meeting House. This shed was 66 feet long by 50 feet wide. Raised galleries were erected, and rough benches set on the ground sufficient to seat about 750.'' Here the men were to assemble; while in the adjoining ''Meeting House, 35x60 feet, to which was attached a shed 15x60'', the women were to gather.[116]

When the appointed day arrived everything was in readiness for the meeting. The Spring Creek meeting-house, once the western outpost of Quakerism, was the center of attention. Though the weather proved inclement, the people gathered from all directions, some coming in heavy cumbersome wagons, some in carriages or buggies, and some on foot. From the five Quarterly Meetings there came the appointed committees,[117] together with large numbers of the members from the many meetings in Iowa. From the Indiana, Western, Baltimore, and New York Yearly Meetings there were likewise officially appointed committees[118] ''to attend the opening and organization of this meeting'' and to give ''comfort and encouragement . . . . in the weighty engagement of conducting the concerns of a Yearly meeting''. In addition to this enthusiastic company the second annual ''Conference of Teachers and Delegates from Friends' First-Day Schools in the United States''[119] was then being held at Spring Creek. Consequently, the ''whole number present was from 1,200 to 1,300. . . . Fourteen ministers were in attendance with minutes for religious service. . . . The Meeting was mostly of young and middle aged Friends of great energy and

6

force of character, and much religious weight existed amongst them.''[120]

How to accommodate and shelter so large a number of people in the open country was a problem. At the Spring Creek Boarding School some fifty or sixty of the visitors from other Yearly Meetings were entertained; while many of the Iowa Friends came in covered wagons, bringing their bedding and their food with them. Dr. J. W. Morgan, at that time one of the teachers in the Boarding School, writes:

These structures [the meeting-house and the school building] were in the edge of about 40 acres of fine timber; and much of this grove was filled, during Yearly Meeting time, with tents for sleeping, cooking, eating, and stalls for horses, as nearly all came with horses and covered wagons, with a *few* carriages; for the nearest Rail Road was about 25 miles away. Yet the great crowds of people were remarkable, and the great interest and earnest devotion shown by all, indicated an abiding faith in *Quakerism*.[121]

To further care for the visitors two regular bus lines with four-horse teams were operated between the then thriving little village of Oskaloosa and Spring Creek, carrying the passengers the round trip of five miles for one dollar each.

The vitality and vigor of western Quakerism was well attested by the amount and character of the work which the Iowa Yearly Meeting of Friends accomplished at its first gathering. In the early part of its session the new Yearly Meeting adopted as its form of church government the ''Book of Discipline

of Indiana Yearly meeting, as revised and approved
by that meeting in 1854, with the alterations and
additions since made'', five hundred copies having
been furnished by the Indiana Meeting for Sufferings for distribution in Iowa.[122]   The problem of the
new meeting-house was then taken up, and with
equal dispatch the plans of the committee were
approved and the erection of a building to cost
$16,000 was directed.   Furthermore, the long and
troublesome dispute over the building site was
finally settled.[123]

With due consideration the various fields of labor
were reviewed, and large and representative committees were selected to have charge of First-Day
Scripture Schools, the work among the ''people of
color'', education, and the proper distribution of
books and tracts.   A survey of the conditions then
existing in the Iowa field was also entered upon and
this proved of special interest to those who were
visiting the West for the first time.   From the two
Quarterly Meetings of Pleasant Plain and Red Cedar
there came requests for the establishment of two new
Quarters, namely: Spring Creek Quarter, embracing
numerous growing settlements in Mahaska and
Jasper counties; and Winneshiek Quarter, now extending as far as Minneapolis in Minnesota and
Baraboo in Wisconsin.[124]   Internally the Society in
Iowa was shown to be in a most prosperous condition.   Harmony and enthusiasm prevailed through-
out the order; and ''those present from other Yearly
Meetings were impressed with the belief that the

establishment of the Yearly Meeting will prove to be a blessing to our Religious Society.''[125]

Then came the close of the gathering, and in the intense spiritual feeling that prevailed the Presiding Clerk was moved to record: ''we feel . . . . our humble but fervent sense of gratitude to the God and Father of all our sure mercies, who from day to day has deigned to own and cover us in our several sittings''.[126]

X

A RETROSPECT OF FIFTY YEARS

OVER fifty years have passed since the first Yearly
Meeting of Friends in Iowa was held, and there are
now few survivors among all those who attended
that gathering.[127] Almost within the life of a single
generation there have been reproduced in Iowa the
salient features of two hundred years of Quaker
history on the American continent. Religious upheaval, sufferings from war, the issue of slavery,
contact with the Indians, and the problems of education, schisms, migration, and decline — all of these
form a part of the annals of Iowa Quakerism.

The future appeared hopeful as the Iowa Yearly
Meeting of Friends began its labors under the direction of a group of the strongest men that this Yearly
Meeting has produced, and with a membership
made up of sturdy, restless emigrants from the East
and South. But there came a time when the incoming migration from the East ceased to exceed or
even to equal the continued movement of the Quakers
to the farther West, and the effect on the Iowa
Yearly Meeting was disheartening. Stretching from
the Mississippi to California there are long chains
of isolated and disconnected communities of Friends,
the founders of which may be traced back to the now

depleted Iowa centers. In Iowa numerous Quaker communities, once strong and flourishing, have entirely disappeared; and in fact, it may be said that with but few exceptions the communities of Friends from the Atlantic to the Pacific coast are engaged in a struggle for existence.

The effect of this draining force on Iowa Quakerism during the last half-century is well illustrated in the case of the Spring Creek settlement, the birthplace of the Iowa Yearly Meeting of Friends. Thomas Stafford was the first of the Quakers to settle in this fertile region, and close upon his heels came numerous other Friends, who quickly built up one of the strongest Quaker centers in the State. Then after a number of years of prosperity came a turn of events.

As early as 1847, in his reconnoitering expeditions in the Des Moines valley, D. D. Owen had discovered the fact that Mahaska County was underlaid with large quantities of excellent coal.[128] This knowledge was put to little use, however, until about 1875 or 1876 when "the Chicago, Milwaukee and St. Paul Railroad Co. opened up a mine . . . . about three miles south of Oskaloosa", under the name of the Excelsior Coal Company, which soon developed its output to 1500 or 1600 tons per day.[129] Mahaska County became the largest coal producing county in Iowa, and with the constantly rising prices of land in their neighborhood many of the Friends became restless, sold their lands, and moved away. The climax came in 1890. The Excelsior Coal

Company, which had exhausted its earlier mines, moved its plant to the very heart of the Quaker community and opened the Carbonado mines. Soon the erection of shacks was begun and a turbulent mining element came to Carbonado. The few remaining Friends could endure no longer the worldliness and profanity encountered on every side, and as soon as possible they departed. Five years passed by; the church property was sold; the meeting-house was moved away; and to-day the crumbling ruins of an abandoned railway, great heaps of waste slate, fields made dangerous by unsightly sink-holes, and a few dilapidated miners' shacks have taken the place of this once thriving Quaker community. An early resident of the Spring Creek neighborhood has said:

At this writing (1912) not a stone or fragment of either building of the school house or old meeting house can be found or identified. The little old grave yard, with many of the lost or unmarked graves, remains as a reminiscence of a once quaker settlement. The nice grove has all disappeared, and even the very ground where the two or three buildings stood is cultivated in growing crops.[130]

Within the State of Iowa there are many such localities where only desolate burying grounds, with their half-covered gravestones, now mark the sites of once thriving Quaker meetings; and there are also in Iowa many other communities of Friends which are now on the verge of extinction.

A brief survey of the field of Iowa Quakerism as it exists to-day reveals a few striking facts. First of all it may safely be said that after a period of three-

quarters of a century there are not now in Iowa more
than ten thousand Friends, including the members
of all branches of the Society. There are in Iowa
the Hicksites, the Wilburites, the Conservative, and
the Orthodox Friends, each almost as separate and
distinct in their outward affiliations (except the
Wilbur and Conservative Friends) as are the
Protestants and the Roman Catholics. Indeed, the
members of these various branches have very curious
ideas concerning each other's beliefs and manners of
life. Again, it may be said that in this western field
there has been in progress one of the most interesting experiments in Quakerism in the history of the
Society.

A superficial glance at the Orthodox body of
Friends in Iowa to-day would convey the impression
that it has had a remarkable period of growth; for
when the Yearly Meeting first convened in 1863
there were but five constituent Quarterly Meetings,
while there were in 1912 some sixteen such meetings.
But a more careful examination of the facts reveals
a situation which is alarming to the members of the
Society. In the first report on the membership of
the Iowa Yearly Meeting, made in 1866, there were
on record 1284 families, and 502 parts of families,
with 3855 males and 3797 females, or a total of 7652
members; while at the same time there were reported
1938 Quaker children from five to twenty-one years
of age.[131] In 1912 the records of the Yearly Meeting
show a total membership of but 8383 persons, 2176
of whom are non-resident and largely non-support-

ing members, while 1130 are associate members, most of whom are under ten years of age.[132] This leaves but 5077 as the active, adult membership of the Yearly Meeting in 1912 and, as is always true in religious orders, the interest of many of these is merely nominal.

One other fact must be borne in mind in this connection. In the early period the constituent membership of the Iowa Yearly Meeting of Friends was confined to a much smaller area than it is to-day and was strongly distinctive in character; while of recent years, with weakened and more numerous centers, its members have come more intimately into contact with the outside world, and have all but lost what might be termed distinctive Quakerism.

The reasons for this retrogression are not hard to find. One of the heaviest contributing causes is, without question, the marked decrease in the birthrate among the Friends in this State,[133] together with the struggle which the Society has had to hold its young people. A second reason for the depleted membership of the Iowa Yearly Meeting is the tendency on the part of those who have in later years migrated to the westward from the Quaker centers in Iowa to either enter the fold of other religious denominations or to drop their membership entirely. Thus their names no longer appear on the rolls of the parent Society.

A third powerful factor contributing largely in producing the present condition has been the movement of the rural population to the towns. The

Friends have always been a rural people in the West, and their churches country churches. In this shifting, therefore, large numbers of Friends who have gone to the towns and cities have been absorbed by those denominations to which they felt most inclined.[134] The extent to which this factor has operated is now beginning to be appreciated. It is perhaps no exaggeration to say that to a large degree the backbone of many of the evangelical churches in the West is made up of people who are Quaker either in ancestry or in training or both; and herein lies one of the greatest contributions of this sect to modern religious thought. At a recent ministerial meeting in one of the cities of Iowa a prominent Methodist pastor said: "Gentlemen, there is no longer any real need for the Friends' Church — we are all Quakers at heart."

A deeper investigation into the present condition of the Society of Friends in Iowa and the West reveals what is believed to be the true source of all its troubles, namely, its inability to early adapt itself to new and changed environment. As has been seen, the Friends who first came to Iowa came from both the East and the South, and they brought with them all of the inherited conservatism of the past. Thus, when thrown into contact with the broad spirit of the West, Quakerism received a great shock. In the mould of this new environment racial differences, political ideas, religious creeds, and institutions of every kind were recast, and out of the process there came forth that broad liberalism which character-

izes the West. When the pressure of such surroundings began to be felt by the Society of Friends and
some of its members were caught in the current
instead of attempting to adjust themselves to their
new environment the leaders undertook to purge the
Society by frequent disownments. In one Monthly
Meeting alone there were no less than one hundred
and thirty-seven of such disownments between the
years 1842–1875. This is but an illustration of the
destructive work wrought by this short-sighted
policy among the Friends in Iowa.

Combining, therefore, the influences of the de-
creasing birth-rate, the westward migrations, the
heavy flow into towns and cities where there are no
Friends meetings, the absorption into other more
progressive denominations, and the wide-spread disownment of members, with the internal dissensions
which arose in 1877 and split the Society into two
irreconcilable factions, the real causes for the
present dormant condition of the Society of Friends
in Iowa are apparent.

To gain a true perspective of what the past half-
century has meant to the Iowa Yearly Meeting of
Friends, that organization must be viewed through
the medium of its western appendages. As was
previously stated, the membership of the Yearly
Meeting in 1863 was about seven thousand, chiefly
located about strong centers within the State of
Iowa. By the end of the succeeding quarter-century,
however, this number had increased to 10,234,[135] and
was scattered over the vast expanse of the entire

West, far out to the Pacific coast. Then began the
lopping-off process. In 1893 the two Quarterly
Meetings of Newberg and Salem in the State of
Oregon were set off as an independent Yearly Meeting with a membership of 955 persons.[136] In 1895
the California Yearly Meeting of Friends, with a
membership of 1166 and two Quarterly Meetings,
was likewise set off.[137] In 1908 the field was again
curtailed by the establishment of the Nebraska
Yearly Meeting of Friends composed of Denver,
Hiawatha, Mt. Vernon, Platte Valley, Spring Bank,
and Union Quarterly Meetings, and with a membership of 1679 persons.[138] Not that the Society in Iowa
has dwindled in numbers under these circumstances
but that it has been able to maintain and, in fact,
increase its activities is the marvel.

The history of Iowa Quakerism during the last
fifty years is indeed checkered. Among the older
members to-day there is a wide-spread uncertainty
as to what the future holds in store. The decay of
so many of the early Quaker centers in this State;
the present scattered condition of the constituent
meetings; the lack of sympathy and coherence
among the various sects of the Society in Iowa; and
the general breaking down not only of denominational but even of church ties in general — all of
these facts are disquieting to the Quaker mind.
Nevertheless, for more than a generation there have
been forces at work within the Society of Friends in
Iowa tending towards the modernization of its
ancient teachings and the construction of a religious
organization adapted to the spirit of the times.

PART II
IOWA QUAKER ORTHODOXY

I

THE RISE OF EVANGELISM IN IOWA

In Iowa to-day few are the places where one can sit down in an old-fashioned Quaker meeting. So great have been the changes among the Orthodox Friends that in manner of worship — not to say in worship itself — little real difference longer exists between them and the other evangelical denominations, aside from the religious rites which the latter in some cases observe. The stranger finds little that is distinctive or peculiar, and nothing to embarrass him in the modern Friends meetings. So completely have the ancient Quaker characteristics been obliterated, that those few members of the ancient or conservative body who still live in Iowa insist that their Orthodox brethren should no longer call themselves "Friends", but that they should adopt some name more consistent with their modernized tendencies. It is of interest therefore to trace the conditions which have produced this new form of Quakerism.

The changes in western Quakerism are due to forces which have been brought to bear upon it both from within and from without. The introduction of the Sunday or "First-Day Scripture Schools", the common patronage of the public schools, the adoption of evangelical methods of church activity, and the transition from the isolation of rural communities to modern social conditions and town life, have been powerful factors in the breaking down of that conservatism which in the early days hedged the Friends about on every side. It would be incorrect to single out any one of these forces as being the important factor in producing present-day conditions, for all of them have acted and interacted one upon the other. The one factor, however, which stands out most prominently and which best lends itself to investigation is the rise and development of evangelism. The presence of so large a number of young people in the Orthodox body to-day is the result of this force. Evangelism was the one solution to the great problem of filling up the yawning gaps in the membership of the Society due to the westward migrations, and in it may be found the origin of those forces which to-day dominate and control the Iowa Yearly Meeting of Orthodox Friends.

To imagine that the rise of the spirit of modern Quakerism as expressed in its evangelistic tendencies was spontaneous and the product of a single event at some given place would be a grave mistake. As is the case with all great movements, its origin is to be found in deep-seated and wide-spread causes.

For many years there had been a growing apathy on the part of the Friends toward a careful and regular study of the scriptures. The belief had become prevalent that people would involuntarily be led into such religious exercises as were in accord with the promptings of the Holy Spirit, and that to have a set time for such acts of devotion was strongly tinctured with an unwholesome formalism, always extremely obnoxious to the Friends. The first step in the modification of this belief, as it prevailed in Iowa, was the appointment of a committee by the Salem Monthly Meeting in January, 1841, to visit each family of the membership and find out how many were "destitute of the scriptures".[139] The nine families not possessing a copy of the Bible were early supplied, and then committees were appointed to continue the visitations in order that "parents and heads of families may be encouraged to the daily practice of calling their families together, and after a solemn pause, let a portion of the Holy Scriptures be read."[140]

This breach having been made in the old order of things, the next step was the setting apart of a special time and place for a group study of the scriptures by both children and adults. Herein is to be found the origin of the "First-Day Scripture Schools" (Sunday schools). Until this time the religious instruction of Quaker children had been almost entirely ignored. This new departure, therefore, was of great importance, for the first Sunday school established at Pleasant Plain in June, 1844,[141] was the basis upon which a very large part of the superstructure of modern Quakerism rests.

The next evidence of internal awakening was the appearance of a spirit of revival in the Quaker

7

schools, not only in Iowa, but throughout the whole
field of Quakerism west of the Allegheny Mountains.[142] In the spring of 1865 "The Christian
Vigilance Band" was organized among the students
of Center Grove Academy, about two miles north of
Oskaloosa, with remarkable results;[143] and in 1869
a similar student organization was formed at Whittier College[144] at Salem. Here and there in various
parts of the Iowa Yearly Meeting similar manifesta-
tions of evangelistic tendencies appeared, only to be
speedily frowned down by those in authority. Then,
almost before the Society at large could realize what
had happened, there came an upheaval which all but
overturned the ancient order. Such men as John
Henry Douglas, Jeremiah A. Grinnell, Dr. Ely Jessup, Benjamin B. Hiatt, and John Y. Hoover stepped
forward to champion the new movement. In some
places rash and unseemly scenes occurred. But the
most regrettable attending result was the splitting
off of the conservative element into a separate and
distinct organization in 1877.

The Iowa Yearly Meeting of Friends was thus
brought face to face with its internal condition in
1877, when the older and more conservative members
refused longer to submit to breaches which were
being made in the ancient faith. Then, freed from
their restraining influence, the Yearly Meeting
responded vigorously to the new movement of evangelism. At the annual gathering in 1883 a committee
of forty-two of the strongest members from all parts
of the Iowa field was appointed to take into its care

the evangelistic work of the Society.[145] The committee organized before the close of the Yearly
Meeting by the appointment of a president, secretary, and treasurer. The whole field was divided
into four districts as follows, with an evangelistic
superintendent in each district: 1st, Oskaloosa,
Pleasant Plain, and Salem Quarters; 2nd, Winneshiek, Minneapolis, and Springdale Quarters; 3rd,
Bangor, Honey Creek, Greenville, and Mt. Vernon
Quarters; 4th, Ackworth, Bear Creek, and Lynn
Grove Quarters. Information relative to needs and
opportunities was gathered from every meeting.
Arrangements were made for financing the work,
and the entire strength of the Yearly Meeting was
enlisted with an enthusiasm which gave promise of
success.[146]

For many years the disconnected local and itin-
erant ministry had labored in the field of Iowa
Quakerism with results that were all but imper-
ceptible. The first report of the above committee
indicates the effectiveness of the new movement. It
reads in part as follows:

In a large number of our meetings there have been
revival meetings held, varying from a few days to four
weeks in length, in which about 2,200 persons have been
converted, renewed, or sanctified. . . . Of the number
converted or otherwise blessed, many were our birth-right
members; but in some instances our revival meetings have
been largely made up of people from outside our church
membership, a number of whom were members of other
churches and many unconverted.

Such a report was very pleasing to the Yearly Meeting. It recalled the days of George Fox and the ingatherings of his time. With redoubled energy the committee again set to work. In the reports which came up to the Yearly Meeting for the two successive years of 1885 and 1886 the results were again gratifying — 1310 and 1888 conversions, renewals, and sanctifications, respectively.[147] These reports mark the end of the first stage of the new era, and indicate the beginnings of that new life and vitality which were to gain for the Society of Friends a place among the more progressive religious denominations of the present time.

The second stage of this evangelistic development not only brought into play the personal supervision of one of the most interesting and powerful ministers that American Quakerism has ever produced, but it is also marked by the adoption of that form of organization under which the Yearly Meeting still conducts its evangelistic and church extension work, and which has served as the pattern for nearly all of its other activities. At the Yearly Meeting held in 1886 the unit of evangelistic activity was transferred from the district to the Quarterly Meeting, each Quarter being requested to appoint an evangelistic superintendent for itself, while a ''General Superintendent'' was placed over the whole field.[148] Fortunate indeed was the Iowa Yearly Meeting of Friends in having at this time such a man as John Henry Douglas for so responsible a position. Some idea of the field thus brought under the direction of one man may be gained from the General Superintendent's report in 1887, which reads as follows:

We have churches in Wisconsin, Iowa, Minnesota, Dakota Territory, Nebraska, Oregon, Washington Territory, California, and Texas, and individual members scattered in all the great Northwest. . . . We have about one hundred churches, with an average membership of one hundred. We have about one hundred and forty ministers; some fifty of these in the active work.[149]

That John Henry Douglas entered upon his task with vigor is evinced by the fact that immediately upon his appointment as General Superintendent he opened up correspondence with the ministers and Christian workers in every part of the field, at the rate of ''a hundred letters per month''. During this the first year of his superintendency he says: ''I have received invitations to hold union meetings from a large number of cities and towns, not more than one-tenth of which I was able to respond to.'' Under his own preaching he saw during that year the ''conversion of over six hundred souls'', some people coming from ''fifty to sixty miles'' across the plains in covered wagons with four-horse teams to attend his meetings. During the four years which he devoted to the supervision of this work in Iowa there were 7430 recorded conversions and 2595 persons added in membership by this means to the Iowa Yearly Meeting of Orthodox Friends.

Since the incumbency of John Henry Douglas there have been four successors to the office of General Superintendent, namely: Isom P. Wooten,

Z. L. Martin, W. Jasper Hadley, and Harry R.
Keates. During the twenty-three years that have
since passed away the ardent vigor of the earlier
evangelical movement has gradually subsided, and
the problems confronting these men have been increasingly those of the organization of the fields
already occupied and of promoting a more healthy
and permanent church extension in those communities where already a sufficient number of Friends
have settled to constitute new Quaker congregations.
The evangelistic meetings still play an important
part in the growth of the Orthodox Yearly Meeting,
but this factor has given place to that much more
powerful institution which grew directly out of it,
the pastoral system.

The two main contributions, then, which the
evangelistic movement made to the Iowa Yearly
Meeting of Friends are: first, a new vision of both
the nature and the purpose of the Quaker message;
and second, that thorough organization which char-
acterizes the work of the Yearly Meeting to-day.

II

THE PASTORAL SYSTEM AMONG THE IOWA FRIENDS

The chief distinguishing feature between modern and early Quakerism is the pastoral system. So marked is this distinction that to-day among the English Quakers, where the original order of things so largely obtains, their more progressive brethren on this side of the sea are commonly known as the "Pastoral Friends".

This system, now so prevalent in American Quakerism, is generally considered as having had its rise contemporaneously with the great awakening throughout the order which was touched upon in the previous chapter.[150] In so far as the Iowa field is concerned, however, the groundwork upon which the pastoral system was to be built was well laid years before the modern tendencies became at all apparent. As early as 1845 the Monthly Meeting at Salem appointed a committee with the assigned duty of keeping in touch with its members who lived "remote from this Meeting", either by "writing to them or by visiting them".[151] Then came an extension of the duties of the committee to the care of the local resident membership; and so successful was the experiment that the plan was speedily adopted by other

meetings, and by 1875 a new amendment was
attached to the discipline of the Iowa Yearly
Meeting directing that each Monthly Meeting have
"a committee on pastoral care over the entire
membership . . . . who will be expected to extend pastoral care towards all the flock, by visiting
each family by two or more of their number from
time to time as they shall think proper, ...
to encourage an establishment and growth in the
divine life."[152] Thus the pastoral idea had been
adopted among the Friends in Iowa even before the
Separation of 1877.

As a new medium of self-preservation this plan
was at once seized upon, and at the annual gathering
in 1876 nine out of the ten constituent Quarterly
Meetings were able to report that they had complied
with the above direction to good effect. But this
system soon proved impracticable. The pressure of
work on the farms made it increasingly difficult for
the members of the committees to perform the
church duties laid upon them, and a demand was
made for some one who could devote his entire time
to the work. Thus was the way opened for the shifting of the burden from the committee on pastoral
care to the shoulders of a single individual: the
"hired" pastor and preacher.

By 1871, before the revival movement had gained
headway in Iowa, two Iowa Quarterly Meetings were
unable to report to the annual gathering that their
testimony concerning a "hireling ministry" was
clear.[153] Three years later (1874) a similar breach

was made in the ancient Quaker principle of a free gospel ministry; and from that time on, reference to this time-honored testimony completely disappears from the answers to queries as recorded in the minutes of the Yearly Meeting.

In 1880 the first open step was taken towards a complete breaking with the past. The Yearly Meeting of that year was forced by the more enthusiastic leaders to consider in joint session (men and women sitting together) the proposition that "this meeting cordially recognizes the right of meetings, ... to invite ministers or other Friends whom the Lord has qualified for that service to reside and labor among them, ... suitable provisions being made for their partial, or entire support." It soon became clear that the project had been thrust forward prematurely, and in the minutes of the meeting it was recorded that "way did not open for its adoption".[154]

Owing, however, to the pressure of the large number of converts from the evangelistic meetings held in every Quarter, the opposition to the new order of things soon began to yield. Confronted by the demands of a young and vigorous membership which was not in sympathy with the maintenance of the original customs and precepts of the Society, the older members found it more convenient to suffer the necessary changes to take place than to undertake the long and laborious process of education that would be necessary if the old order were to be maintained. As a result, though not directly chargeable

to the pastoral system, the present generation of
Orthodox Friends in Iowa is surprisingly ignorant
of the ancient and fundamental religious tenets and
teachings of the Society.

The committees on pastoral care and evangelistic
labor now united and worked hand in hand for
a given end. By 1886 the Yearly Meeting was
brought to reconsider its action on the pastoral
system. On the 8th day of September the Ackworth
Quarterly Meeting introduced two carefully worded
propositions on the subject which were at once referred to a committee composed of twenty-four men
and twenty-four women, all prominent members.[155]
Three days later the propositions were favorably
reported and on September 11, 1886, the pastoral
system was recognized by the Yearly Meeting in the
following terms:

1.   That it is advisable for each particular meeting to
have a regular ministry; and that meetings be encouraged
to call and support ministers in laboring among them as
pastors, as far as in their judgment may seem wise and
practicable.

2.   That the Evangelistic Committee of Iowa Yearly
Meeting be authorized to provide as far as possible for the
supply of ministers and workers in meetings desiring such
help, and that they be instructed to give such pastoral advice and aid to any needy places within their knowledge as
the Lord may lead them to see advisable.[156]

Having thus committed itself to the new policy,
the Yearly Meeting entered upon its minutes a
lengthy ''Explanation'', stating its reasons for so

doing. "One of the chief reasons for this action", reads this statement, "is the deplorable fact that many individuals brought to Christ through the labors of our evangelists have been left almost immediately to themselves, and in many instances have fallen away from lack of care and instruction. . . . . Our pastoral oversight has not kept pace with our evangelistic ingathering." Following this explanation the Yearly Meeting proceeded to define as follows the intended bounds of its action — bounds which, as will be seen, have since been largely disregarded:

The action of the Yearly Meeting is not to be construed as giving its Evangelistic Committee general jurisdiction over all individual meetings so as to interfere with their independent self-direction. It is simply to assist as far as possible those meetings desiring help, to give advice and assistance to small needy meetings and little remote companies of believers that they find to be in need of the larger wisdom of the superior body.[157]

The rapidity with which this new system spread throughout the Iowa Yearly Meeting of Friends is to be seen by the fact that one year after its adoption it was reported that three meetings were supplied with pastors who were fully supported, six with pastors who had two or more appointments each, and fourteen with pastors having one appointment each. By 1889 the number of acknowledged pastors had increased to fifty-one, fifteen of whom were receiving full support from the meetings which they served, while thirty-two received partial support.

In 1889 the fifty-one ministers received the total sum
of $6,411.69; in 1900 the amount paid throughout the
Yearly Meeting for pastoral support was $13,305.96;
while in 1912, with sixty pastors in service, the
amount paid for their support stood at $23,677.07.

Although the pastoral system has become firmly
established in the Iowa Yearly Meeting, it still presents many intricate and perplexing problems, and
may safely be said still to be in the early stages of
evolutionary development.[158] Throughout the Yearly Meeting there is apparently a groping after the
right course for the future, based on the unsatisfac-
tory conditions of the present. In the homes, on the
farms, in places of business, on the trains, and
everywhere among the Friends of Iowa the problems of the church are being discussed. The advantages of system and centralization are almost
universally acknowledged. But with the growing
professional tone and formality of the modern
ministry, the manifest decline of congregational
interest and responsibility in the meetings for
business and worship, the marked disappearance of
Quaker simplicity in manner of dress and personal
conduct, and the ever-tightening grasp of a system of
church government which threatens to stamp out the
independence of the various local meetings, many
Friends are filled with forebodings for the future.
Nevertheless, as has been said of the pastoral system
in general, ''it is not clear that equal progress could
have been made under any other form of procedure,
or that without it we would not have lost, e'er this,
most of what was gained through the revival.''[159]

III

THE IOWA ORTHODOX QUAKER MINISTRY

I~ his apology for the "Principles and Doctrines of the People called Quakers", Robert Barclay enumerated the fundamental principles of the Quaker ministry as follows:

As by the *light* or *gift* of God all true knowledge in things spiritual is conceived and revealed, so by the same, as it is manifested and received in the heart, ... every true *minister* of the *gospel* is ordained, prepared, and supplied in the work of the *ministry;* and by the leading, moving, and drawing hereof ought every *evangelist* and *Christian pastor* to be led and ordered in his labour and work of the gospel; both as to the place *where,* as to the persons *whom,* and as to the time wherein he is to *minister.* Moreover, they who have this authority may and ought to preach the *gospel,* though without *human commission* or *literature;* as on the other hand, they who want the authority of this *divine gift,* however learned, or authorized by the *commission* of *men* and *churches,* are to be esteemed but as *deceivers,* and not true *ministers* of the *gospel.* Also they who have received this holy and unspotted gift, *as they have freely received it, so are they freely to give it,* without hire or bargaining, far less to use it as a *Trade* to get money by.[160]

Such was the early Quaker conception of the ministry, and such it remained to a very large extent

109

even among the Friends in Iowa until the pastoral
system was ushered in with all of its attendant
changes. Then came the gradual transition from a
form of religious service in which all the members of
the meeting had equal privileges and responsibilities,
and where the only impelling force to vocal utterance
for either minister or people was the direct leadings
of the Holy Spirit, to a form in which the pastor, as
the remunerated servant of the congregation, was
the chief spokesman and religious guide on all occasions. At the present time a strong tendency
toward formality in the religious services prevails:
when the given hour arrives the minister ascends
the pulpit, a hymn is announced, the organ or piano
begins to play, the choir sings, the scriptures are
read, prayer is offered, the sermon prepared for the
occasion is delivered, another hymn is sung, the bene-
diction is duly pronounced, and the service ends — a
service which is in strange contrast with the simple,
silent meetings which universally prevailed among
the Friends in former days.

That it was not intended by the Yearly Meeting
in Iowa that the introduction of the pastoral system
should thus reduce its meetings for worship to a one-
man ministry and a set routine is made clear by the
statement which opened the explanation accompanying the adoption of the proposed system in 1886:
"By a regular ministry is not meant that a single
person should be placed at the head of a meeting and
do all the preaching, nor that there should neces-
sarily be preaching in every single instance". But

the very conditions which were thus guarded against now prevail almost universally among the Orthodox Friends in Iowa. The religious responsibility of the individual member in the congregation has largely been shifted to the shoulders of the pastor. Under ordinary circumstances he is expected to preach a sermon both religiously instructive and intellectually interesting. If the sermon approaches an hour in length, uneasiness and restlessness is frequently observed. Periods of "waiting silence", once so precious to those who deemed reflection and deliberate thought the best medium for worship, are often periods of embarrassment for both the congregation and the minister.

It is true that there are many meetings among the Orthodox Friends in this State where periods of silent worship are scrupulously observed and where every encouragement is offered for vocal prayer or testimony on the part of members of the congregation; but there is now a strong tendency throughout the Yearly Meeting to sacrifice this, an essential characteristic of the old-time Quaker meeting, to the growing idea that a religious meeting, to be successful, must be kept moving, with no long and embarrassing pauses. It has been pointed out that there is "in the comparatively aggressive attitude we have assumed of late years . . . . a constant temptation to adopt methods less pure, less severely disinterested, than those to which we are pledged by all our traditions."[161] This breaking away from time-honored tenets and customs is one of the great-

est problems which now confronts the Quaker
ministry not only in Iowa, but throughout the entire
country.

Since it is the set policy of the Society of Friends
that "Whatever may be the talents or Scriptural
knowledge of any, unless there be a distinct call to
the ministry, our Society cannot acknowledge it; and
except there be a sense of the renewed putting forth
and quickening influence of the Holy Spirit, we believe it to be utterly unsafe to move in this office",[162]
it is of interest to note the manner in which the
Friends single out those who have this divine gift,
and how they are recognized as ministers. "When a
member, man or woman, has spoken as a minister
. . . . so that the meeting is edified and spirit-
ually helped thereby," the ministers, elders, and
overseers of the local Monthly Meeting are to "carefully consider whether he has received from the
Head of the Church a gift in the ministry which
should be officially recognized." Once this local body
of officers is favorably disposed the matter is taken
up by a committee purposely appointed by the Quarterly Meeting of which the party concerned is a
member, which committee is charged with the duty
of obtaining "information as to the evidence that the
person has received spiritual gifts; as to his manner
of life; his doctrinal views; his mental capacity; and
his general qualifications for the ministry." If the
results of such inquiry prove satisfactory, the
Quarterly Meeting returns the request with its consent to the Monthly Meeting from which it has come,

with authority to "act in the case according to its judgment."[163]

Such in general has for many years been the plan of recognizing ministers in the Society of Friends; but as the result of long prevailing looseness in this important matter, the Orthodox Friends in Iowa have now proposed that the Yearly Meeting appoint five of its most responsible members to act as a "Board on Recording Ministers" to take into its care, in the manner heretofore described, the examination of all persons proposed for the ministry throughout the Yearly Meeting. Under this plan it is expected that more careful and thorough investigation will be made in each case, and thus a higher standard for the ministry will be maintained. The Yearly Meeting itself, in open session, becomes the final acting authority; while the persons concerned are to receive from the hand of the Clerk of the Yearly Meeting "a certificate stating the action of the meeting".[164]

A second set of problems which confront the Iowa Friends in this connection are those which center around the practice of employing a paid ministry. In the light of its traditions there is but one ground upon which the Society can justify this practice, namely, the ground of modern economic and social necessity. In former days the Friends repudiated the idea that men should be remunerated for preaching the truths of a gospel message which was intended to be as free as the air. If, however, in the adjustment of things religious to suit the condi-

8

tions of present-day society it becomes necessary for a man to devote his entire time to ministerial duties, it is the modern view that society in turn should see that such a person be supported, and that without embarrassment, at his highest point of efficiency.

Until a generation ago the Society of Friends at large was tenacious in its opposition to an ''hireling ministry''. In the early days most of the Quaker ministers in Iowa were holders of land which they had acquired by settlement, and they stood on equal terms with all other members of the community, sharing with them all of the hardships common to pioneer life. They cleared their fields, harvested their crops, and gained their livelihood as did their neighbors; and then on Sunday morning they went to meeting to sit in silence or to speak in an impromptu manner as the Spirit gave them utterance. This done, the duties of their station were performed. But such is not the case with the pastoral body of to-day. With but few exceptions, the pastors among the Friends in Iowa are a landless class, dependent for their daily bread, at least in a large part, upon the salary received for their pastoral labors.

That they have been placed in this condition by modern developments is readily apparent. The pastor of to-day is not only considered as the mouthpiece of the community on all religious occasions, but in times of trouble or misfortune he is also looked to as the natural comforter. When difficulties arise, he is expected to be the adviser. When nuptial ceremonies are to be performed he is a necessary guest. When death comes, he is called upon to perform the last rites in honor of the departed. In all matters of uplift in the community his is the part of a leader and guide. Under such conditions a minister's time is entirely taken up with pastoral duties, leaving him little opportunity to gain a livelihood by engaging in other pursuits.

In viewing the Iowa field in 1909 the Meeting on Ministry and Oversight of the Iowa Yearly Meeting drew up the following statement of the conditions then existing:

Our ministers, especially our pastors as a whole, have good educational qualifications. They are thoughtful, industrious and helpful to those under their pastoral care. We have just grounds, however, of fear that some of our ministers are not as successful in soul winning, soul feeding, as possibly they might otherwise be. And what is said of ministers and pastors may in a subordinate sense be said of the members of our meetings on ministry and oversight.[165]

This is a clear statement of the present situation; but for the real causes few people are sufficiently concerned to diligently seek. In the face of an expenditure of $20,546.69 for the maintenance of a pastoral system during the year 1910–1911, during that same year the membership of the Iowa Yearly Meeting decreased from 9029 to 8578; and while there were but forty-one members received from other denominations there were eighty-nine certificates of membership issued to persons wishing to enter other denominations. Of the seventy-one meetings reporting to the Iowa Yearly Meeting in 1912, sixty per cent had less than one hundred members, over eighty-eight per cent fell below two hundred, while but one could boast a membership of five hundred persons. Moreover, about twenty-five per cent of the members of the Iowa Yearly Meeting reside outside of the State.

A few reasons for this condition of affairs present themselves. In the first place, strong leadership is apparently lacking. Twenty-five years ago the Iowa Yearly Meeting of Friends was guided by such strong leaders as John Henry Douglas, Cyrus Beede, and Laurie Tatum. To-day, with the exception of one or two persons who are hampered by adverse conditions, men of this stamp are not forthcoming. In the second place, the starvation wage upon which the ministers among the Friends in Iowa are compelled to subsist makes it almost impossible for a man to enter this field of labor with the fair expectation of raising a family and maintaining a home in keeping with the average standard of living in the community.[166] In the third place, the system of constantly changing pastors is destructive of permanency along the line of church activity and prevents the carrying out of far-reaching policies by the ministry.[167] In the fourth place, as has been seen, most of the meetings of Friends in Iowa are small, and consequently they do not present a strong appeal to young men of ability who are looking for a place for the large and permanent investment of their energies. Finally, the almost universal scarcity of available church funds blocks at every turn the progress which might otherwise be made by the present ministry.

These are some of the causes for the stagnant condition of the Iowa Yearly Meeting of Friends; and these are some of the problems which must be met and solved if in the years that are to come Quakerism is to hold its own in this State.

IV

THE GENERAL SUPERINTENDENT

THE one office which to-day stands out in importance above all others in the Iowa Yearly Meeting of Orthodox Friends is that of the "General Superintendent of Evangelistic, Pastoral, and Church Extension Work". This office had its origin, as its name would indicate, both in the evangelistic and pastoral systems and in the modern demand for a careful supervision of the whole field of the work of the Yearly Meeting. Its history is the record of the labors of the five men who have held the position.[168]

Born at Fairfield, Maine, in 1832, John Henry Douglas, the first General Superintendent among the Iowa Friends, was in the very prime of life when he assumed the responsibilities of this new office. He was trained "according to the strictest sect" of the Quaker faith, receiving his early education at St. Albans and at Hartland Academy in his native State, and later spending three years at the Friends' School at Providence, Rhode Island. By 1858 he was recorded as a minister in the Society of Friends in Clinton County, Ohio; and from there he came to Iowa.[169]

Douglas arrived in Iowa about the time that the evangelistic movement was getting well under way. He entered into the work with an energy and enthusiasm which gave the movement a great impetus. Keen of mind, eloquent in speech, magnetic, and tireless, as the first General Superintendent among the Iowa Friends, John Henry Douglas left his indelible stamp upon the church in a firmly rooted pastoral system and a new membership which to-day constitutes the backbone of the Society in Iowa.

Worn out by ceaseless toil, at the end of four years Douglas's health failed him and he was compelled to give up the superintendency. Before long, however, he was again at work in other fields. Twenty-nine times he has crossed the Rocky Mountains in the course of his labors, and now after sixty years in the ministry[170] he is able to write from his California home that his interest in the work is unabated.

In looking forward to the man who might be chosen to take his place Douglas wrote to the Yearly Meeting in 1889: "I would suggest that my successor should be a man of God, full of the Holy Ghost and wisdom. He should be a man of large experience in both the evangelistic and pastoral work, ... and he should be a man capable of representing the church before the world".[171]

It was upon just such a man that the choice fell. Much like his predecessor, Isom P. Wooten was filled with a zeal for evangelistic work. For five years he labored with a vigor that commanded respect on every hand. Evangelism, pastoral needs, and the internal organization of the fields already occupied, all received his constant attention. For the first

year he reported that throughout the Iowa Yearly
Meeting there were sixty-six ministers who devoted
at least a part of their time to evangelistic work;
while during the five years of his administration the
records show the conversion of 6251 persons through
this means, with 3878 names added to the membership rolls of the church.

The labors which had overtaxed the strength of
John Henry Douglas, likewise proved too much for
Isom P. Wooten and he also was compelled to retire
from the work. At the annual gathering in 1895
Zenas L. Martin[172] was called by the Iowa Yearly
Meeting to the General Superintendency. While the
five years which followed show the same evangelistic
activity which had been displayed under the two
previous administrations, it is to be remembered
that the problems confronting the General Superintendent were rapidly changing. The evangelistic
movement, so far as the Society of Friends in Iowa
was concerned, had spent its force; and the real
problem of the church was that of holding the ground
already taken and the development of a strong life
within. This problem Martin undertook to solve.
He repeatedly called the attention of the Yearly
Meeting to the necessity not only of building up its
pastoral service by the increase of salaries and the
construction of comfortable parsonages,[173] but also
of providing ''homes for our aged ministers, some of
whom in giving their whole time to the ministry
have been unable to provide for the needs of their
declining years.''

Like those who had served as General Superintendent before him, Zenas L. Martin gave a definite
bent to the policy of the Yearly Meeting. In pointing out the fact that "most of our churches, for
years, have followed with studied regularity their
methods, time and place of holding annual evangelistic meetings", he ventured to recommend the
uniting with other denominations where feasible,
both for the salvation of souls and for the upbuilding
of the communities where Friends found themselves
brought into contact with other churches. This plan
has frequently been tried, but of late years with
little or no success so far as Friends are concerned.

Having "received a call from the American
Board of Foreign Missions to take charge of the
mission work in the West Indies", Zenas L. Martin
resigned the superintendency of the Iowa Yearly
Meeting on April 1, 1900, and William Jasper Hadley, then acting as the President of the Executive
Board of the Evangelistic Committee, was appointed
to fill out the unexpired term.[174]

When William Jasper Hadley read the report of
the Evangelistic Committee in the fall of 1900 it was
clear to all that he was the logical successor to the
superintendency. As pastor of several of the most
important congregations in the Yearly Meeting,[175]
as clerk of Monthly, Quarterly, and Yearly meetings,
and as President of the Mission Board he had
known the problems and conditions of the home and
foreign field probably better than any other man in
Iowa. He accepted the office, and for eleven years

he performed the tasks of the position with a devotion and with results which place him alongside of John Henry Douglas for the services which he rendered to the Society.

While the first General Superintendent labored chiefly in the work of evangelism, Hadley concentrated his efforts on the perfection of a more effective form of church machinery. The extent to which the former succeeded has been noted; while to appreciate the full measure in which the latter accomplished his purpose, one must view the organization through which the Superintendent does his work to-day. Hadley persistently urged the consolidation of rural meetings into circuits, the centralization of authority in the hands of the Evangelistic Board, and the establishment of permanent funds for the care of aged ministers and for church extension. He aroused a deeper appreciation of the problems confronting the church.

William Jasper Hadley resigned the office of General Superintendent in the fall of 1911, and Harry R. Keates,[176] a man of wide experience and great energy, became his successor. Evangelistic in his methods, the type of ministry which Keates is bringing to bear upon the home field appears in the following statement from his first annual report to the Yearly Meeting in 1912:

The preaching demanded today is the same that has been blessed of God in the past to the salvation of souls. Man's utterly lost condition, the penalty for sin, the Divine provision for salvation, man's responsibility for accepting this on Divine terms, its results here and hereafter are fundamentals which cannot be ignored.

The vigor with which the new Superintendent entered upon his work surprised and almost alarmed many members of the Society. For some time the meeting at Marshalltown, Iowa, had been torn and rent with factions to such an extent that it was on the verge of breaking into pieces. In a manner that in the light of ancient Quaker democracy seemed arbitrary, the Evangelistic Board intervened and enforced its right to adjust the difficulties. A storm was raised, and the Yearly Meeting was asked to give its ruling in the case.[177]

Keates has also grappled with the problem of re-energizing the ministry of the Yearly Meeting on an evangelical basis. Constantly moving from one Quarterly Meeting to another, he has throughout the field called the ministers and workers into special conferences to discuss the problems of each particular charge. Here again adverse criticism has found expression. Undaunted, however, at passing obstacles, Keates has continued his work with an enthusiasm which promises to put new vitality into the Society.

V

THE CHRISTIAN WORKERS' ASSEMBLY

In 1890, at the Iowa Yearly Meeting on Ministry and Oversight, a project was launched for a ministerial training school by one who felt "a concern for young ministers and workers, that they have the right kind of training, preparation and instruction for their important work." Fully appreciating the fact that the majority of its ministers came from the common walks of life, without having had the advantages of a college education,[178] the Meeting on Ministry and Oversight at once took up the matter. A representative committee was appointed to consider the subject; and in consequence a "Summer School" of four or five days duration was held for such workers at Le Grand, Iowa, in June, 1892.

From the very first the undertaking was a success. So enthusiastic were the forty or more persons who attended the school at Le Grand that plans were made for the holding of a similar school at Earlham, Iowa, the following year. This in turn proved of like benefit to the large number of ministers and workers who assembled; and that fall the movement was officially endorsed and encouraged by the Yearly Meeting. In the fall of 1895 the Yearly Meeting appointed a managing board of six of its prominent members to assume the responsibility of carrying on the work;[179] and at the same time the name "Summer School" was changed to that of "The Christian Workers' Training School", which it continued to bear until 1903, when it was again changed to "The Christian Workers' Assembly"—a name which it still bears.[180]

The Christian Workers' Assembly, throughout the two decades of its development, has found its chief importance in the coming together of the active forces of the orthodox body for mutual consultation over the problems of the church before the convening of the regular sessions of the Yearly Meeting, where the press of business leaves but little time for the thorough discussion of the less tangible concerns of the Society. Here the ministers and church workers from the entire field come more intimately into touch with each other. Here the detailed problems of the ministry are taken up and threshed out in the light of the experience of the whole body. Here new friendships are formed; ministers new to the field are introduced; and a fresh interest, earnestness, and enthusiasm are almost invariably developed. Thus the gathering serves well its purpose in the onward movement of the church.

Since 1893 the "Assembly" has been held at New Providence, West Branch, Oskaloosa, Indianola, New Sharon, Lynnville, and Marshalltown — each time with a program planned to meet the urgent needs of the hour. Such subjects as "Missionary Work, Christian Endeavor, Sabbath School, Church Loyalty, Power of Prayer and Bible Study, Personal

Work, Holiness, Family Religion, Call to the Ministry, Social Life, Moral Issues, Church Literature, City and Country Problems, Music and Militarism"[181] are assigned to capable members of the Iowa body for formal discussion; and usually there are in attendance upon the invitation of the Assembly prominent persons from other Yearly Meetings to lecture on subjects with which they are particularly familiar.

The stand which the ministers as a whole have taken on the tendency toward centralizing control in the hands of a Board on Recording Ministers is clearly set forth in the following resolution, adopted by the Christian Workers' Assembly in 1912:

Resolved, That we believe the final act in recording of ministers should be in the Yearly Meeting and that we ask the Yearly Meeting to request the permanent Board to consider the proposition from Honey Creek Quarterly Meeting referred to them in 1910.

Indeed the resolution went one step further than this in recommending that there be "a clause added requiring a course of reading and an examination on the same".[182]

In meeting the modern demand for a strong, efficient, educated, and spiritual ministry, it is unquestionably true that, aside from Penn College, the Christian Workers' Assembly must be the chief source of supply for the future. It has made itself of vital importance in the modern program of progress outlined by the Iowa Yearly Meeting of Orthodox Friends.

VI

MODERN QUAKERISM IN IOWA

MANY of the fundamental testimonies for which the Friends still seem to stand out in the public mind had served their purpose long before the first Quakers came to Iowa. But during the last three-quarters of a century the Friends in Iowa have had ample opportunity to assert their position upon the problems of justice to the Indian and freedom to the negro, and to express their hatred of war.

Against the evils of the past the people called Quakers were persistent and courageous in their opposition. But an entirely new set of problems now confronts the American people. Social immorality, economic injustice, civic unrighteousness, and ecclesiastical formalism — these are among the evils which are claiming the attention of churches and of reformers at the present time.

In view of the conditions which prevail throughout the entire field of Iowa Quakerism it is not surprising that on every hand thinking Friends are asking themselves the question whether or not the Quakers any longer have a distinctive message. Still to a large extent rural in its membership, the Society of Friends in Iowa has not been brought into direct contact with those forces of economic discontent which are disturbing our large industrial centers. The Quakers have been inclined to hold aloof from the political conflicts which have from time to time convulsed the country[183]— except in their opposition to the liquor traffic. Usually well trained in the home, few Quaker children find their way into the criminal,[184] pauper, or socially degenerate classes of society. Few in numbers as they are in comparison to the whole population of the State, and gifted with a natural religious inclination, the Society of Friends has been comparatively successful in preserving its religious integrity, in spite of the worldliness which has invaded even the most obscure country districts.

Almost universally the Friends in Iowa, including even the Conservatives, have brushed aside those external eccentricities which once marked them out as a peculiar and seclusive people. The orthodox body, as has been seen in the preceding chapters, has adopted modern methods of church activity, if not with the same degree of energy which some other denominations show, still with results which are in marked contrast with their earlier policy of seclusion. To be specific, the Orthodox Friends in Iowa have launched boldly into foreign mission work, spending large sums of money in the enterprise, and sending many of their strongest leaders into the field. They are continually placing greater and greater emphasis upon the importance of higher education, thus preparing their youth to meet the competition of modern life. And they are insisting through every possible channel upon the maintenance of the purity of their ministry and religious doctrines. But with all these changes the question still remains: has the Society of Friends a message for the world to-day?

Until about ten years ago there was little evidence in this country that any satisfactory answer to this question was forthcoming.[185] But now it is safe to say that Quakerism is being given a new meaning in terms of modern life. The ideal of social service has been developed in its midst; and this religious society, which once so scrupulously refrained from contact with the "profane" world, is now preparing itself to take an active part in the work of uplifting humanity. The fact is gradually being recognized that the great need of the world is not more religion, but that religion as it is should touch the common plane of the common man's daily life.

PART III
THE MINORITY BODIES OF FRIENDS
IN IOWA

I

THE ANTI-SLAVERY FRIENDS IN IOWA

In the year 1688 the Friends of Germantown, Pennsylvania, drew up the famous "Germantown Friends' Protest Against Slavery";[186] and from that time on until the last vestiges of the slave power had been banished from America, the Society of Friends stood in the forefront of the struggle for human freedom. The Quakers had been firm and outspoken in their position on this great question for generations. But as the first half of the nineteenth century drew to its close, the Society stood charged by the Abolitionists with having changed its colors and turned pro-slavery.[187]

As has been seen in a previous chapter, most of the Friends who early came into Indiana were from the southern States, where they had come into direct contact with slavery. Having moved into the Old Northwest for the specific purpose of getting away from slavery, these Friends might well have been expected to champion the cause of abolition; but such was not the case. Reserved in manner of life, it had never been "the practice of Friends to make a parade before the public of their efforts in the cause of humanity". "Silently and steadily to persevere in the path of duty, unawed by the frowns of the world'', was, and ever had been, their characteristic attitude. It is not strange, therefore, that in spite of their deep desire to see the complete overthrow of the institution of slavery, the Society of Friends as a whole in America refused to ally itself with the Abolitionists.

In 1838, however, within the Society there began a movement of immense importance to the Indiana Yearly Meeting and to the Quaker settlements growing up about Salem in Iowa. In that year a few interested members convened at Newport, Indiana, to consider what should be their rightful attitude towards the growing anti-slavery movement of the day. Before adjournment twenty-five dollars were subscribed for the purchase of anti-slavery books, tracts, and papers, to be circulated throughout the community. About two years later this work received a decided stimulus by the visit of Arnold Buffum, a Friend and one of the original founders of the American Anti-Slavery Society, who, with the aid of Levi Coffin and others, labored for several months in various parts of the Indiana Yearly Meeting. The New Garden Quarterly Meeting, near Newport, became the focal point for the anti-slavery activities of the Friends in the West, much to the chagrin of the leaders of the Y ·ly Meeting.[188]

Passing from mere abolition sympathizers to active propagan lists, some of the bolder spirits among the avowed Quaker abolitionists undertook to force the Indiana Yearly Meeting for Sufferings into the same activity; but they were at once frowned down

by those in authority. The crisis came at the Yearly
Meeting in 1842. It was in the early autumn, and
the great American compromiser, Henry Clay, was
in Richmond, Indiana, on an electioneering campaign. Upon hearing that the Indiana Friends were
in attendance at their annual gathering, Clay let it
be known that he would like to visit the meeting;
and soon the desired invitation was forthcoming.
Fearing the effect which the presence of so distinguished a slave-holder might have upon their cause,
the anti-slavery leaders called upon him with a
petition signed by about two thousand of their
number, requesting him to free his slaves. In his
adroit manner the petition was put aside; while on
the morrow (Sunday) Clay was conducted to the
Yearly Meeting by its chief clerk, and was given
"one of the most conspicuous places in the house".[189]
On that day, says an eye witness, "Colonization
triumphed over Abolitionism in a large Yearly Meeting of Quakers" and "Henry was informed, that
Friends had neither part nor lot with the Abolitionists!!"[190]

Events led rapidly to disruption. Eight prominent members of the Yearly Meeting for Sufferings
— among whom was the well known Thomas Frazier
of Salem, Iowa — were summarily proscribed for
having "unhappily joined in with these [abolition]
views, and opposed and rejected both privately and
publicly, the advice of that body". When about one
hundred of these dissatisfied members undertook to
hold a meeting in the yearly meeting-house "to con-

sider what course it would be proper for them to pursue'', they were ruthlessly thrust from the building. A committee was also appointed to visit all Quarterly, Monthly, and Preparative Meetings composing the Yearly Meeting for the purpose of reading to each community the "direction" that all members refrain from uniting with any abolition societies, or even allowing their meeting-houses to be used for anti-slavery meetings upon pain of being dealt with.[191]

It was now clear to all that any who desired to array themselves openly against the slave power must do so outside of the Indiana Yearly Meeting of Friends. There was, therefore, but one thing for the abolitionist Friends to do, namely, to organize independently of the parent body. This they did; and at their chief stronghold, Newport, on February 7, 1843, there was founded the "Indiana Yearly Meeting of Anti-Slavery Friends",[192] with four Quarterly Meetings (of which Salem, Iowa, was one) and with a membership which soon numbered about two thousand.

Unique, indeed, in the history of the Friends is this schism over the question of slavery. By setting aside the intense bitterness and the charges and counter-charges flung back and forth between the two factions it is now clear that the real differences lay not so much in the question of the final abolition of slavery, as in the manner by which this end was to be accomplished.

Naturally a disruption within the Society of

Friends on this question attracted wide attention. The London Yearly Meeting, long committed to the cause of abolition, took a deep interest in the affair, and in 1845 sent a deputation of four of its prominent members to the Indiana Yearly Meeting to bring about a reconciliation. The deputation, after a long and wearisome journey, arrived in Richmond, Indiana, on September 29th, just in time to attend the sessions of the Yearly Meeting. Here they perceived the real situation and decided to visit ''these dear *soi-disant* anti-slavery friends in their own respective neighborhoods.''

Immediately upon the close of the Yearly Meeting the four English Friends set out for Salem, Iowa, the most western settlement whither the disaffection had spread. For two long weeks these messengers of good will journeyed westward. On the 26th day of October they reached the village of Salem and from there, on the following day, William Foster, a member of the committee, wrote to his wife:

Here we are, twenty miles west of the Mississippi, 1140 from New York, and, as far as I know, we have now arrived at the most remote point of our travels.

Having crossed the river late Saturday evening, the party arrived at the New Garden meeting on the following morning, ''before Friends were all assembled''; and of the place Foster writes: ''A log house in the open prairie . . . . pretty well filled with new settlers and their children; such a lot of babies as I had never before seen in so small a meeting.''[193]

Upon entering Salem, these English visitors had, as will be seen later, reached the chief station on the "Underground Railway" in southeastern Iowa. Owing to its close proximity to the Missouri border, there had appeared almost at the beginning of the settlement at Salem a line of cleavage between those members of the Society who stood for open defiance of the slave power and those who insisted upon the necessity of working under the cover of secrecy. Unable to conform to the latter policy, a number of the prominent members — among whom were Aaron Street, Jr., Thomas Frazier, Elwood Osborn, Henderson Lewelling, Marmaduke Jay, James Comer, Eli Jessup, Nathan Hammer and Jonathan Cook — early withdrew from the Salem Monthly Meeting, set up a monthly meeting of their own, built a new meeting-house, purchased a five-acre tract of land for a burying ground, and termed themselves the "Abolition Friends".[194]

In accordance with the strict orders of the Indiana Yearly Meeting concerning the Anti-slavery Separatists, complaint against Jonathan Cook and Elwood Osborn was on March 25, 1843, laid before the Salem Monthly Meeting because of their "neglecting the attendance of our religious meetings and for detraction".[195] Care was extended to these two Friends, and after a period of several months Osborn was brought to retract his position, presenting to the meeting the following statement:

Dear Friends I have given way so far as to unintentionally be guilty of detraction and also for taking a part in setting up a separate meeting and attending the same; for which deviation I am sorry and desire friends to pass by the same and continue me a member as long as my future conduct may deserve.

[Signed] ELWOOD OSBORN [196]

From this time on, as the anti-slavery feeling became more and more intense at Salem, scarcely a monthly meeting convened without one or more members being complained against for joining the "Separatists". Jonathan Cook, refusing to acknowledge that he was sorry for the course he had taken, was disowned; and before the year 1845 had drawn to its close, no less than fifty of the most vigorous members of the Salem Monthly Meeting had been dealt with, most of them being disowned.

Having spent Sunday, October 26th, at New Garden, the visiting deputation of English Friends drove into Salem toward evening. There they found rest and comfort; and on Tuesday, the 28th, in response to a call which had been issued by them, they met in conference with the Anti-Slavery Friends in their little meeting-house. "After the meeting had been gathered a few minutes, George Stacey arose to his feet, made a few remarks explanatory of their mission, read the Minute of their appointment, and then the Address from London Yearly Meeting", which, in part, runs as follows:

To those who have recently withdrawn from Indiana Yearly Meeting of Friends:

Dear Friends — This meeting has from time to time been introduced into a feeling of much brotherly concern and interest on your behalf, in consequence of your having withdrawn from the body of Friends in Indiana Yearly Meeting; and those feelings are attended with an earnest and affectionate solicitude for your re-union with them.

.   .   .   .

The considerations which have led us to address you are confirmed on reflecting on the comfort and strength which have arisen from that Christian fellowship and harmony which have prevailed in our religious Society to so large an extent from its rise to the present period; which we can only ascribe to the power of the Holy Spirit, so conspicuously manifested at its first gathering; and every interruption to which blessings must be regarded as a very serious evil.

.   .   .   .

Trusting that on the fundamental doctrines of the Gospel, and on the spirituality of divine worship, there exists no essential difference between you and the body from which you have withdrawn, we have felt much concern and sorrow on hearing that you have discontinued assembling with them to present yourselves together before the Lord. Accept, we beseech you, our earnest and affectionate entreaty that you will relinquish your separate meetings for this purpose — will wholly discontinue them, and again assemble for the public worship of Almighty God with those with whom you have been accustomed thus to meet.

.   .   .   .

With sincere desires that the wisdom which is from above, which is pure, peaceable, gentle and easy to be entreated, may be granted to every one of you on the perusal and calm consideration of this our affectionate address, we are your friends:

Signed in and behalf of the Meeting by

GEORGE STACEY

Clerk to the [London Yearly] Meeting this year.[197]

At the close of this address of admonition and appeal each of the visiting Friends had something to say concerning the occasion. "William Foster", says one who was present, "expressed, in a feeling manner, his gratitude for the opportunity with us, and bore testimony to the precious solemnity which covered the meeting". In response to the "Address", the "committee were informed that our English brethren did not know what they were asking of us, when they required our return to those from whom we have separated, without a removal of the causes of the separation".

After a "full and free expression of sentiment" by those present on the contents of the London "Address", the London Friends withdrew; and the meeting further discussed the matter and appointed a committee to draw up a proper reply on the subject. Early the next morning the following statement, signed by six men and four women, was presented to the deputation:

Esteemed Friends, William Foster, Josiah Foster, George Stacey, and John Allen.

Upon duly considering the advice contained in the Address to us from London Yearly Meeting, to discontinue our meetings for worship, and attend the meetings for worship of those with whom we were formerly associated in religious fellowship, we believe it right to inform you, through this medium, that we cannot accede to the proposition, for the following reasons:

First, because we occupy our present position more from necessity than choice, having no alternative left us, if we would enjoy the benefit of religious society [they had al-

ready been disowned]. Second, because we believe it would
be a virtual surrender of our A. S. [Anti-Slavery] principles. Third, because by so doing we would not be securing
to ourselves the benefits of religious society, nor the fellowship and unity so desirable, unless we are acknowledged by
those you advise us to return to, as Friends in unity, with
full privilege to continue our active exertions in the A. S.
cause, as Truth may dictate, being accountable to the
Society for violations of the discipline only. . . .
Fourth, because by so doing our influence in a society
capacity will be lost, and thus, instead of advancing the
cause of truth and righteousness on the earth, we would
become a hindrance. And fifth, because we are in unity
with Indiana Yearly Meeting of A. S. Friends, and believe
the Advice should claim the attention of our Meeting for
Sufferings.

And, in conclusion, we would further state, that we can
but view the course of London Yearly Meeting, and your
course as a committee, as very extraordinary. That without
ever entering into an impartial examination of the causes
that led to the difficulty that exists between us, and those
we were formerly associated with in religious fellowship,
you enter into judgement, and require us to return, without
an effort to remove the causes of the difficulty that separates
us; which removal would open the way for us to return on
principles that would have a tendency to restore the unity
that is so desirable, but which cannot be restored without
the removal of those causes.

In love we remain your friends.[198]

Having thus failed in their mission to the Anti-
Slavery Friends at Salem, the deputation prepared
to leave for Nettle Creek, Indiana, where they would
pursue the same course. Before their departure,

however, on October 31st they attended the regular Salem Monthly Meeting, which recognized their presence in the following significant statement:

Our Beloved friend William Foster, a minister in company with his brethren George Stacey, Josiah Foster and John Allen, all from England in the prosecution of their visit in passing through these parts have acceptably attended this meeting & produced a copy of a minute from our yearly meeting directing them to the attention of Subordinate meetings whose company and labor of Gospel love amongs[t] us have been satisfactory & edifying.[199]

A last attempt at conciliation on the part of the Anti-Slavery Friends at Salem was made on Saturday morning, November 1st. In response to the urgent request of these Quakers, the English deputation again convened with them to review the situation. The Salem Friends undertook to explain the causes for their separation and the situation in which they were placed; but the commission at once let it be known, positively and clearly, that they had not come to America for the purpose of investigating the right or the wrong in the separation, but that they had come with the specific purpose and under directions to summon the Anti-Slavery Friends, in the name of the London Yearly Meeting, to disband and to return unconditionally to the parent body.

Now came the final clash. Realizing the highhanded manner in which this representation from across the sea proposed to crush them, Quakers though they were, the Anti-slavery leaders exhibited something of the spirit and pioneer courage of their forefathers. The London Friends were plainly told that their mission in America must inevitably widen rather than heal the breach between the two bodies of Friends in the West, and that it would ·likewise have a strong tendency "to retard the work of emancipation in the United States, by throwing the weight of the influence of the Society of Friends in England and America, against the honest laborers in the cause". But such advice was utterly disregarded, and, having visited each of the separatist families at Salem, the visiting deputation left Iowa for the other Anti-slavery Quaker centers to the eastward, displaying at every point the same indisposition to enter into the merits of the controversy, and in turn being met each time with the same unflinching opposition.

The remaining history of the anti-slavery movement among the Friends at Salem and in the Indiana Yearly Meeting can be briefly told. In Iowa these vigorous Friends made Salem one of the most hated spots to the Missouri slave-catcher in the southeastern part of the State. Here, as in Indiana, they gradually drew into their ranks the most energetic spirits of the main body, and forced the whole Society into a more open and sympathetic attitude towards the abolitionists. Gradually throughout the North the term abolition lost its stigma; the leaders of the Indiana Yearly Meeting abandoned their proscriptive measures; and a change was made in the Discipline, making it easy for their brethren to return to the fold. At Salem the Anti-slavery meeting gradually declined through the death of some of its members, the removal of others to other communities, and the return of most of the rest to the main body. The meeting-house was finally abandoned and sold for a dwelling before the opening of the war; and in 1862 the Salem Monthly Meeting purchased the Anti-Slavery Friends' burying ground for the sum of twenty dollars.[200] In Indiana by 1857 scarcely enough was left of the Indiana Yearly Meeting of Anti-Slavery Friends to keep up a Monthly or Quarterly Meeting, and in this year it, too, was abandoned.

10

II

THE HICKSITE FRIENDS IN IOWA

WHILE the difficulties arising out of the Anti-slavery separation were being worked out at Salem, another settlement composed of Hicksite Friends, with which the Salem Monthly Meeting had no connection, was forming in the northern part of Henry County.

For nearly a century and a half after the Friends came to America almost unbroken harmony reigned among them. Then, as outside persecution and oppression of this peculiar people ceased, disruption took place within their ranks which split the Society into two irreconcilable camps, each nursing its animosities down to the present time. This upheaval had its origin in the preaching of Elias Hicks, a strong, eloquent, and powerful minister from Long Island, New York, who traveled far and wide, spreading religious views which to the heads of the church seemed to be unitarian and unorthodox. The movement focused at the Philadelphia Yearly Meeting in 1827, where amidst intense feeling, antagonism, and commotion, the Hicks sympathizers effected a separation from the main body and organized independently. The disaffection, already widespread, was carried to a similar issue in the Yearly

Meetings of Baltimore, New York, Ohio, and Indiana. In places there was great disorder and confusion, followed by appeals to courts of law for the possession of lands, meeting-houses, and schools which each faction claimed. The Yearly Meetings of Genesee, held at Coldstream, Ontario, Canada, and the Illinois Yearly Meeting, held near McNabb, Illinois, to which the Iowa Hicksite Friends belong, did not figure in the bitter scenes of this early separation, but were largely the result of later migration and expansion.[201]

This movement, which so violently disrupted American Quakerism, came to Iowa as a spent force. The first Hicksite Friends to appear in Iowa, so far as there is record, came from the Monthly Meetings of Hopewell, Goose Creek, and Fairfax, in Virginia; and in the northern part of Henry County (Wayne Township) they planted their settlement in 1855 or 1856, giving to it the appropriate name of Prairie Grove.

With an acknowledged minister in their midst, and with some who in their earlier home had occupied the station of elder, these Friends opened up a meeting in a neighboring schoolhouse and made application through their respective monthly meetings to the Fairfax Quarterly Meeting for the establishment of a new Monthly Meeting among them. This request, ''expressing in touching language and great tenderness their painful situation in being deprived of an opportunity of attending religious meetings'', awakened in the Quarterly Meeting ''a feeling of deep sympathy with our absent brethren and sisters, in their remote and tried situation.'' A committee was first appointed to correspond with those making the request; but in November, 1856, the plea was granted, and in the dead of winter, 1856–1857, a committee of five members made their way to this far distant settlement, to assist in officially opening the desired Monthly Meeting.

Providing themselves against the scarcities of the new West, the ''Committee took out with them books, suitably prepared, in which to keep a register of their members, and a record of births and deaths amongst them, to record the minutes of the Monthly Meeting, to record certificates of removal, and marriage certificates. They also took out several copies of our discipline for the use of the members of that meeting.'' They arrived at their destination in safety; and on the 6th day of December, 1856, opened the Prairie Grove Monthly Meeting with all due solemnity.

The one problem which gave the Virginia committee concern in its work of organizing the new Monthly Meeting was the fact that there was no regular meeting-house. The schoolhouse could, as before, be used for First-day services; but the midweek and business meetings, in consequence of the regular school which was conducted during the week, were left unprovided for — a grave matter in point of the Society's discipline. This difficulty, however, was obviated by the gift of three acres of land as a site for a meeting-house and burial grounds by two

resident Friends; while the construction of a meeting-house, estimated at a cost of $1300, "including
sliding partitions, and seats", was also provided for,
the Prairie Grove Friends and the Fairfax Quarterly Meeting each paying half of the expense.[202]

While the Hicksite Friends from Virginia were
thus building their settlement in Henry County, a
prosperous community of the same sect was develop-
ing about West Liberty, in Muscatine County, to the
northward. Among the earliest and most prominent
Friends settling in that neighborhood were John
Wright from Ohio in 1845, Nehemiah Chase from
Ohio in 1848, Witham Haines prior to 1853, Joseph
M. Wood from Ohio in 1853, Stephen Mosher from
Ohio in 1853, and George and Reuben Elliott, both
from Maryland, in 1855.[203] Before long a meeting
was established at West Liberty by the name of
Wapsinonoc,[204] which in June, 1866, united with
Prairie Grove to form the Prairie Grove Quarterly
Meeting, then under the Baltimore Yearly Meeting
but now under the Illinois Yearly Meeting of
(Hicksite) Friends.

By way of comparison, the Orthodox and Hicksite
bodies of Friends in Iowa now present an interesting
subject for study. While the former are progressive
in spirit and modernized in outward appearance; the
latter are more conservative, though not eccentric,
attempting to preserve the distinctive features of
Quakerism in their manner of worship and home life.
The Orthodox Friends in this State have for the last

twenty-five years placed great emphasis on evangelistic activities, upon a developing pastoral system,
and upon both home and foreign mission work; while
the Hicksite Friends have at no time adopted popular evangelistic methods. They have no pastoral
system or paid ministry, and they maintain no
distinct missions, either home or foreign, although
they most energetically support works of general
philanthropy. In the various departments of activity in the Illinois Yearly Meeting, such as ''Rescue
Work'', ''Indian Affairs'', ''Lotteries, Gambling,
etc.'', ''Peace Arbitration'', ''Prison Reform'',
''Temperance'', ''Education and Equal Rights [for
women]'', and ''Interests of Colored People'', the
Hicksite Friends resident in Iowa usually hold
prominent places and take an active part.

In like manner the fields of labor, the numerical
strength, and the problems confronting these two
bodies in Iowa present an interesting and striking
comparison. As has been pointed out, the Orthodox Friends have seventy-one Monthly Meetings,
with a total membership in 1912 of 8383; while
the Hicksites are limited to three Monthly Meetings,
with a membership of 191 persons. As has been the
case with the Society in America as a whole,[205] the
Hicksite Friends in Iowa show almost a steady
decline from 393 members in 1893, to 191 members
in 1912.[206] The causes for this decline are in many
respects identical with those which are responsible
for the decline among the Orthodox Friends. The
increase of death-rate over the birth-rate, the sift-

ing of their young people into the more progressive
denominations, the migratory tendency of their
people — all these are causes for the present pre-
carious condition of the Society. During the decade
1903 to 1912 the records of the Prairie Grove
Quarterly Meeting show but three births. In 1912
less than ten per cent of the membership was made
up of minors; while in the same year almost fifty-
two per cent of the membership of the Quarterly
Meeting was non-resident, scattered over various
parts of Iowa and the States of Alabama, Arkansas,
California, Colorado, Idaho, Illinois, Indiana, Kansas, Louisiana, Minnesota, Missouri, Montana,
Nebraska, North Dakota, Oklahoma, Oregon, and
Washington.[207]

As the older members of the Hicksite Friends in
Iowa now assemble on Sabbath mornings at their
little meeting-houses to sit down together in quiet
and peaceful worship, they have the consciousness of
a past that is full of rich labor; but before them lies
an uncertain future. Like their Orthodox brethren,
they too are located in agricultural communities, far
removed from contact with the life and issues of the
modern world. To-day they seem to have little part
in the world's work. At the same time the results of
years of simple living, linked with a devoted religious faith, are evident among them. Clear of
features, clean of soul, natural in manner, open of
heart, these Friends, few though they are in numbers, may be said to have more nearly preserved the
true characteristics of the primitive Quaker than

have the other sects going by that name in the State
of Iowa, with the possible exception of the Springville settlement of Conservative Friends in Linn
County.

In view of the common Quaker name which the
Hicksite and Orthodox Friends bear, the question is
often asked by the present generation: "Why do not
these two religious sects reunite and combine their
efforts upon grounds that are common to each?"
The impossibility of such a reunion because of the
divergent religious teachings of three-quarters of a
century ago has been pointed out in the pages of the
Evangelical Friends.[208] but it is safe to say that
these religious differences exist more in imagination
than in fact between the two sects in Iowa to-day. In
the most simple phraseology, the Illinois Yearly
Meeting of the Society of (Hicksite) Friends states
the essence of its religious position as follows:

The Society of "Friends" had its origin in 1647–1648
with George Fox, who was educated in the doctrines of the
"Church of England," but who, at an early age, became
dissatisfied with its teachings, and its interpretations of the
Bible; and being led into periods of solitary meditation and
prayer, there came times in which the truths of this book
were opened clearly to his spiritual vision.

The doctrines of the universality and efficacy of what he
termed the "Inner Light;" that consciousness within, that
tells us when we do right, and when we do wrong; the
"still small voice" that spoke to Elijah of old, which has
ever been the watchword of the true Friend, was revealed
to him with such power, that he felt it to be his mission to
proclaim it to the people at large, calling them from de-

pendence upon priests and preachers for instruction in religious duties, to this inner guide.

While we believe in the inspiration of the Bible, and that it is a record of God's dealings with men in the past, and is a treasure house of sublime truths, which, if heeded, will be a great help to us, we believe the spirit that inspired their writing to be superior to them, and to it we look for guidance. We believe that the Spirit of Christ in the soul of every individual is most efficacious in governing action, and saving from sin.

We believe Religion to be a *life* as well as a *belief;* a *practice* more than a *creed.*

We believe in the baptism of the spirit of Christ, of which water baptism is but a symbol.

We are firm believers in the divinity of Christ, which spirit has been always in the world, manifesting itself at different times, and in different degrees, and to different individuals, but in its fullness in Jesus, making him preeminently the Son of God, our elder brother and great exemplar.

As to the manner of our worship we believe in silent communion with our Heavenly Father, during which times of quiet, if the Spirit prompts, we will give utterance to the Truth, as it has been presented to our minds.[209]

A careful survey of this clear and simple declaration of beliefs reveals the fact that there is in it scarcely a line which the Orthodox Friends could not accept as their own; and furthermore, there is scarcely one of their cardinal religious principles which is here omitted. The chief differences which now separate these two religious sects are, therefore, not differences in religious belief, but rather a mass of traditions and a lack of personal acquaintance.

III

THE WILBUR FRIENDS IN IOWA

THE Wilbur-Gurney controversy had its origin in the attacks made by John Wilbur[210] of New England against Joseph John Gurney,[211] a prominent minister of the London Yearly Meeting then traveling in America, for unsoundness in doctrine and for making a religious visit under credentials not properly authorized. The contention first resulted in a separation in the New England Yearly Meeting in 1845. The disaffection then spread to the Ohio Yearly Meeting; and from there it was carried westward to individual centers, such as Red Cedar, Iowa. Concerning the essentials of the controversy it may briefly be said that Gurney undertook to emphasize the authority of the scriptures and the necessity of a thorough knowledge of the same;[212] while Wilbur magnified the direct promptings and revelation of the Holy Spirit, and in addition, held that an absolute knowledge of personal salvation was impossible.[213]

In 1851 two brothers named Hampton, both Friends, settled near the present site of Springville in Linn County, Iowa. Soon afterwards Joseph Edgerton, Francis Williams, Jesse North, William P. Deweese, and William P. Bedell, with their families, also settled in the same neighborhood; and at once they organized a meeting among themselves, under the direction of the Red Cedar Monthly Meeting.[214] These Friends, nearly all from the counties of Belmont, Monroe, Jefferson, Columbiana, Morgan, and Washington in eastern Ohio,[215] had been intimately connected with the contentions then disrupting the Ohio Yearly Meeting of Friends, and they were generally in sympathy with the Wilbur element.

In the spring of 1853, Caleb Gregg, a recognized minister of some force, likewise moved with his family from the same locality in Ohio to Iowa, intending to make his home among his former neighbors. Some of the Friends at Red Cedar had taken an interest in this new community; and soon a certain member called informally on Caleb Gregg, and in the course of conversation inquired ''what he [Gregg] would do, in case a separation should occur in Ohio Yearly Meeting, on the ground of the New England difficulty.'' To this inquiry Gregg candidly replied that ''he should maintain the position he had taken, even if he should stand alone''.[216]

By some channel this information reached the ears of the overseers of the Red Cedar Monthly Meeting, who, feeling that the undercurrent of discontent must be checked, planned to take action at once. A formal complaint was drawn up against Gregg and forced upon the attention of the Lynn Preparative Meeting, of which he was a member. Somewhat astonished by this extraordinary procedure, the meeting proceeded to consider the case, but finally ordered placed upon its records the following minute:

We have given close attention to the subject, have heard the Overseers in all they alleged against him [Gregg], and after conferring together were united in judgment, that there is no just cause for such complaint, or ground on which such charge can be sustained. We find that he is firmly attached to the principles, the doctrines, and testimonies of our Society, as upheld by Fox, Penn, Barclay, and others of our standard writers, and closely united to all our members in the different Yearly Meetings who are concerned to support them. We therefore think it best and right to dismiss the subject.[217]

Disappointed in their first attempt, the overseers now appealed directly to the Monthly Meeting; and through three of their number, on August 9, 1854, they presented to that body a statement which reads:

Caleb Gregg has manifested in one of our monthly meetings and at sundry times elsewhere disunity with the body of Friends and has endeavored to alienate the minds of our members from unity with proceedings and decisions of our Yearly Meeting —, Also in the same meeting and at divers times in other places he has manifested himself to be in unity with the separatists in New England called Wilburites. And at one time in the presence of several Friends he explicitly avowed himself to be in unity with the aforesaid body called Wilburites, for which he has been visited by some of the overseers.

A complaint against him for his deviations was presented to Lynn Preparative Meeting by some of the overseers in 6 mo. last — but said meeting declined to enter the complaint on their minutes; and nominated some of their members to investigate the case; whereupon one of the overseers requested the preparative meeting to direct those nominated to assist the overseers in perfecting the complaint if they should find it necessary; but the meeting declined acceding to the request — And in their last preparative meeting they refused to enter any charge on minute against him.[218]

The Monthly Meeting listened attentively to the reading of these charges and then relapsed into a period of meditative silence. Then followed the appointment of two committees, one to treat personally with Caleb Gregg ''for the aforesaid deviations'', and one to visit the Lynn Preparative Meeting, there to labor ''as ability may be afforded & way opens''.[219]

When the Monthly Meeting again convened in regular session in September the reports of both committees were ready; but Caleb Gregg being present and ''refusing to withdraw'', the presiding clerk called upon the meeting to adjourn. Numerous of Gregg's friends were present and confusion ensued. One elderly woman proclaimed aloud: ''Mark Friends — if you proceed in the course you are now taking, you will be scattered as sheep without a shepherd''.[220]

Amid great commotion an adjournment was carried; and the clerk, gathering up his books and papers, stalked from the building, followed by the main body of the membership. The Gregg party, however, remained in their seats until their brethren

had departed; and when all was again quiet they
appointed a new clerk of their own and at once
proceeded with business under the name of the Red
Cedar Monthly Meeting of Friends, as though
nothing serious had happened.

On the following day, September 7th, the main
body assembled again without disturbance. The
committee appointed to deal with Caleb Gregg
reported him "not in a disposition of mind to make
Friends any satisfaction"; while the second committee reported that "further care" would be
advisable in the case of the Lynn Preparative
Meeting. A month later Gregg was summarily
disowned and judgment was reached that because of
its insubordination the Lynn Preparative Meeting
should "be laid down and the members thereof
attached to Red Cedar preparative."[221]

A few years after this disruption (about 1860) a
number of Wilburites from Ohio, among whom were
Jeremiah Stanley, Benjamin Bates, and Evan Smith,
and their families, settled along Coal Creek in the
northwestern part of Keokuk County, Iowa, and
there built up a prosperous Quaker community.
This meeting, together with the meetings at Red
Cedar (now Hickory Grove) and Whittier, near
Springville, soon united to form what is now known
as the Hickory Grove Quarterly Meeting, by authority of the Ohio Yearly Meeting of (Wilbur) Friends,
which meets at Barnesville, Ohio.

If either the Hicksite Friends in Iowa, or that
body which separated from the Iowa Yearly Meeting

in 1877 may to-day be called conservative, the Wilbur Friends here represented may well be classed as ultra-conservative. In almost every particular and to the minutest detail they have succeeded in preserving the peculiarities, not to say the eccentricities, of Quakerism as it appeared three-quarters of a century ago. Now numbering some seven hundred in all, in spite of the changes which have taken place about them on every side, they have been able to maintain the integrity of their organization to a remarkable degree. While scarcely any members have been added from the outside for more than a generation, and while death and resignation have removed some, still through births within the organization their membership has remained about stationary.

Although almost identical in religious and disciplinary beliefs with their Conservative brethren of the Iowa Yearly Meeting, and although repeatedly encouraged to unite with that body, still the Wilbur Friends have refused to do so officially.[222] They attend the Conservative Yearly Meeting, serve on its committees, and take part in its deliberations, but in reality they do not belong to it. On Sunday morning members of the Conservative body drive from the vicinity of Hickory Grove to their little meeting in West Branch, and in turn numbers of the Wilburites drive some two miles from West Branch over the same road to their small meeting at Hickory Grove, greeting each other kindly as they pass, but holding aloof from union.

The true spirit of this interesting and conscientious religious sect has been well shown in their management of "Scattergood Boarding School", owned and controlled by the Hickory Grove Quarterly Meeting. The school, discontinued in 1913, was situated in the open country about two and one-half miles southeast of West Branch, and was under the care of a committee appointed by the Quarterly Meeting. It was declared to be "intended for the education and especial benefit of members of that religious society"— this statement being strictly construed. The management of the institution was turned over more specifically to a Superintendent and a Matron, who, together with from two to three teachers, provided for all of the needs of the students, numbering in late years from twenty to thirty-five. The following quotations from the catalogue of the school for the year 1909–1910 will show something of the rules and regulations which governed the institution:

The pupils are expected to attend meetings at the Meeting House nearby, and collections on First Days for reading the Holy Scriptures and other religious works.

It is requested that all unnecessary noise, such as whistling, singing, or loud, boisterous laughing, or hallooing be avoided by the pupils.

.   .   .   .

Pupils are not expected to take newspapers or other periodicals while attending school.

.   .   .   .

Finger rings, class pins and other jewelry should not be brought to the school.

FOR BOYS.

Two or three suits of plain, substantial goods; if of figured or plain goods the figure should be small and inconspicuous. A rolling or falling collar shall not be allowed on either coat or vest; sweaters, if worn, of solid black or brown, or grey, without cape.

.   .   .   .

FOR GIRLS.

Three or more suits to be made of plain worsted or other materials of small figure and not so light as to require frequent washing, and made with plain waists. No ruffles or unnecessary trimming on any garment. Silk not allowed.

.   .   .   .

The girls are expected to part their hair in the middle and comb it down plain and smooth. If ties are worn, plain colors, black, white, or brown. No useless ribbons allowed on any occasion. As head dress, a hood of plain make and color is recommended for ordinary use, and a plaited or plain drawn bonnet for other occasions. Hats are not to be worn.

.   .   .   .

Pupils are tenderly advised to check the arisings of pride in their hearts, and cherish instead a true regard for the truth, that no desire may be fostered to imitate the ever-changing fashions of the world inconsistent with that simplicity heretofore enjoined.[223]

Such a system and set of rules, when applied to the younger generation seem strangely in contrast with modern ideas relative to the government of boys and girls; and yet, in actual practice in this specific instance, it is safe to say that the Wilbur Friends in Iowa need not be ashamed of the results

11

produced. Though naturally somewhat narrow in general outlook, what with wholesome food, exercise, and rural surroundings, together with their strict application to mental and religious training, it is believed that the young men and women there developed have generally surpassed in stability and strength of character the average product of the neighboring public schools.

IV

THE CONSERVATIVE FRIENDS IN IOWA:
THE SEPARATION OF 1877

THE Iowa Yearly Meeting of (Conservative) Friends, now numbering in all about four hundred members,[224] meets alternately in its annual gatherings at Earlham, Madison County, and at West Branch, Cedar County, Iowa, usually during the second and third weeks of September. This independent body of Friends is, as has been elsewhere indicated, the result of the separation which took place in 1877 between the conservative and the more progressive members of the Iowa Yearly Meeting of Friends, principally upon the grounds of the introduction of evangelistic methods and upon the departure of the majority from the primitive precepts of the Society. This separation had its counterpart in other Yearly Meetings and marks the last of the important schisms among the Friends in America.

The troubles which culminated in the separation of 1877 were years in developing. With the rise of a new generation of Quakers in Iowa, together with the gradual loosening of the rigid bonds of custom in many of the Quaker homes in this State, conditions developed which soon became intolerable to those who stood for the old order of things. In the year

1867, at the Bear Creek Meeting in Madison County, there occurred the first serious contest, so far as has been discovered, between these two growing factions.

In that year, two Friends, Stacy Bevan and John S. Bond, both ministers with minutes for religious service from the Honey Creek and Bangor Monthly Meetings, respectively, stopped at Bear Creek on their way to visit among the Friends in Kansas, and there held a meeting. Of this occasion Stacy Bevan writes:

We made a brief stay at Bear Creek and held one public meeting at least, where the power of the Lord was wonderfully manifested. Many hearts were reached and all broken up, which was followed by sighs and sobs and prayers, confessions and great joy for sins pardoned and burdens rolled off, and pressious fellowship of the redeemed. But alas, some of the dear old Friends mistook this outbreak of the power of God for excitement and wild fire and tried to close the meeting, but we kept cool and held the strings, and closed the meeting orderly.[225]

During the ten years following this incident "general" or revival meetings became more and more prevalent in various parts of the Iowa Yearly Meeting. For a time no attempt was made to control these meetings; but by 1872, because of irregularities and occasional disturbances which had occurred here and there, a conviction had come upon the Yearly Meeting that "the time has come for this meeting to engage in such a work, by setting apart a committee to arrange for, and have the oversight of, General Meetings for worship, and the dissemination of the principles of the Christian religion, in conjunction with similar committees of the Quarterly and Monthly Meetings.'' This official recognition of the new system, so sweeping in its extent, aroused a storm of opposition and marks the beginning of the end of unity in the Yearly Meeting.

The four succeeding annual gatherings of the Yearly Meeting which assembled at Oskaloosa seemed peaceful enough; but beneath the surface there was a growing discontent which but awaited a favorable opportunity to give vent to its pent up force. The break came in one of the most conservative centers in the Iowa field, namely, the Bear Creek Quarterly Meeting.

Immediately upon the close of the sessions of the Bear Creek Quarterly Meeting in February, 1877, a revival was opened in the meeting-house by Benjamin B. Hiatt and Isom P. Wooten, both ministers of great power. The meetings began on a Sunday evening, continuing with an ever deepening interest through the morning, afternoon, and evening sessions of Monday and Tuesday. On Wednesday morning to a crowded house the call was made ''for all those who wished to forsake sin and lead a different life to come to the front seats.'' Despite the fact that of all things repugnant to the Quaker mind mourners' benches and religious excitement were the worst, when the call was made ''about twenty arose at once and came. Others followed, some not waiting to reach the isles but stepped over seats. Great confusion followed. Some who did not come forward were visited at their seats where prayer groups were formed. Some were praying, others weaping aloud, some pleading, and occasionally a stanza of a hymn would be sung.''

To those who all along had been displeased with the revival methods, such a scene in their quiet meeting-house was simply intolerable; and in utter astonishment and consternation they arose and abruptly left the meeting. ''One elderly woman, before departing, standing in front of the 'mourners bench,' declared that the Society of Friends was now dead, that this action had killed it.'' On the following day the revival came to a close, with a session which ''continued over five hours without intermission'' in which the ''feeling was intense''. When the meeting broke up with the shaking of hands ''some wept [while] others laughed''; and in the midst of it all a deep consciousness prevailed that a breach had been made which would inevitably result in a separation.

Three months passed by as the offended Friends cautiously thought their way through the painful difficulties which now confronted them. On the 29th day of May they reassembled at Bear Creek to solemnly consider the ''present and sorrowful condition of our beloved and once favored society''. Under what they believed to be the guidance of the Holy Spirit, and with an eye to the future in justification of the course which they were about to take, the assembly drew up the following statement relative to the conditions then existing in their midst:

The prevalent practice of endeavoring to induce dependence upon outward means, thereby drawing away from the spirituality of the gospel, and to settle down at ease in a literal knowledge and belief of the truths of the Holy Scriptures.

To set individuals at work in the will and wisdom of the natural man to comprehend and explain the sacred truth of religion to bring them down to the level of his unassisted reason and make them easy to the flesh.

The running into great activity, in religious and benevolent undertakings showing an untempered zeal by taking up one particular truth and carrying that to an extreme to the exclusion of other important truths.

A tendency to undervalue the writings of ancient Friends, and to promulgate sentiments repugnant to our Christian faith. . . .

The introduction into meetings for worship much formality in the way of reading and singing and in the character of the ministry and prayer.

The manner in which general meetings are conducted, leaders being selected to conduct the exercises who many times point out and dictate services, also the introduction of the mourner's bench and the manner of consecration the disorder and confusion and ex[c]iting scenes attending many of them wherein the young and inexperienced are urged to give expression to their over-wrought feelings in a manner inconsistent with our principles.

In a word, the whole procedure and spirit of the old-time Quaker meeting had been overturned; and in the process those who stood for the old order of things had gradually been displaced from positions of authority. It was to meet this situation, therefore, that those in conference were moved to declare:

We believe that the time is now fully come when it is incumbent upon us to disclaim the appointment of all the offices imposed upon us by the nondescript body now in the seat of church government and replace them by those in unity with the doctrine and in favor of supporting the ancient principles and testimonies of our society.

So clear was this declaration that no one could mistake its meaning. Sympathetic leaders in each of the subordinate meetings of the Bear Creek Quarter were given copies of the statement, with instructions to carry it into effect as best suited the condition in their individual localities. On Saturday, June 16th, the North Branch Monthly Meeting assembled for business, and the project was there first launched. Such confusion attended the attempt of the Conservatives to displace the regular clerk that in dismay they finally withdrew to the yard and in a brief conference decided to reassemble for separate organization on the following Wednesday; while the Friends within continued their meeting as though nothing had happened. At Bear Creek the Separatists, if they may be spoken of as such, took the precaution to assemble separately from their brethren, and at the schoolhouse on June 30th they organized an independent Monthly Meeting. At Summit Grove a similar plan was followed with no attendant friction.[226]

On August 12th the three Monthly Meetings thus segregating themselves united; and when the Iowa Yearly Meeting convened at Oskaloosa on September 5th there were two sets of reports presented from

Bear Creek, each purporting to be from that Quarterly Meeting. The subject was at once referred to the representatives present from all the Quarterly Meetings — Bear Creek excepted — for action; and in their report on the following day they said that parties to each side of the controversy had been present and made their statements, "which we considered to the best of our judgment, and we were entirely united that the reports signed by Jesse W. Kenworthy and Catherine R. Hadley as clerks [representing the progressive sect], are the reports of Bear Creek Quarterly Meeting." The representatives further suggested "that a committee be appointed by the Yearly Meeting, to labor within the limits of Bear Creek Quarterly Meeting, with a hope, that through the blessing of our Heavenly Father there may be a restoration of the harmony that appears to be interrupted in that Quarterly Meeting."[227] This recommendation was approved and the committee was duly appointed.

Those determined upon separation had secured two distinct advantages by this action of the Yearly Meeting. In the first place, they had gained widespread publicity for their cause through this treatment of their case by the representatives from all of the Quarterly Meetings; and in the second place, the refusal by the Yearly Meeting to recognize their reports and delegates gave them strong justification, so they considered, for withdrawing from that body. They accordingly issued a general call for all who were in sympathy with them to meet in a building at

Oskaloosa which had been secured for the purpose;
and on September 7th, under the following minute,
the Iowa Yearly Meeting of (Conservative) Friends
was organized:

In consideration of the various departures in doctrine
and principle and practice brought unto our beloved Society
of late years by modern innovaters who have so revolution-
ized our ancient order of the church as to run into views
and practices out of which our Early Friends were led, and
into a broader and more self pleasing and cross shunning
way than that marked out by our Saviour and held by our
ancient Friends and who have so approximated to the un-
regenerate world that we feel it incumbent upon us to bear
testimony against all such doctrines principles and practices and sustain the church for the purpose for which it
was peculiarly raised up, and in accordance therewith we
appoint Zimri Horner clerk for the day.

Thus arose the Separation of 1877 which was
soon to complete itself by spreading into two additional Quarterly Meetings in Iowa.

V

THE CONSERVATIVE FRIENDS IN IOWA: SEPARATION AT SALEM AND SPRINGDALE

Upon the adjournment of the two rival Yearly Meetings at Oskaloosa, the Friends in attendance returned to their homes in all parts of Iowa and related the story of what had transpired. For days and weeks in almost every Quaker home in Iowa separation was the common topic of discussion. Many there were who had long felt dissatisfied with the course affairs had for years been taking but who still were not ready to break from the meetings they loved; while there were others who were led at once to aid in promoting the separation.

At Salem, naturally a strong center of conservatism, a separation was not long in being effected. Side by side in the minutes of the Salem Monthly Meeting for August 2, 1879, it is recorded that meetings were being held in the surrounding country by the students of Whittier College, and that "about 20 of our senior members who neglected Mtgs. for a year or more and manifested their disunity with the Church at large organized a separate society under the name of 'Friends' ".[228] In the same month the report sent to the Quarterly Meeting from Pilot Grove gave notice that forty-three of its members had withdrawn and established a separate meeting.[229]   Under the leadership of such men as Peter Hobson, Ephraim B. Ratliff, Thomas Nicholson, James Pickard, John R. Brown, and Mathew Trueblood a new Salem Quarterly Meeting was organized and a report was made to the Iowa Yearly Meeting of (Conservative) Friends in 1879.

Separation next appeared in the Springdale and West Branch neighborhoods; and although slow in its development, it proved to be unique both in the manner in which it took place and in the way in which it has since persisted. The first recorded evidence of the rising discontent at Springdale is to be found in the resignation from membership of Thomas Montgomery, a prominent and influential member of that meeting. The manner in which he met the committee appointed by the Monthly Meeting to treat with him on the subject illustrates well the spirit in which the whole separation was conducted in this Quarter, much in contrast to the more violent scenes that transpired at both Bear Creek and Salem. The report of the committee rendered on May 21, 1881, reads:

We have had an interview with Thos. Montgomery on the subject of his resignation, in which he gave us in a kind Christian spirit, the reasons for the step he has taken. As chief among these reasons he mentioned changes in our manner of worship, which seem to him to be gaining ground, such as singing from books & in companies; & the practice of calling on one another to pray, & responding to such calls, in public, which he spoke of as admitted & practiced by ministers & others among us. Regarding such practices as inconsistent with the doctrines of Early Friends, while expressing warm attachment to our ancient principles & to his neighbors & friends, he is best satisfied to release himself from responsibility for these things by withdrawing from membership with us.[230]

At West Branch, near Springdale, Archibald Crosbie, Clarkson T. Penrose, and Jesse Negus led the movement looking towards separation. Those who were among the discontented met on January 1, 1883, and organized an independent meeting, arranging for the use of the Baptist church as their future place of meeting.[231] It was not until April 21st, however, that cognizance was taken of the fact; when the West Branch Preparative Meeting complained to the Springdale Monthly Meeting of the first two persons named above for assisting "in setting up a meeting for worship contrary to our discipline."[232]

In the Baptist church this growing group of Quakers devoted to the principles of their ancient faith, continued to meet Sunday after Sunday during the spring and summer months, entirely independent of, and out of touch with, any other organized religious body in Iowa. Conscious of their isolated position four of their number attended the Yearly Meeting of (Conservative) Friends held at North Branch, Iowa, in the fall of 1883 for the purpose of feeling their way towards a union with them. So hearty was the welcome which they received and so congenial were the conditions which they found there

that when they returned to their friends at West
Branch it was with the recommendation that such a
union be perfected at the earliest possible time.
Action was taken accordingly, and when the Iowa
Yearly Meeting of (Conservative) Friends convened
in 1884 there appeared a new Quarterly Meeting
upon its roll, namely, Springdale (now known as the
West Branch Quarterly Meeting), with Jesse Negus,
Clarkson T. Penrose, Abram Wilson, James Hawley,
Erick Knudson, and James Hadley as its repre-
sentatives.[233]

VI

THE NORWEGIAN FRIENDS IN IOWA

ALONG the southeastern border of Marshall County, in Le Grand Township, and almost mid-way between the railway stations of Le Grand on the Chicago and North-western, Dunbar on the Chicago, Milwaukee, and St. Paul, and Dillon on the Minneapolis and St. Louis railroads, there is one of the most unique and interesting Quaker settlements in Iowa. It is the Norwegian community bearing the name Stavanger.

The first of these Friends from the land of the midnight sun to appear in Iowa came with a group of their fellow-countrymen, who founded the settlement of Sugar Creek, Lee County, in 1840. Soon, however, a dissension arose in the settlement. Some of the company adopted the Mormon faith, then spreading in the southeastern corner of Iowa; while the Quaker members of the settlement moved northward into Henry County, near Salem, and there built a Norse meeting-house for their use on the farm of Omund Olson in 1842.[234] Free from the ecclesiastical oppression and compulsory military service of the home-land, and from contentions among themselves over religious differences, they lived here in peace and plenty for a time. Before long, however, the rigor of long winters was missed,

the news of better and cheaper lands to the northward came to their ears, and once again they moved
on to build new homes and settlements, leaving
Sugar Creek to decline and disappear.

The first of these Norwegian Friends to find their
way to Marshall County were Soren and Anna
Oleson. Having made the acquaintance at Salem of
Thomas McCool and his wife, Julia Ann (a minister
of prominence in the Society of Friends), both of
whom were much away from home in their religious
travels, the Olesons were induced to take charge of
the McCool farm in Marshall County, near LeGrand.
They moved there in 1858, and found a climate that
was delightful and a soil surpassed in fertility by
none in Iowa. They early purchased a small tract of
land and then sent word to their friends concerning
their attractive new home.[235] Within a year an old
neighbor, Thore Heggem, came with his family direct
from Norway and settled to the south of Le Grand.
In 1861 Christian Gimre came with his family from
Wisconsin; while in 1864 Mathias Huseboe and
family, together with a number of young people,
came from Norway and settled in the neighborhood.[236] Thus began the settlement of Stavanger,
named after the community in Norway, from which
most of its members had originally sailed.[237]

For a time the Friends at Stavanger regularly
attended the recognized meeting at Le Grand; but
being unable to understand much of what was said
in English, they requested the privilege of holding a
meeting for worship among themselves. In 1864 the

request was granted, and under the care of the Le Grand Monthly Meeting an ''Indulged Meeting'' was set up at Stavanger.[238] At first, as was common in the West, the meetings were held in the nearby schoolhouse or at private homes. Later, about 1870, ''an old building was purchased'' for meeting purposes; and finally, this gave place to the present more attractive though strictly plain structure which preserves all of the primitive features of a Quaker house of worship.[239]

An episode of peculiar interest in connection with the history of the Stavanger settlement was the arrival in 1869 of about fifty newcomers direct from Norway. In the year 1853, Lindley Murray Hoag, one of the most powerful and widely traveled ministers among the Friends in Iowa, had an impression that he should make a religious visit to the Friends in Norway; and in connection with this impression he claimed to have been given a clear mental image of the place he was to visit, though its name and location were entirely unknown to him. True to his inner promptings, he made the long journey. Upon his arrival in Norway, the Friends there ''received him most kindly, and several of them, among whom was the able interpreter, Endre Dahl, went with him to all places where Friends were found''. Dahl finally informed him that they had now made the rounds, but Hoag did not feel satisfied. ''A map of Norway was placed before him, but that did not give him any help.'' He became uneasy, fearing that his mission was a failure, when suddenly, looking out

12

from a little window across the mountains to the eastward, he exclaimed: ''There, over there, is the place where I must go.'' Dahl led the way; and among the mountains, in the valley of Roldol, they found a people who, although they had never heard the Quaker message, responded eagerly to the simple religious truths which fell from the lips of their strange American visitor.

Soon after the visit of Lindley Murray Hoag to this mountain fastness in Norway, many of the people of Roldol Valley united to build a church and joined themselves with the Society of Friends at Stavanger. Almost at once persecution arose over the questions of military service and their relation to the priest; but rather than give up their new found faith, some fifty of them banded together, ''left Stavanger in a sailing-vessel bound for Quebec, Canada,'' in search of a refuge in the New World. From Quebec they continued their journey to the westward; and, ''one day'', says John Marcussen in writing for the *Friend's Intelligencer,* ''all these people came to Le Grand, Marshall County, Iowa.'' They had not forgotten their visitor from America, and though they knew but little of the English language the one word ''Iowa'' was very familiar to them.[240]

Foreign by birth and conservative by nature, the Stavanger Friends early found some things not to their liking in the meetings to which they were subordinated. In 1871 they entered protest against the ''mode of raising money by apportionment'';[241] and by 1885 so discontented had they become with their church connections that they withdrew from the Orthodox body and united with the Iowa Yearly Meeting of (Conservative) Friends.[242]

As unremitting toil soon won for this sturdy Norwegian folk the blessings of material success, they set to work to provide for their children the means for a better education than they themselves had had. In 1888 they submitted to their newly adopted Yearly Meeting a project for founding a school of advanced grade in their midst.[243] The Yearly Meeting's committee on education, to which the subject was referred, at once took action. In the fall of 1891 this committee reported that a two-acre tract of land had been purchased for a campus, that "a building twenty-six by thirty-six feet, two stories high, with a stone basement for dining and cooking purposes" had been nearly completed, and that a school was in operation with Anna Olson as matron and Anna Yocum as teacher. The expenditures, amounting to $2,741.25, had been nearly all met by subscriptions, and there was an indebtedness of but $81.50.[244]

The new "Yearly Meeting Boarding School" at once became popular. When the educational committee presented its report in 1890 there were in the Yearly Meeting 121 children of school age, thirteen of whom had, during the year, attended schools which were under the care of the Friends. By 1892 this number had increased to 128 children of school age, sixteen attending the Boarding School, and

thirteen attending other Friends' schools; while of
the 146 children reported in 1893, thirty-six were
attending Quaker schools, and the enrollment at the
Stavanger school had increased to sixty-three
students for the year.[245]

No exertion was spared to create for the Stavanger institution a healthful religious environment
and a strong moral tone.[246]   For a time it gave
promise of a considerable growth; but with the rise
of neighboring high schools and the removal and
death of many of its most ardent supporters, there
has come a marked decline of late years.   For the
academic year 1910–1911 there were but twenty-one
students in attendance; and at the Yearly Meeting
held at West Branch in 1912 it was a grave question
whether the Stavanger School should longer be
continued.[247]

To-day, it is true that Stavanger has lost much
of its unique and distinctive character.   Many of the
first settlers have either died or moved away; while
a new generation, untutored in the ways of the
fathers, has arisen.   But still there is much of
interest about the community.   There on the prairie
still stands the quaint little meeting-house, sombre
and silent; while here and there within the un-
pretentious homes of this congenial folk, one may
find some aged Friend still clinging to his mother
tongue and to the ancient customs of the Quakers.

VII

QUAKER CONSERVATISM AND ITS FUTURE IN IOWA

In view of what has been said in the foregoing pages it must now be clear that unless some great change takes place, the Friends of whatsoever branch in Iowa are not likely to become a numerous or influential body in the immediate future. This is an age of progress. The spirit of modern life has penetrated to the most secluded communities. For any people to avoid contact with the outside world is well nigh impossible under existing conditions.[248] Herein lies the struggle of the Conservative Friends in this State.

For the most part those who withdrew from the Iowa Yearly Meeting of Friends on the ground of departure from the primitive customs of the Society were the middle-aged and elderly members. Out of harmony with the free spirit of the rising generation, they have from year to year, like the Wilburites, received almost no additions to their membership. Almost every year one or more of their leaders pass away, there is a gradual thinning of the ranks of the older members, and the attachment of the young people to the order steadily declines.[249]

The first serious blow to their cause came in 1891,

when in the following words came the request that
the Salem Quarterly Meeting be closed:

After deliberate consideration on the subject, we are
united in requesting that this Meeting [Salem Quarterly
Conservative] be discontinued, and that its members be
attached to West Branch Quarter. Our greatly reduced
numbers by death, removals and resignations, together with
the remoteness from Meeting of the most of our members
are the reasons for our making the request.[250]

With the death of their two most prominent
ministers, Harvey Derbyshire and Ephraim B. Ratliff, the spirit of the Conservative body at Salem,
weak from the beginning, was broken; and in response to the above request their meeting was
discontinued.

Among these Conservative Friends there is a
grave feeling of uncertainty and anxious care relative to the years that are to come. The records of
their Yearly Meeting in Iowa from 1880 to 1912
seem almost wholly concerned with matters of
internal interest. There is little reference to broad
lines of religious activity, such as home or foreign
missions, temperance reform, the men and religion
forward movement, or social service. Their roll of
meetings is annually called and responded to with
little change. Epistles are received from the Yearly
Meetings with which they correspond, and these are
answered after the accustomed style. But of the
world at large and the great issues of the hour they
appear unconscious and unconcerned. They seem
little to realize the great lesson of unprogressive

Quakerism, or the truth of the ancient proverb that "Where there is no vision, the people perish."[251]

In conclusion, it may be observed that while a persistent spirit of conservatism has led the smaller body of Orthodox Friends in Iowa into a state of stagnation and apparent decline, a growing disregard for its original tenets now threatens to leave the larger Yearly Meeting little that is distinctive in character except its denominational name. Is there not somewhere between these two extremes a happy medium, which would be advantageous to both? It is possible that the rising generation in both sects, freed from old-time prejudice and imbued with the broader spirit of the twentieth century, may find sufficient common ground on which to reunite. Indeed, the trend of events would seem to point in that direction.

PART IV
BENEVOLENT AND EDUCATIONAL ENTERPRISES

I

THE IOWA QUAKERS AND THE NEGROES

AMONG the Quakers there had long prevailed the feeling that of all "the various calamities which flow from the ambition and cupidity of man, there are few productive of more extensive and distressing evils, or which give rise to greater degrees of human misery and wretchedness . . . . than the African Slave Trade"[252] and the great institution of slavery.

ON THE MISSOURI BORDER

Hardly had the members of this religious sect planted their homes upon the free soil of Iowa before two families arrived at Salem, direct from Virginia. One of these families brought to the frontier community an old negro mammy who had for years been in the family as a domestic slave. Such an arrival was of course unwelcome at Salem; and in no uncertain manner and with no waste of time, the newcomers were made aware of the fact, their attention being called to the prohibitory clause of the Ordinance of 1787. As a result, a part of the company disappeared for a time, only to return before long with "one beast of burden, and the remnants of an old store", which they had somewhere received in exchange for their human chattel.[253]

With the rapid settlement of the Iowa country, its rise to the stage of an organized Territory, and the bitter dispute over the southern boundary question,[254] the troubles of the Missouri slaveholders began. As water percolates through unknown passes in the rocks, so the news of a possible escape from their bondage in some way reached the ears of negroes across the border, and raised within their breasts the hope of freedom. Taking his life in his hands, some unknown slave made his way to safety, then another, and another, each opening wider the way for those who were to follow. Salem, but twenty-five miles from the Missouri line, and surrounded by numerous wooded streams well adapted for hiding, proved for the negro a most advantageous place at which to stop for food. The unfailing help which they there received soon became widely known. Could he but reach the town where lived the people of plain grey clothes and broad brimmed hats, the fugitive was assured of safety.

Having noted the separation among the Friends at Salem on account of the anti-slavery agitation, the reader is prepared for a recital of the events which transpired in that quiet little village. What with the heavy loads of human freight concealed within hollow loads of hay or beneath grain sacks filled with bran, and the strange proclivity of this Quaker folk for midnight drives to unknown mills or markets, large numbers of fugitive slaves were spirited away to safety by that mysterious route which justly gained the name: "Underground Railway". Month after month and year after year with Quaker-like precision this work went on at Salem — not a single slave being retaken, it is said, once he had reached this community. The children in the homes were trained to ask no questions, much less to answer any asked by strangers. They were supposed to have no eyes and no ears concerning this solemn business. Among the adults vague but well understood terms were used in conversing on the subject; and while it is certain that this grave concern was frequently the subject of guarded discussion in the two Monthly Meetings, still on the records no written reference to the subject is to be found.

Fruitless were the patrols which the Missourians kept on the road to this Quaker center. At last, stung by their failure to uncover the nest of "nigger thieves", they determined to destroy the entire community. The specific event which led them to this drastic decision occurred at Salem in 1848.

About June 2nd of that year, nine slaves owned by one Ruel Daggs of Clark County, Missouri, made their escape into Iowa; and being pursued, they were found hidden among the bushes about a mile to the south of Salem by two slave-catchers, Messrs. Slaughter and McClure. The captors at once seized their prey, and were in the act of leading them back to bondage when they were met face to face by three stalwart Salem Quakers, Elihu Frazier, Thomas Clarkson Frazier, and William Johnson. One of the Quakers demanded that the negroes be taken to Salem, and there before a Justice of the Peace be identified as fugitive slaves before they be returned to Missouri; while a second declared that ''he would wade in Missouri blood before the negroes should be taken.''

Apparently there was nothing the Missourians could do but to comply with the demand, so to Salem they went. As they neared the Quaker village, the strange sight created the wildest excitement; and it is said that almost as a single man the people of the town abandoned their work and rushed down the road to meet the approaching strangers. In the confusion that followed some of the slaves disappeared; while the crowd proceeded to the great stone house of Henderson Lewelling where Justice Gibbs had his office.[255] The room proved too small, and by common consent the trial was transferred to the abolition meeting-house. On the way thither Henry Dorland, the village school-master, mounted a pile of lumber and harangued the crowd, while all about him the shouts and threats of the men were intermingled with the prayers of the women. When the church was reached and quiet obtained, Aaron Street and Albert Button came forth as counsel for the negroes. The plaintiffs were unable to show warrants for the arrest of their captives, and so Justice Gibbs dismissed the case. Seizing the opportunity, and with apparent meaning for the slaves, a member of the crowd, Paul Way, called out: ''If any body wants to foller me, let him foller.'' Two of the negroes obeyed the impulse and in a moment were on horseback and on their way to freedom. Foiled and outraged at their treatment, Slaughter and McClure made their way back to Missouri, uttering threats of vengeance on the Quaker settlement.[256]

A few days later Salem was startled by the approach of a large band of Missourians, variously estimated from seventy-two to three hundred in number, armed to the teeth and bent on searching every "nigger-stealing house" in the town, and, if necessary, burning them to the ground. The streets were blocked and the village surrounded, while small squads went forth to make the search. One of these squads made straight for the home of Thomas Frazier, the most vigorous abolitionist in the settlement. Hearing of their approach, Frazier hurried the negroes then in hiding on his premises into the neighboring timber, and when the boisterous gang arrived he with his family sat quietly eating dinner. The Missourians came tramping in with threats and oaths, declaring that they proposed to search the house. Frazier quietly told them to do so. Other homes were entered, and where a stand was made wild confusion reigned. Finally the Missourians abandoned their attack and made for their native State, having accomplished little either in recovering escaped property or in frightening the Quakers of Salem.[257]

THE SPRINGDALE QUAKERS AND OLD JOHN BROWN

Active as was Salem in the cause of aiding fugitive slaves, other Quaker communities as they arose in Iowa were not to be outdone in this work. The settlements to the northward in Muscatine, Cedar, and Linn counties constituted new links in the growing chain of Underground Railway stations, and with Springdale as a center they played a part second to none. All went well, until one day Old John Brown of Kansas fame made his appearance, with results long to be remembered. Often has the tale been told, but until now, not from the Quaker point of view.

John Brown's connection with this interesting Quaker settlement began late in October, 1856, when, astride a mule, weary and travelstained, he rode into the little town of West Branch, halted before its only tavern, "The Travelers Rest", and from the proprietor, James Townsend, received a Quaker welcome which until his death he never forgot.[258] Learning of the strong abolition sentiment in the neighborhood and of the activity of these Quakers in the transportation of fugitives by means of the Underground Railway, Brown at once realized the advantages of such a place for maturing the schemes he then had in mind. Turning from the scenes of his exploits in "bleeding Kansas", plans were fast forming in his mind for another attack on the institution of slavery — this time in the East.

A little over a year after his first visit to the Springdale neighborhood, Brown reappeared late in December, 1857 — this time with some ten companions[259] and for purposes which he seemed not anxious to have known. The men were lodged with a

Quaker, William Maxon, about three miles northeast of the village of Springdale, Brown agreeing to give in exchange for their keep such of his teams or wagons as might seem just and fair. Brown himself was taken into the home of John H. Painter, about a half-mile away; and all were welcomed with that unfeigned hospitality for which the Friends have always been known.

Not many days passed by until suspicions were aroused concerning this group of men; for the word was spread that strange maneuvers, much like military drill, were daily being conducted on the lawn at the Maxon home. Much as these Quakers sympathized with and aided in the escape of fleeing slaves, there was one thing they could not sanction: an appeal to force. If Brown had this in mind he could expect no sympathy or support from the Springdale Friends — a fact which other writers seem to have failed fully to appreciate.[260] Some there were of this Quaker sect, however, more charitable and less suspicious than their brethren who believed that these men gave signs of being Mormon missionaries; while John H. Painter and William Maxon alone had any definite information as to what John Brown actually had in mind.[261]

During their stay in this pleasant community, many friendships were formed between Brown's men and the young people of the surrounding country; and when the 27th of April, 1858, arrived, the day when these men were to depart for unknown scenes and adventures, among those who came to bid

13

them "farewell" scarcely a dry eye could be seen —
though it may safely be asserted that "flirting with
the fair young Friends" and the kissing of "a very
handsome young school teacher" in "the confusion",[262] as depicted by one writer on the subject,
had neither place nor sanction among this Quaker
folk of sober mind.

The months passed swiftly by with only an
occasional line from the men whom Brown had led to
Canada; when suddenly, and much to the surprise of
the Springdale Friends, Brown himself reappeared
on February 25, 1859, with some twelve slaves res-
cued from Missouri. With their usual avidity, his
Quaker friends found hiding places for the slaves;
but fearing the approach of a United States Marshal,
Brown felt insecure, and so he departed in haste for
Chicago and Canada.[263]

Nothing more was heard from Brown until the
middle of July, when, in accordance with their
previous promise, the two sons of Ann Coppoc,
Edwin and Barclay, received from John Brown a
summons to meet him at Chambersburg, Pennsylvania, at the earliest possible moment. Unhesitatingly they prepared to depart, and on July 25th
Barclay Coppoc said to his mother: "We are going
to start for Ohio to-day." "Ohio!" said his mother,
"I believe you are going with old Brown. When you
get the halters around your necks, will you think of
me?"[264]

The Coppoc boys departed, and soon the affair
was half forgotten. The summer passed quietly as

the Springdale Quakers busied themselves with the humdrum of daily cares. Autumn had begun, when one day there came to this peaceful village, like a clap of thunder from a clear sky, the startling news of Brown's attack on Harper's Ferry. In the act of treason Edwin Coppoc had been captured and thrown in prison, with sure death staring him in the face; while his brother Barclay, pursued by men and dogs, was fleeing for his life through the Pennsylvania mountains.[265]

Haggard and worn with his long flight,[266] with a price upon his head, and hunted by an official with a requisition from Governor Wise of Virginia upon Governor Kirkwood of Iowa for his immediate rendition to justice,[267] Barclay Coppoc reached his home in Iowa on December 17th.[268] On the day before, his brother Edwin, loaded with chains and shackles, had yielded up his life upon a Virginia scaffold. Thus the mother's parting prophecy was fulfilled.

When it had become clear what had actually transpired in their midst, the Friends at Springdale made haste to state their position. On November 9th, three weeks after the disastrous raid on Harper's Ferry, the Springdale Monthly Meeting convened; and among its most important actions was the appointment of a large and representative committee[269] to investigate the report that there "appears to be an impression abroad that Friends in this neighborhood have improperly encouraged a war spirit."[270] The committee at once took the matter vigorously in hand, visited each of the members of the Society who had been connected in any manner with Brown and his men, and on December 7, 1859, rendered the following significant report:

We have endeavored to consider the subject confided to us in all its bearings, & are united in the conclusion, that any publication [in the way of a defense] on the part of the Mo. Mee. [Monthly Meeting] is unnecessary. While we believe that our principals of peace were never dearer to most of our members than now, we feel it to be cause of deep regret that those engaged in the late deplorable outbreak at Harpers Ferry, have been entertained, & otherwise encouraged by some of our members.

While brought under a deep concern we desire to establish a forgiving feeling towards those who may have been overtaken in weekness, & would tenderly admonish all to an increased watchfulness in the precepts of our Redeamer.[271]

For the sake of accurate history, it now seems necessary to make plain the real relation which the much-eulogized Coppoc boys bore to the Society of Friends at the time of the events in question. Early in life both of the boys developed wayward tendencies, discomfiting to their mother and to the church. Edwin took to dancing, and though repeatedly dealt with in the "spirit of restoring love" by the Monthly Meeting, he spurned all advice, refused to "condemn his course", and was in consequence duly disowned from membership in the Society on May 6, 1857.[272] Barclay, also, about this same time gave the Springdale Friends grave concern. Fresh from the stirring scenes in Kansas,[273] he had engaged in a fight soon after reaching home, and a month after his brother's disownment the complaint was entered on the records of the Monthly Meeting that "Barclay Coppoc has used profane language, and struck a man in anger."[274]

Coppoc gave the proper satisfaction for this first offense, and the meeting "passed it by". But immediately upon his return from Harper's Ferry his conduct called for new attention. With the officers close upon his heels Coppoc sought his home in Cedar County; and upon his arrival there a large number of the young men in the vicinity united as a military guard to prevent his capture, while he himself went heavily armed. His presence of course attracted wide attention, and the overseers of the Preparative Meeting called upon him. Action seemed necessary and on January 11, 1860, a report was made to the Monthly Meeting that "Barclay Coppoc has neglected the attendance of our religious meetings & is in the practice of bearing arms."[275] The usual care was extended to him, but with no avail. Two months later Barclay, like his brother, was formally disowned; and thus came to a close this interesting episode in the history of the Iowa Friends.

ORGANIZED WORK FOR THE FREEDMEN

The work of aiding fugitive slaves, however, practically came to an end with Lincoln's Emancipation Proclamation,[276] and so the Iowa Friends turned to the freedmen with a view to helping them adjust themselves to their new conditions and responsibilities.

For years various of the Monthly and Quarterly Meetings in Iowa had maintained standing committees on the welfare of the "people of color", and when the Iowa Yearly Meeting of Friends first convened in the fall of 1863 strong efforts were made by interested parties to consolidate this important work for the entire field. The Yearly Meeting concurred in the plan, and on September 11th appointed a committee of nine members with instructions "to embrace every opening for the relief and benefit of that much injured people".[277]

The committee at once took up the work with a vigor that brought results. An appeal was issued to every part of the Yearly Meeting for help, and during the ensuing year in response to this appeal the committee received subscriptions to the amount of $3,181.74 and clothing valued at $1,691.90, all of which was despatched to the destitute freedmen at given points in the South. When the Yearly Meeting heard the report of the new work in 1864, there was great enthusiasm. "During the consideration of this important subject", reads the record, "our hearts have been dipped in sympathy with the distressed condition of our colored brethren of the South now being freed from bondage". Proposals were made for the extension of the work, and with hearty accord the Yearly Meeting now appointed a larger and more completely organized committee, termed the "Executive Committee on the Relief of the Freedmen'', with the charge to labor for ''the physical necessities of the Freedmen, and to their advancement in knowledge and religion.''[278]

While the Quakers in Iowa were thus inaugurating their new project, the Friends in the East were engaging in the same work and with similar enthusiasm. Upon learning this fact the Iowa Executive Committee immediately combined its resources with those of similar committees of the Ohio, Indiana, and Western Yearly Meetings for united effort. Schools, mission stations, and posts for physical relief were opened up in various parts of the South, the Iowa committee alone contributing to the work $4,451.19 for the year 1864–1865. Such a united organization, though not permanent, was of immense importance in connection with activities which were undertaken later.

During the year 1865 it seemed best to the Friends of the western States to again divide the work, allotting specific fields to the several Yearly Meetings. Under this arrangement the work in Missouri and Kansas was turned over to the Iowa Yearly Meeting. The Iowa committee at once secured Isaac T. Gibson of Salem, then a man in the very prime of life, as the ''General Agent'' to take personal charge and devote all of his time to the work. This he did, and with an enthusiasm that won for the undertaking immediate success. He appealed for aid to the Quakers at large, to the Northwestern Freedmen's Aid Commission, to the railroad and steamboat companies of surrounding States, and

to the negroes themselves. From every quarter, and
with a readiness that was almost beyond belief, there
came response to the call. With the money at hand
he began the organization of negro schools, and in
his report to the Iowa Yearly Meeting in 1866 he
was able to say that the following schools had been
opened and maintained with Iowa Quaker teachers
in charge:

In Missouri: at Weston, eight months, two teachers, 127 enrolled; at St. Joseph, eight months, two
teachers, 350 enrolled; at Sedalia, four and one-half
months, one teacher, 140 enrolled; at Columbia, five
months, one teacher, 70 enrolled; at Springfield,
eight months, two teachers, 450 enrolled; at Mexico,
five months, one teacher, 60 enrolled. In Kansas: at
Atchison, six months, two teachers, 160 enrolled.

The total number of pupils enrolled in these
seven schools was 1367, and with the scripture
schools maintained on Sunday, which old and young
alike attended, the total number of negroes reached
was over two thousand.[279]

It was difficult both to meet the white man's
prejudice and to dispel the negro's ignorance; but
the teachers worked devotedly and the blacks responded to a surprising degree. Beginning with
A. B. C. classes the negroes advanced to the first,
second, and third readers, and then to arithmetic,
geography, and history. Practical courses in manual
labor and farming were introduced; and throughout
all these activities a strong religious tone was
maintained. With ever growing magnitude the work

went on. As the State of Missouri gradually took
over the work, the Friends continued their labors in
the public schools. In 1871 a certain County Superintendent wrote the following concerning their
efforts:

> The young ladies who came here from Iowa to teach in
> our colored schools, have *all* done unusually well; they were
> faithful as teachers; bore themselves well as ladies, and have
> done the black people of this county much good, and I can
> report nothing but unqualified praise of all they have
> done.[280]

In 1880, due to unfavorable local conditions, the
school so long maintained at Sedalia was abandoned
and a new site was chosen at Parsons, Kansas, where
the "Hobson Normal School" was established. The
purpose of this school was the training of negro
teachers for work among their own people. Under
its first principal, D. W. Bowles, the enrollment of
prospective teachers reached seventy-five for the
year 1883–1884.[281] In 1890, A. W. Hadley took up
the work for which Bowles had given his life,[282] and
with the same spirit of devotion and self-sacrifice, he
labored in this field until his health gave way. In
1898 the school was sold,[283] and for a time the interest on the proceeds was given to Southland
College to be used as tuition for needy children; but
in 1901 the entire principal was turned over to that
institution.[284] Thus the work for the freedmen,
better known to the Friends as the "people of
color", came to its close.

It is interesting, in view of the long and helpful relation which the Friends of Iowa have borne towards this people, to observe that but very few negroes have ever been taken into membership in the Society of Friends in this State.

II

THE IOWA QUAKERS AND THE AMERICAN INDIANS

FROM the year 1672, when George Fox, the founder of Quakerism, began his wanderings among the Indians along the Atlantic seaboard,[285] until the present time, the Quakers have been the consistent and abiding friends of the American Indians. Strange as it may seem, something in the untamed nature of the red man has always attracted the Quaker to him; and in turn, something in the attitude of the peaceful Quaker has ever made the Indian his trusting friend.[286]

EARLY CONTACT WITH THE INDIANS

Aside from their early contact with the roving bands of Indians in the West, the first direct interest of the Iowa Friends in "Our Red Brothers"[287] appeared in 1851 when Thomas Stanley of Salem informed his brethren at the Monthly Meeting in November that he felt led "to go among the Kansas Indians for the purpose of instructing them in the art of Agriculture and civilization". Two Friends, John Hockett and Enoch Beard, volunteered to accompany Stanley on his proposed visit, as was the custom; and the Monthly Meeting drew up a message which reads in part as follows:

To our brothers, the Kansas Indians, and all whom it may concern,

Brothers, Our dear brother Thomas H. Stanley, believing it required of him by the Great Spirit to pay you a visit, in order to confer with you on a concern, which has for a long time rested with weight upon his mind; of endeavoring, with your consent, at some future time, to give you some instruction in the arts of agriculture, and civilization, and in the doctrines of Christianity, as way may open, and as he may be enabled to do, and as may appear right in further feeling after the mind of the Great Spirit . . . . is fully united with by his friends and brethren . . . . and he [is] left at liberty and encouraged to attend thereto.[288]

On the evening of March 27, 1852, Thomas Stanley and his companion Enoch Beard arrived at the chief village of the Kansas Indians — Council Grove, on the Neosho River;[289] and on the following day they met the objects of their mission in an impressive council. In typical Indian fashion, silence reigned for a time; after which the message from the Salem Monthly Meeting was read aloud and translated into the Indian language by an interpreter. Breaking the stillness which had followed this friendly salutation, Stanley then proceeded to explain in detail the purpose of his coming; in reply to which there came from the Indians many speeches and expressions of good will and welcome.

Owing to the fact that the Methodists had already established a mission station among these people it did not seem best for Stanley at this time to remain; but by the spring of 1857 the way was clear, and so, with his brother James, he returned to undertake a permanent work among this tribe.[290]

The larger work of the Iowa Friends for the Indians of the West came some ten years after the Stanleys had begun their labors in Kansas, and at a time most opportune for the red men. The Indians had gradually been driven beyond the Mississippi and on to the westward.[291] Then came the movement to the Oregon country, the mad rush of the ''forty-niners'' to the gold fields of California, and the building of the first trans-continental railway. The Indian saw the buffalo and other game everywhere recklessly slain or driven from the prairies; and everywhere encroachments were being made on his hunting grounds. At last, thousands of the tribesmen of the plains arose in a desperate and final attempt to stay the advance of the white men. The war-whoop resounded along the entire frontier. At once, from various parts of the nation there came a demand for the complete extermination of the Indian race by the military arm of the government. It was at this juncture that the Friends, with their program of peace, stepped in.

On September 3, 1867, the subject of the ''present condition of the Indians'' was introduced for discussion into the ''Representative Meeting'' of the Iowa Yearly Meeting of Friends. After some consideration it was referred to a committee composed of David Morgan, James Owen, Lindley M. Hoag,

David Hunt, Enoch Hoag, and Brinton Darlington, with instructions to report "the result of their deliberations to a future sitting". Two days later they produced the following statement:

After a full interchange of views, we are united in recommending to the Representative Meeting, the appointment of a committee to labor for the promotion of peace between the Indians & whites, as well as the general protection of the aborogines in all their rights, & to encourage their advancement in civilization & Christianity, by memorializing the proper authorities, or otherwise to labor as way may open for the prosecution of the concern. And we would suggest the invitation of all the Representative Meetings of Friends in the United States, with which we correspond, to cooperate with us if way should open with them.[292]

Having already joined forces with other Yearly Meetings in the work for the freedmen, the Iowa Yearly Meeting in adopting this report was but suggesting that the same plan of action be extended to the work among the Indians. The clerk of the Representative Meeting forwarded copies of the above report to each of the other Yearly Meetings as suggested; and the New England, New York, Baltimore, Philadelphia, Ohio, Indiana, and Western Yearly Meetings all readily united in the enterprise. A body composed of two representatives from each Yearly Meeting, and known as "The Associated Executive Committee of Friends on Indian Affairs", was organized and became one of the most effective instruments for accomplishing a given purpose that the Friends have ever produced.

The bill then pending before Congress "to restore the Bureau of Indian Affairs to the Department of War"[293] was most vigorously attacked by this compact Quaker organization. The Senate and the House of Representatives were petitioned and memorialized; and the "Associated Com't proceeded in a body to Washington & obtained a hearing before the committees of the two Houses of Congress". The President-elect, Ulysses S. Grant, was called upon in person by a deputation of the committee and interviewed on the subject. The great warrior received his Quaker guests with marked respect and cordiality. He listened attentively to all they had to say, as they pleaded that he might use his influence for the appointment of religious men, who in turn would secure religious employees, so far as practicable, for the Indian agencies; and then in his characteristic manner he replied:

Gentlemen, your advice is good. I accept it. Now give me the names of some Friends for Indian agents and I will appoint them. If you can make Quakers out of the Indians it will take the fight out of them. Let us have peace.[294]

Of all the departments of the government service the one most honeycombed with corruption for years had been the Bureau of Indian Affairs. Grant eagerly seized upon the plan suggested by the Quakers, and upon his inauguration he turned over to the Society of Hicksite Friends the care of the Northern Superintendency, including some 6480 Indians, and to the Society of Orthodox Friends the Central Superintendency with twenty different

tribes numbering 16,379 Indians.[295]   Thus originated
Grant's "Peace Policy", of which he remarked in
his first annual message to Congress on December 6,
1869: "The results have proven most satisfactory."[296]

THE CENTRAL SUPERINTENDENCY

While the Hicksite Friends in Iowa took little or
no part in the work assigned by Grant to their branch
of the Society, the Orthodox Friends in this State
bore a share in the new enterprise out of all proportion to their numbers.

The Associated Executive Committee of the
Orthodox Friends, to whom the President turned
over the care of the Central Superintendency, at
once cast about for the proper persons to take charge
of the work.   Enoch Hoag, who had been a leader in
the movement from the start, a member of the
Bloomington Monthly Meeting near Muscatine, and a
man of remarkable ability, was chosen as Superintendent, with headquarters at Lawrence, Kansas,
and with ten Indian agents under his supervision.
Of the agency appointments, the Iowa Friends were
given the most difficult fields.   Laurie Tatum of
Springdale was sent to the blanket Kiowas and
Comanches, about 4500 strong, located near Fort
Sill; Brinton Darlington of Muscatine was despatched to the Cheyennes and Arapahoes, numbering about 3400, along the Canadian River near Camp
Supply; and Isaac T. Gibson of Salem was given
charge of the four thousand troublesome Osages.

Of his own call to this work Laurie Tatum says:

I was living on a farm in Iowa, and knew nothing about
being nominated for an Indian agent until I saw my name
in a newspaper with others who had been appointed Indian
agents, and confirmed by the Senate. . . .
After my appointment I soon received official notice of
it, with instructions to meet Colonel W. B. Hazen at Junc-
tion City, Kansas, May 20th, 1869, and he would convey me
to my agency. I knew little of the duties and responsibilities devolving upon an Indian agent. But after considering the subject as best I could in the fear of God, and
wishing to be obedient to Him, it seemed right to accept the
appointment.[297]

Brinton Darlington, however, was not so taken by
surprise. Intimately associated with Enoch Hoag
as a friend and neighbor, he had served side by side
with him on numerous committees in furthering the
new plan. The following statement appears in a
brief sketch of Darlington's life, published in 1872:

For several years our friend felt impressed with the
prospect that some service would be required of him as a
Christian missionary, among some of the Indian tribes.
The *duty* grew into the cherished *desire* of his heart. And
when at length the door into that field of labor was set open
by our Government to the Society of Friends, he was ready
to offer himself to enter in, though it should be to lay down
his life there.[298]

Under interesting circumstances Isaac T. Gibson,
the third of the agents from Iowa, began his long
connection with the Osages on September 27, 1869.
Superintendent Hoag had been directed by the Com-

missioner of Indian Affairs to go to the Osage
Agency and straighten out, if possible, certain difficulties arising out of a treaty made with the tribe a
year before. With him he took Jonathan Richards
as special clerk, Major G. C. Snow, the former agent,
and Isaac T. Gibson, the new agent. In opening his
address on this occasion, for which "nearly the
whole nation assembled", Hoag said:

> My brothers! I am happy to meet you. I have long
> desired this opportunity to talk with you, but my duty to
> other tribes has prevented my being with you till this day.
> I call you brothers because we have all one common father.
> The Great Creator of all made the white man, the red man
> and the black man equal. He gave to the white man no
> more natural rights than He gave to the red man; and I
> claim from you no rights and privileges but such as I
> extend to you, and you should claim from me no more than
> you extend to me. I have long wanted to have a plain talk
> with you, and am glad to see so many here to-day.[299]

After Superintendent Hoag closed his speech
Isaac T. Gibson made it plain to the Indians that he
was their friend, saying: "I left the plow in the field
to come and stay with you."

On account of the heavy responsibilities and the
difficulty of securing the proper employees from
among the Friends the Associated Executive Committee undertook to stimulate the interest of the
Society by turning over to the several Yearly Meetings the care of specific agencies. In 1873 the
subject was presented to the Iowa Yearly Meeting,
which at once endorsed the plan, took over the Osage

Agency, appropriated $800 to carry on the work, appealed through the Indian Committee to the membership of the Yearly Meeting, and before the close of the year received contributions to the amount of $1251.15.[300]

THE OSAGE AGENCY

In his last report on the Osages before the Friends took charge in 1869, the Commissioner of Indian Affairs said:

> *Osages* number about 4,000 and were, before the late rebellion, making fair progress in civilization, being the possessors of a large number of cattle, horses, and hogs, and cultivating fields of corn, and having an interest in education, manifested in sending their children to the excellent manual labor school established in the nation under the Catholics. But between the contending armies they were despoiled of their property, which greatly demoralized them, and they are now in a deplorable condition.[301]

Restless, dissatisfied, and pugnacious as they were on account of being shifted about from place to place by the government and on account of the encroachments of the whites upon their lands, the Osages were extremely difficult to handle; but Isaac T. Gibson took hold of his task in a manner that won the confidence of the Indians, and as soon as a permanent reservation was located[302] he at once set to work marking off fields, building houses and schools, and laying the basis for a successful agency. Writing to the Indian committee of the Iowa Yearly Meeting in 1874, he declared:

The Osages have in cultivation about 3000 acres of land on the Reservation where they have been two years; during the past year over 100,000 rails have been split by those not used to labor, and they have been assisted in building about fifty houses, and if no preventing Providence, there will certainly be a much greater advancement the coming year than ever before. We have had about one hundred white employees to aid and instruct the Indians and do the Agency work. Among the industries are four black smith shops in different parts of the Reservation, a saw and grist mill, shoe and harness shop, wagon shop, carpenter and cabinet shop at the Agency. With these vast interests to promote and protect, surrounded by 3000 Indians, who are a terror to the Kansas border, no force is used to preserve order nor weapons carried by any employees for defense.

This was in accordance with Quaker principles, and, as Gibson said, "it would be difficult to find a more striking demonstration of the power of the principle of peace."

In this same report Isaac T. Gibson makes mention of the "Osage Agency Manual Labor Boarding School" with an enrollment of over eighty pupils, under the care of Benjamin and Elizabeth Miles from Iowa, and describes its workings as follows:

The children rise at six o'clock a. m., make their beds and prepare to breakfast at seven. By detail the boys arrange, wait upon, and clear their table, have the care of the school room and boys' sitting room, and assist in the care of their lodging room. By detail, the girls attend to their dining room duties, washing dishes, sweeping halls, girls' sitting room and lodging room. At 9 o'clock collection in school room, singing a hymn by the school, repeating in concert the Lord's prayer or some text of scripture. Bible reading by teacher, a short session of devotion, then the ordinary school exercises, reading from charts, blackboard exercises, recitations, writing, object lessons, oral instruction of various kinds, and gymnastic exercises. Dinner at noon. . . . Collection again at 1 p. m. Exercises as in the forenoon, except the Bible reading. Supper at 5, children assisting in doing the evening work. At 7:30 again collected, singing, general advice, reading from the scriptures, and season of devotion.

By such a process, in 1875 Benjamin Miles was able to report that "24 Indian children are now able to express themselves in English, and as many more can understand what we say to them and are beginning to talk."[303]

Year after year numerous members of the Society of Friends in Iowa have served at the Osage Agency and in other parts of the Indian country with results that have indeed been gratifying. After nine years of most successful labor in this great cause, owing to the unremitting opposition of those who disliked the Quakers' peaceful policy, together with the personal hostility and interruptions on the part of the Commissioners of Indian Affairs under President Hayes, the Friends, through their Associated Executive Committee, felt it incumbent upon them in 1878 to withdraw from the responsibility for the superintendencies which they had assumed, although they continued to maintain their organization to assist the government in the selection of agents.[304] The last of these men to give up the work was Laban

J. Miles of Iowa, who resigned as agent of the
Osages in 1885. Since that time the work of the
American Friends, and of the Iowa Yearly Meeting
in particular, has been centered about the various
schools and private mission stations on the Indian
reservations.

III

WHITE'S IOWA MANUAL LABOR INSTITUTE

In the fall of 1850 Josiah White, the founder of the famous Lehigh Coal and Navigation Company and the chief pioneer promoter of the rich beds of anthracite coal in Pennsylvania, visited the Indiana Yearly Meeting of Friends with the thought in mind of founding somewhere in the West a manual training school where ''poor children, white, colored, and Indian'' might receive a religious education in accordance with the teachings of the Friends. Short of stature, corpulent in build, and dressed in the full Quaker garb, Josiah White was much in evidence at this annual gathering.[305]

When the purpose of White's visit was made known, every inducement was brought to bear to persuade him to lend his aid to the Yearly Meeting Boarding School (Earlham College) which was then struggling for existence; but all to no avail. His mind was fixed, and nothing now could turn him from his course. More than satisfied with what he had seen and heard of the western country, he returned at once to Philadelphia, his home, and included in his written will an endowment of $40,000 for the establishment and maintenance of two schools under the care of the Indiana Yearly Meeting, directing that "the land for these schools be bought where I am now in negotiation to purchase, if they can be, viz: a tract one and a half miles square in Iowa, near Salem and a tract of two miles square in the Indian reserve, Indiana".[306]

Such a generous sum seemed for a time to disconcert the western Friends; and it was with some hesitancy that they accepted the trust with its attendant responsibilities. Two committees were appointed — one for each of the schools — and in 1851, in the heart of the growing Quaker settlement about Salem, 1440 acres of prairie land were purchased in a single tract in the northwest corner of Lee County as a site for what was to be called "White's Iowa Manual Labor Institute".

EARLY YEARS

The purchase having been made, the Indiana Yearly Meeting appointed a board of trustees, with Joseph D. Hoag as president, to look after the interests of the school. Fortune seemed to smile upon the project in the opening days, for in his second annual report (for the year 1853–1854) Hoag informed the Yearly Meeting that five hundred acres of the prairie sod had been broken and enclosed, and an orchard of six or seven hundred apple trees had been set out on that part of the tract designed for the school buildings; while arrangements had been made for having five eighty-acre farms with good dwelling houses ready to rent by March 1, 1855.[307] Thus, at the outset the prospects were bright; but hardly had fortune smiled until disaster followed. With an abundance of fertile lands to be had on every hand almost for the asking, satisfactory renters were not easily found; drouths caused a failure of crops; and the panic of 1857 brought about a shortage of funds for building. Finally, in 1864 the Indiana Yearly Meeting proposed to the newly established Iowa Yearly Meeting of Friends that the latter take over this important trust, and after due consideration it was so arranged.[308]

A new board of trustees now took control. The $8400 worth of building materials and the $2600 in funds collected by the former trustees were put to use and the construction of a two-story brick school building seventy-four by thirty-five and one-half feet in size was begun in the spring of 1866.[309] As the walls rose to completion and materials were needed for roofing it became clear that unless some source of revenue other than the income from the farm were secured the building could not be completed for want of means. In this predicament the board laid the situation before the Yearly Meeting in 1867 in the following statement:

Owing to the extreme high prices of labor and material, the cost of thus enclosing the building will so far exceed original estimates, as to incur an indebtedness of $1500, or $2000, which is a source of deep regret to us, and we earnestly hope that Friends generally may feel the necessity of carrying on the work so nobly begun by our late dear friend Josiah White, and cast in their several mites into the treasury towards the completion of the structure.[310]

But it so happened that at this time most of the Iowa Friends were more concerned in casting ''their several mites'' into the treasury for the erection of a new $16,000 yearly meeting-house, and in consequence paid little attention to the appeal from the trustees of White's Institute. The trustees soon reached the limit of their credit, and then, rather than see the entire project fail, they turned to means little contemplated in their appointment by the Iowa Yearly Meeting of Friends or in the will of Josiah White.

WHITE'S INSTITUTE UNDER STATE CONTROL

With an accumulated debt of nearly $3200, and with no available funds with which either to complete the building or open the school as contemplated by the donor, the trustees of White's Institute appealed to the State legislature in 1868 for assistance.[311] For ten years or more the Iowa State Teachers' Association had urgently called the attention of the legislature to the need of some sort of a school for juvenile offenders in the State.[312]   When the appeal for aid came from the trustees of White's Institute, it was suggested that the State lease the property and there conduct such a school — thus fulfilling, in a way, the will of Josiah White.

In consequence, on January 17, 1868, Senator John A. Parvin introduced ''A Bill for an act to establish and organize a State Reform School for juvenile offenders'';[313] and on January 25th Representative Charles Dudley introduced a similar bill in the House of Representatives.[314] Thorough investigation of the subject was made; and on March 31st the proposed measure received its final approval and was published as required by law. By the provisions of this act the State of Iowa was to lease from the trustees appointed by the Iowa Yearly Meeting of Friends the buildings and grounds of White's Iowa Manual Labor Institute for a period of ten years or less for use as a reform school, and an appropriation was made amounting to $15,000, of which $2,500 was to be applied in liquidating the debt already incurred by the Institute. A board of trustees appointed by the State was to open the new institution as soon as practicable.[315]

In accordance with the provisions of the act the trustees met and organized on April 28, 1868. The board chose Senator Parvin as its president, M. A. Dashiell as secretary, and Isaac T. Gibson of Salem as treasurer. A formal lease was entered into with the Quaker trustees of the institution, and plans were made for completing the necessary construction work as rapidly as possible. So marked was the progress that on September 21st the board announced through the newspapers of the State that the Iowa Reform School was ready to open its doors; and on the seventh day of October the first boy to be committed to the institution came from Jasper County.[316]

In his first annual report to the Board of Trustees (for the year 1868–1869) Joseph McCarty, the Superintendent of the Reform School, reported that

there had been committed to the institution during
the year forty-six youths, ranging from nine to
eighteen years of age and coming from twenty-two
of the counties of the State. Among the causes for
commitment, twenty-five were for larceny, five for
incorrigibility, five for vagrancy, three for burglary.
Furthermore, the facts showed that seventeen of
these youths came from homes where the father was
deceased, six from homes where the mother was
deceased, five from homes where neither father nor
mother was living, and five from families where the
parents had separated.[317]

The rules inaugurated to govern this group of
juvenile offenders were neither harsh nor rigid. An
honor system prevailed, and in so far as possible the
principle of the "family" was maintained. Aside
from the mental and moral training obtained in the
regular school work, every evening the boys were
required to attend assembly where the scriptures
were read and prayer was offered. A Sunday school
was conducted with organized classes; and during
the year ten thousand texts were committed to
memory by the boys. Regular preaching services
were conducted by ministers from the surrounding
country or by officers of the school. "Many of the
boys", said the Superintendent, "have very fine
voices for singing, and take great delight in these
exercises."

Though the joint committee appointed by the
legislature to visit and inspect the Reform School
reported in 1870 unanimously that "the institution

is no longer an experiment; that its adoption, as one of the permanent institutions of the State, is not only wise but an absolute necessity for the public good'',[318] it early became apparent that the site of White's Institute was not well adapted to the ends which the State had in view. As pointed out by Senator Parvin, it seemed unwise for Iowa to make permanent improvements on land which the State could not own, the Friends having no power to convey title to any part of the property. The Superintendent also pointed out the fact that the school was not only ''down in one corner of the State'', but that the ''nearest railroad point now is about fourteen miles distant, Fort Madison, twenty-five miles, and Burlington and Keokuk, thirty-five miles. To all these points the roads are quite rough, and during a great portion of the year very disagreeable.''[319]

Notwithstanding these disadvantages commitments to the school increased, the number for the two years from 1869 to 1871 reaching ninety-one. Of the conditions then existing Superintendent McCarty said: ''We have but one family building, and its capacity will accommodate comfortably about fifty inmates. Into it are now crowded *eighty-five* boys, and still they are coming.'' He further called attention to the fact that ''the law under which the school was organized, provides just as much for the reception of *girls* as it does for boys; yet for want of accommodations, we have been compelled not to receive them when brought to our door.''[320]

Thus it was apparent that the need for extension

was imperative; and so, in 1872 the legislature passed an act carrying an appropriation of $45,000 for a new and more centrally located reform school for the boys, to be owned by the State, and another appropriation of $5,000 for organizing a school for the girls where the boys were then kept.[321]   The commission charged with carrying the new arrangement into effect, early located the boys school at Eldora, in Hardin County, where it still remains; and in April, 1873, they opened the girls' school on the White's Institute farm, with L. D. Lewelling and wife, Quakers of Salem, as Superintendent and Matron.[322]

In his report of November, 1875, Superintendent Lewelling states that since the opening of the girls' department forty-seven girls had been committed to his care, under the following charges: incorrigibility, fifteen; vagrancy, thirteen; prostitution, seven; larceny, six; immoral conduct, four; manslaughter, one.   Of these forty-one girls, the Superintendent declared that "only eight are of families living in normal conditions." "One little girl fourteen years old with a sweet face and gentle manners" was brought to the institution as a "common prostitute". The parents had separated and the girl was an outcast.[323]   Firmly, and yet with tender care and affection these girls were taken in hand, everything that was possible being done to turn them back into the healthful channels of society.   The far-reaching results of this important work, in all probability, will never be known.

During the years that the State thus held control of the Institute, little was known of the work in detail by the Iowa Friends at large, the annual report of the trustees to the Yearly Meeting concerning itself only with the gradually accumulating indebtedness. As the lease drew to a close, however, and the State applied for a short extension, a new interest was awakened among the Friends. During the early years of occupation by the State extensive improvements were made and the land was well tilled; but when the boys were removed to Eldora less acreage was needed, and the farm, with little consideration, was rented and the property allowed to run down. When the Yearly Meeting's trustees assembled at the Institute in the fall of 1877 to consider the proposed extension of the lease, they "found the buildings and fences very much out of repair, and the farm grown up to weeds". Instead of again turning it over to the State they "determined to ask an appropriation from the State Legislature of a sum sufficient to put the farm in as good repair as it was when leased."[324]   In consequence, early in the spring of 1878 the girl's department of the State Reform School was transferred to a location about one mile west of Mt. Pleasant,[325] where it remained until May 25, 1880, when it was moved to its permanent location at Mitchellville in Polk County.[326]   It now became necessary, therefore, for the Friends to make new arrangements for the conduct of White's Manual Labor Institute.

WHITE'S INSTITUTE AS AN INDIAN SCHOOL

As soon as the control of the Institute property reverted to the trustees appointed by the Yearly Meeting[327] they had the articles of incorporation renewed and amended, and then set about to bring the farm out of the dilapidated and thriftless condition into which it had been allowed to fall while leased by the State. During the year 1879–1880 about a mile of new barbed wire fence was built; some five hundred rods of hedge fence, "which had been long neglected", was trimmed; and an orchard of one hundred and fifty apple trees, thirty cherry trees, and fifty grape vines was set out. In addition, the trustees paid off the debt that had been hanging over the institution for more than a decade, and in 1880 reported to the Yearly Meeting that they would "soon be in a condition to start a school on a small scale in accordance with the will of the founder."[328] It was not until a year later that the funds at hand warranted the opening of the school. With John and Abigail M. Fry as Superintendent and Matron, the institution started on its new career on the first day of October, 1881.

Two years passed by with small though encouraging results, when there came an unexpected turn of affairs. Benjamin and Elizabeth B. Miles, who had long been in charge of the Indian "Government Boarding School" at the Osage Agency, resigned their positions, and in 1881, "with the approval and encouragement of the officers of the Indian Department [Bureau]", they opened up, at a cost to them-

selves of some $8,000, a ''Training School for Indian
Children'' at West Branch, Iowa. The project was
an immediate success, the government paying to Mr.
and Mrs. Miles the sum of $167 per year for the keep
of each Indian boy or girl sent to the school. Soon
the requests for admission outnumbered the capacity
of their buildings, and in consequence they turned to
the trustees of White's Institute with a request to be
allowed to lease that property. So thoroughly in
accord with the will of Josiah White was the request,
that the trustees unhesitatingly leased to Benjamin
Miles and his wife for a term of three years from
November 1, 1883, the Institute ''school building,
barn, and 480 acres of land'', with the understanding
that the lessees were ''to board, clothe, and educate
the eleven white children for the use of said building
and land.''[329]

The West Branch school was speedily moved to
Lee County; and the rooms and halls of the large
building, which ten years before were filled with the
juvenile wards of the State, were now turned over to
Indian children. The results were indeed pleasing,
for to the Yearly Meeting in 1886 Mr. and Mrs. Miles
were able to report that seventy-five Indians and
thirteen white children were enrolled in the school,
and that of this number forty-eight had made application and been received into the membership of the
Society of Friends.[330]

It was in the midst of such success that there
came a disaster from which the institution has not
yet recovered. On May 27, 1887, in some unknown

15

manner the main building caught fire and was completely destroyed. Every effort was put forth to
hold the students together until arrangements could
be made to continue the work; but within a month
after the fire there came an order from Washington,
directing that all but three of the Indian children be
sent to Haskell, the government Indian school at
Lawrence, Kansas. This having been done, Isaac N.
Miles and wife took charge of the twelve white
children remaining, and in a small frame building on
the farm continued the school; while Benjamin Miles
and his wife Elizabeth, broken in health, retired from
the work.[331]

AN ATTEMPT TO FULFILL WHITE'S WILL

Not since the disastrous fire of 1887 has White's
Iowa Manual Labor Institute given promise of any
real success until within the last few years. What
with the continuous wrangle of certain local persons
interested alone in selfish gain, the distance from
convenient markets, and the rise in recent years of
first-class public schools and charitable institutions,
the school has had a hard struggle to maintain its
place.

Immediately after the Indian school broke up, the
trustees set to work to erect a new building. By an
extended lease of 960 acres of the farm to Charles
and Matthew Lowder, they received in advance
$3,500 with which to begin. Isaac N. Miles and his
wife remained in one of the cottages on the farm
with the twelve white children belonging to the

Institute, holding the school together as best they could while the new quarters were being constructed. The new building, a two-story brick structure, though not completely finished, was opened in the fall of 1888, with Silas and Mary T. Taylor as Superintendent and Matron.[332] But the success of former years did not seem now to attend the enterprise. Gradually the number of pupils increased from twelve in 1888 to twenty-five in 1896. Then came a steady decline until 1903, when but eight children could be reported as belonging to the institution.

To devote a fourteen hundred acre farm to the maintenance of so small a school seemed indeed preposterous; and so, in their desire to administer to the best advantage the trust confided to them, the trustees closed the doors of the Institute and during the year 1903–1904 applied $1,365.60 of the proceeds from the farm in helping needy students to attend other Friends' schools as follows: "five at New Providence Academy, three at Penn College, twenty-three at Whittier College and six at Central City, Nebraska."[333] But certain disaffected persons had watched with jealous eye this attempt to utilize the income from the Institute farm in other schools; and with the avowed purpose of blocking the plan they brought suit at law to have the trust taken from the Yearly Meeting. In connection with the annual report of the trustees, submitted in 1904, the following "Original Notice" confronted the Iowa Friends:

You [the trustees] are hereby notified that there will be on file September 26th, 1904, in the office of the Clerk of the District Court of Lee County, State of Iowa, at Fort Madison, a petition of......(names of petitioners)......, claiming of you that you as Trustees, Superintendent and Manager of White's Iowa Manual Labor Institute . . . . created by the last will and testament of Josiah White, deceased, and claiming that you are violating said trust and diverting the trust fund and violating and wholly disregarding the trust created by said will and asking that you be removed as Trustees. . . . And that the management of said trust fund and institution, be taken out of your hands and management, and out of the hands and management of the Iowa Yearly Meeting of Friends.[334]

Much as the Friends have disliked to engage in legal proceedings, it was apparent that a contest was inevitable; and so the trustees were instructed "to take such steps as may be necessary to safeguard the interests of the heirs of Josiah White, the donor, and of the Yearly Meetings." On the grounds that the plaintiffs were members of the Yearly Meeting, and in consequence could not sue the body to which they belonged, the attorneys for the Yearly Meeting demurred; but the plaintiffs were sustained, and the case came to trial in the District Court at Fort Madison in June, 1908. Upon the hearings in the case the court gave as its finding "that it was the intention of Josiah White, deceased, to establish and maintain perpetually a manual labor school on the farm . . . . in controversy"; "that it is a diversion of the funds of said trust, and contrary to the intent of said Josiah White . . . . that any of the income of said farm should be used for the purpose of paying the tuition of pupils while attending or entering at any other school or institution of learning''; and ''that the defendants should [again] start said school upon said farm as soon as practicable and as soon as pupils may be obtained, after the buildings have been put in the proper condition to receive them''.[335]

It was now made clear that the Iowa Yearly Meeting of Friends must, if it expected long to retain control of White's Institute, administer the trust both in accord with the terms of the will and to some practical effect. That the investment was sufficient for the purposes intended was apparent, for during the year 1906–1907 the rents from the farm alone amounted to $4,947.47; while during the seven years from 1902–1909, when Newton Branson served as the managing member of the board of trustees, the funds which accumulated, over and above all current expenses, amounted to $12,879.90. To save permanently this important trust, now valued at nearly $175,000, it was apparent that the Yearly Meeting must awaken to its responsibility in the matter, for the court had spoken in no uncertain terms.

Fortunately, at this critical juncture James B. Bruff, a prominent Quaker attorney living at Atlantic, Iowa, was appointed a member of the Board of Trustees in 1908. Bruff appreciated the seriousness of the situation, was appointed president of the board, and took hold of things in a business-like manner. With a full treasury at hand he first set to work clearing away the rubbish about the institution, and putting the buildings, schoolhouse, and farm into good condition. The main brick building, so inadequate and ill-adapted for housing both boys and girls, was remodeled, and in addition a contract was let for a new and up-to-date dormitory for the girls, which was rapidly pushed to completion. For a time the money in the treasury rapidly dwindled, the disbursements for the two years from 1909 to 1911 amounting to over $21,000. Then, abandoning his lucrative practice in Atlantic and with a determination to make the project succeed, James Bruff and his wife Jessie moved to the Institute and assumed personal control as Superintendent and Matron. In this capacity their first annual report to the Yearly Meeting stated that ''a school on the Institute premises'' had been successfully conducted during the year just passed with twenty-four students enrolled, and that there was ''a surplus on hand after paying the year's obligations, of something over $1,500.''[336]

After many years of ups and downs, White's Iowa Manual Labor Institute now gives evidence of approaching that usefulness and efficiency so long maintained by its twin sister institution in Indiana. Thirty-eight students were enrolled during the last school year, 1912–1913. Ten of these were day pupils from the surrounding country; three were enrolled as resident students, paying for the year's board and tuition $100 each; and twenty-five were children under written contract by parent or guardian to remain in the entire custody of the institution until of legal age. Of these latter no fee of any kind is charged. They are made to feel that the services rendered during the latter years of their stay will be ample compensation for their care and keep while young; and, says the Superintendent, "this thought thoroughly pervades the children." Here all work together on a common plane, the drudgery of labor being lost in the pleasantness with which tasks are assigned and done. In this, again says Superintendent Bruff, "we have thus far admirably succeeded."[337]

To-day the fourteen hundred and forty acres are dotted here and there with fields of grain and browsing cattle. Cosy farm cottages and a little Quaker church nestle among the groves and orchards; while in the center of the broad expanse stand the large school buildings. The voices of happy children are heard in this healthful country home, where under the kindly influence of those in charge boys and girls are growing into strong and healthy manhood and womanhood. Surely now, if ever, Josiah White's hopes are being realized.

MISSIONARY ACTIVITIES OF THE IOWA FRIENDS

CLOSELY allied with their efforts in behalf of the freedmen and the American Indians are the activities of the Iowa Friends along other philanthropic lines, particularly their missionary work in the island of Jamaica. After the first appearance of missionary zeal among the early Friends in England it will be remembered that a strange apathy seemed to pervade the new religious order. This decline in zeal continued until the Quakers, in the new world at least, "actually came to find a satisfaction in the thought that they were not a proselyting people"[338] and so withdrew from all evangelistic or missionary effort. But there came a reawakening. The progressive or orthodox branch of the Society throughout America heard the call to world-wide evangelization, and arose to meet the call under the direction of the American Friends' Board of Foreign Missions, in the work of which the Iowa Yearly Meeting of Orthodox Friends has borne a prominent part both with men and means.

Before the Separation of 1877 took place in the Iowa Yearly Meeting, a so-called "Missionary Association" had been organized among the membership, with a president at its head and vice presidents in each of the several Quarterly Meetings. The work of the association seems, for a time, to have been purely local, consisting of "tract reading, temperance and sabbath school work, visiting the families of the poor"[339] and such like; but it was not long until its activities were extended to the founding of "mission schools", the "assisting to reform and find homes for the outcast and destitute", and the holding of open air meetings in county jails — a work similar to that carried on at present by the Salvation Army.[340] This organization proved successful and led to the establishment of what was called the "Home and Foreign Missionary Board."

Provided with a minute for religious service from the Stuart Monthly Meeting and the Bear Creek Quarterly Meeting, a minister named Evi Sharpless laid before the Iowa Yearly Meeting of Friends, in 1881, "a concern that had been resting on his mind for some years, to visit in gospel love some of the West India Islands, and to labor there as an evangelist". The request was heard in a joint session, men and women sitting together, and after "prayerful deliberation" on this new departure Sharpless was liberated for the service.[341]

Those who were acquainted with the early history of Quakerism were well aware of the rôle which the founders of the faith had played in those western seas: as early as 1662 two Quaker ministers, Ann Robinson and Oswell Heritage, had preached the Quaker message on the island of Jamaica, and nine years later George Fox himself was there. By the beginning of the eighteenth century it is said that on this island alone there were nearly ten thousand followers of the Quaker faith. But long before Sharpless or the Iowa Friends had ever dreamed of these fields for personal service almost every trace of the Quakers on the island had been obliterated.[342]

Accompanied by William Marshall of Bangor, Sharpless sailed from New York early in November, 1881, and after a six days' voyage landed in Jamaica. Marshall soon returned, but Sharpless remained and itinerated from place to place, preaching and working in company with the Presbyterian, Baptist, and Wesleyan missionaries on the island. In the spring of 1883, however, he launched out for himself, and high up among the mountains in a temporary booth covered with green banana leaves as a shield from sun and rain he established his first Quaker mission at Cedar Valley.

While Sharpless labored thus, Marshall, at the Iowa Yearly Meeting in 1883, told in such forceful language of the Jamaica field that his hearers were deeply stirred. The following resolution, first unanimously adopted by the "Missionary Association", was in turn approved by the Yearly Meeting, thus bringing the Iowa Yearly Meeting of Friends into definite relations with the work of foreign missions:

Resolved, That in view of the demand for missionary work in Jamaica we feel that the time has come for Friends to establish and support a Mission Station on that island,

and we recommend that Friends of Iowa Yearly Meeting consider it their special field.[343]

Among the listeners on this occasion were Jesse and Elizabeth R. Townsend, two Friends living at Iowa City, who had long meditated on a religious call to labor, as they thought, among the Indians; but learning of this open door, they volunteered for the work in Jamaica. The Yearly Meeting sent them forth, and on December 14, 1883, they arrived at their chosen field of labor. Sharpless gladly received them at Cedar Valley and turned over to them his mission station, while he set out again on an evangelistic tour.

In the forepart of January, 1885, Sharpless, for a second time, entered the home of his friend Dr. Waldron at the extreme end of the island; and on the following Sunday morning, with hymn book and Bible in hand, and with two of the Waldron boys at his side, he marched down the long street of the village announcing his intended service at the other end of the town. A crowd soon gathered out of the huts and from over the palm-clad hills. Then, with a "high moss covered rock" for a pulpit, he preached his sermon, and within two weeks thereafter, it is said, the people had built a meeting-house of "sticks from the mountains" and "a roof of cocoanut leaves", and called it Happy Grove.[344]

During these years a missionary spirit, no doubt largely aroused by the evangelistic movement at home, seemed to be developing among the Iowa Friends. Side by side with the Missionary Associ-

ation, the women of the Yearly Meeting organized a
Women's Foreign Missionary Society, on identically
the same plan, for aggressive missionary work. The
Sunday schools, also, caught the spirit, and by 1884
out of a total of eighty-two such schools in the
Yearly Meeting fifty were contributing monthly to
the missionary fund, which collections for the year
amounted to $969.93.[345] The Christian Endeavor
also took up the work, and with the combined
strength of all these agencies the funds raised for
the Jamaica field rose from $2381.63[346] in 1887 to
over $14,000[347] in 1906. For the entire period from
1883 to 1913 the Yearly Meeting through all of its
agencies has expended over $143,000 in the work.

In 1893 the Iowa Yearly Meeting sent Gilbert L.
Farr of Oskaloosa to Jamaica to superintend the
Friends' mission stations and to extend the work.
Fortunately, some months before, Arthur H. Swift
of Worcester, Massachusetts, then a young man of
power and deep devotion, arrived on the island to
take charge of the Seaside School and mission.
Hand in hand these two men worked, aided by the
other missionaries. Meeting-houses and schools
were built and out-stations located at advantageous
points. Moreover, valuable properties were bought
as investments to provide a means of future support.[348] Through persistent effort the ignorance
and immorality prevailing on every hand[349] gradually gave way and scores of natives came into the
Quaker fold.

Worn with ceaseless toil and anxious to educate

their boys, Gilbert L. Farr and his wife returned to
Iowa in 1903, leaving in the island Arthur Swift,
who had earlier taken over the superintendency. In
that same fall the Mission Board gave to the Yearly
Meeting the following statement of the work:

> We thankfully report a year of great blessing in the
> Jamaica work. There are now 569 members in the three
> Monthly Meetings [Glen Haven, Amity Hall and Seaside]
> — a net increase of 39 the past year. There are 1040
> scholars enrolled in the Sabbath Schools, about 200 mem-
> bers, including Juniors, or the Christian Endeavor soci-
> eties, and over 500 scholars in the day schools.

Furthermore, the funds raised in the island itself
for the work during the year amounted to $1,950.[350]

With that zeal which marks the true missionary
Swift grappled with his problems, inspiring those
about him to increased effort through his own
example. In order to bring about more united and
more efficient work, a weekly council of all the workers, both American and native, was held at Seaside,
where reports from the various stations were read
and discussed.

On Saturday, June 26, 1909, Swift responded to a
call to address a large union missionary gathering at
Morant Bay, some twenty miles from his home. For
many days he had been under a nervous strain, and
in his address that day those present seemed to perceive a peculiar touch of pathos.[351] When descend-
ing from the pulpit as the sermon closed, his sight
seemed to fail, a strange malady came upon him,
and with all speed he was taken to the nearby parson-

age, where medical assistance was summoned. The word despatched to his wife brought her to his side but two hours before he passed away. ''The bell tolling in the night'', says one writer, ''was the first intimation to many of his illness. A company of Seaside Friends started immediately to walk to Morant Bay. Four miles from Seaside they met Mrs. Swift and a company of Friends from Amity Hall and Golden Grove who had already joined her, returning with the corpse. Reaching Hector's River just after day light the people thronged out of their houses and wept aloud as the company passed, many following to the mission yard which was already filled with the sorrowing ones. All day crowds of people came from far and near to express their sorrow and sympathy.'' ''His death'', says the writer, ''has produced a wonderful effect upon people and many lives have been consecrated to God's service as a result.''[352] The news was received with dismay by the Iowa Friends.

It was a sad council meeting of the missionaries on the island of Jamaica on July 5th. With rare courage, however, ''H. Alma Swift supplied the vacant place'';[353] and by unanimous consent has continued to fill it, crowning the work of her husband with complete success. Under her immediate direction as Superintendent the following missionaries are at work at present in the Jamaica field, in addition to Alsina M. Andrews, Matron of the Happy Grove School for girls: Mary E. White, Sada M. Stanley, Alice Kennedy, Jefferson W. and Helen F.

Ford, Lizzie Allen, Anna Sherman, and Charles and Anna Kurtzholz. The field itself, and the various centers with their respective memberships in 1912 stood as follows: "Seaside, 711; Amity Hall, 278; Orange Bay, 73; Glen Haven, 126; Annotto Bay, 68; Middle Quarter, 83; St. Maria, 21; total, 1360."[354]

While the Orthodox Friends of Iowa had thus for years been working out their foreign missionary problem,[355] other Yearly Meetings had developed fields in Asia, Africa, and in many islands of the sea.[356] Owing to their earlier experience with the advantages of coöperation in the negro and Indian work, the consciousness gradually grew that here, too, a union would give added strength. To that end a move was made in 1879;[357] but not until 1894 was the "American Friends' Board of Foreign Missions" established.[358] By this means the mission work of the Friends was brought into harmonious unity and into touch with the greater world movements of the day. In 1911 the Iowa Yearly Meeting authorized the transferrence of its Jamaica charge to the management of the American Board.[359] According to the present plan the Iowa Friends, still responsible for the maintenance of the Jamaica field, work through a "Foreign Missionary Committee" appointed by them,[360] which committee is subordinate to the directions of the American Board.

V

EDUCATIONAL WORK AMONG THE IOWA FRIENDS

THE history of the Society of Friends has been adorned with the names of men eminent in almost every field of scholarship. The number of Friends who have thus distinguished themselves has been "large in proportion to the small body with which they are connected".[361] Two factors seem chiefly to be responsible for this fact: first, the thoughtful and meditative form of worship among the Friends; and second, their unfailing provision for a "guarded education" of their youth. Wherever the Quakers have planted new communities in the West, there side by side are found the home, the church, and the school.

By a "guarded education" the Quakers did not mean an exclusively religious one; but believing, as they did, that a human being found his highest expression in things religious, they realized the necessity of both intellectual and spiritual training in the making of a man. As is still the case, rarely did the public schools of the early days afford religious training; and to meet the need, the Friends evolved a system of education which to them seemed complete. It was expected that each Preparative or Monthly Meeting would maintain within its borders one or more elementary schools, presided over by a Friend and in which the scriptures would be taught daily. Above these schools were the academies or seminaries with their secondary courses, likewise maintained by Monthly, or Quarterly Meetings, or by holding associations in which members of the Society owned the controlling stock. Then, as the final step, came the colleges, of which the Friends have in America at the present time no less than ten, stretching in a chain from the Atlantic to the Pacific coast.

SALEM AS AN EDUCATIONAL CENTER

Hardly had the Quakers become settled in their Iowa homes before the Salem Monthly Meeting appointed a committee to "endeavor to have schools put in operation"[362] in their midst. In its report in 1841 the committee stated that there "are 212 Children of suitable age to go to School" in the Monthly Meeting; that there "are 185 of our children who have received Education the past year in schools taught by Friends"; and that there "are none of our children growing up without education."[363] Typical, indeed, is this report of the conditions which prevailed almost universally among the Iowa Friends for the next half century, for well did they carry out the disciplinary provisions on this important subject.[364]

The real advancement began in 1845, when Reuben Dorland, a highly educated Friend, came from Poughkeepsie, New York, and on his own

16

responsibility founded Salem Seminary. By the winter term of 1851 he had built up his enrollment to over two hundred students, coming from far and near; and with his staff of three teachers besides himself, was offering courses in the following subjects: reading, spelling, grammar, geography, history, astronomy, chemistry, physiology, mineralogy, botany, algebra, geometry, surveying, book-keeping, mercantile correspondence, and intellectual and moral philosophy.[365] In the very midst of success, however, Dorland's health failed. He was forced to abandon his school, and on March 4, 1852, while enroute to California, he died and was buried in the sea.[366]

For a time Salem Seminary was neglected; but realizing the value of the institution to the church, the Salem Monthly Meeting took up the work in 1854, built a brick structure twenty-five by thirty feet in size, and reopened the school. But these accommodations soon proved insufficient, and to meet the growing demands in the spring of 1867 a number of interested persons banded together as a joint stock company, and organized the ''Whittier College Association''.[367] John W. Woody was secured as president, and on April 20, 1868, Whittier College opened its doors. The school met with immediate success; and with an enrollment of over two hundred students in 1869, Salem again took on the appearance of an educational center. Further increase in the number of students created a demand for larger space, and in 1874 the old brick meeting-house was remodeled for a school building, and the Friends sought other quarters for their religious gatherings.[368]

Buoyant with hope, the Salem Quarterly Meeting of Friends now launched a campaign for an endowment fund of $15,000; but in the midst of the undertaking there came the panic of 1877, which blighted the hopes of Whittier College. What with the foreclosure of mortgages and failing crops the enrollment dwindled, and in their attempt to keep things running in hope of a brighter day, the trustees plunged the institution into debt. Then came the second blow, from which it never recovered. On the night of December 4, 1885[369] came the call of fire, and in a short time thereafter the main building of Whittier College lay in ashes. With a courage typical of the Salem Friends they built anew; and in 1887 the present brick structure, two stories high, was erected. But with these set-backs, Whittier College was not able to regain its former prestige. Without good railroad connections, with little financial backing, surrounded by public high schools and denominational colleges, and in competition with Penn College with its superior equipment, Whittier College could have little hope of success. For years it struggled along as a Friends' academy, but in 1910 gave up and closed its doors.

QUAKER SEMINARIES OR ACADEMIES IN IOWA

The same desire for independent schools shown by the Salem Friends has at various times and in various ways expressed itself in almost every Quaker center in the State, so that among this religious sect there have existed a number of academies, each characteristic of its time. A typical example of the establishment and subsequent history of these church schools is to be found in Springdale Seminary.

At the opening session of the Red Cedar Monthly Meeting in 1853 the subject of education was taken up and the founding of church schools was urged; but owing to the heavy public school taxes already assessed upon them, many of the Friends were more inclined to the policy of gaining control of the public schools and conducting them to their liking. As a result it appears that in 1859 of the two hundred and thirty-two children of school age in the Monthly Meeting but thirty-five were in attendance at the school maintained by the Monthly Meeting's committee, while one hundred and seventy attended the public district schools in which eleven Quakers served as teachers.[370]

Soon, however, a school of higher grade was needed, and to meet this need the Friends built a small academy in 1860. Seeing that this would not long suffice, a plan for uniting with the school authorities of the ''Independent District of Springdale'' for better instructional facilities was evolved. Thus under an agreement, peculiar on the part of Friends, Springdale Seminary was founded in 1866.[371] To assist in the construction of the necessary building the Monthly Meeting pledged three hundred dollars, in return for which it was to be represented by three of its members on the board of directors in the selection of teachers and in administering the affairs of the school; and as a special concession, the Friends were to be allowed to hold a religious meeting "of short duration" in the building once each week for the benefit of the students.[372]

Springdale Seminary at once pushed its way to the front, occupying a place second to none of the same rank in the State of Iowa. Its graduates were for a time admitted to the State University without examination. But friction soon arose over the question of special privilege. The Springdale Monthly Meeting, feeling that its rights had been ignored, withdrew in 1877 from its official relation with the school. As a Quaker community, however, the Friends have down to the present time exerted a controlling influence over the institution. While not strictly a Quaker school, its teachers with few exceptions have from year to year been Friends, and it has administered largely to the interests and needs of the church.

Other academies conducted by the Friends in Iowa have each had a history unique and interesting; but only a passing reference can be given to them in this connection. About five miles to the east of Indianola, in Warren County, through the energetic efforts of J. W. Morgan a school called Ackworth Academy, with a two-story brick building costing about $6,000, was founded in 1867.[373] In 1881 the officers of the institution reported an enrollment of one hundred and thirty-one students in the academic courses and seventy-four in the preparatory courses;[374] but in succeeding years for various reasons there was a gradual decline, and in 1910 the building was remodeled and is now used by the Sunday school and church alone.

Contemporaneous with the beginnings of Ackworth Academy was the founding of West Branch Academy, in Cedar County; Lynn Grove Academy, in Jasper County; and Stanford Seminary, in Marshall County. Each of these schools flourished for a time after 1869[375] and then disappeared.

LeGrand Academy, in Marshall County, founded by the LeGrand Monthly Meeting in 1872;[376] Pleasant Plain Academy, in Jefferson County, founded by a "Stockholders' Association" in 1876;[377] and New Providence Academy, in Hardin County, also founded by a "Stockholders' Association" in 1882,[378] all have had interesting careers, productive of much good to hundreds of young men and women in their respective communities. Earlham Academy, in Madison County, the last of these Quaker schools established in Iowa, opened the doors of its $10,000 building in 1892.[379] For seven years, under the direction of the Bear Creek Quarterly and Earlham Monthly Meetings, it did excellent work; but during the winter of 1899–1900 an epidemic of smallpox closed its doors. In the fall of 1900 the Academy and Earlham High School were combined, and thus the institution passed from under the control of the Friends.[380]

Having briefly traced the history of these various schools, a statement should be made as to the causes of their general decline. First stands the fact that, aside from the attempt on the part of the academies themselves of late years to so adjust their courses of study as to meet the entrance requirements of the higher schools of learning, little or no correlative effort or general control has prevailed, each school, for the most part, following out its own peculiar policy. Secondly, in Iowa no successful attempt has been made to endow these schools and place them on a sound financial basis; but year after year the instructors have been expected to shift for themselves, generally having to depend for their compensation on the tuition received or on whatever bonus fund might be contributed by interested persons. Finally, because of the growth of the public high schools there has of late years been a marked decline in interest in these church schools on the part of the Friends whose efforts have been shifted to the maintenance of their growing college at Oskaloosa.

PENN COLLEGE

Penn College, the pride of the Orthodox Friends in Iowa, is the product of the fusion of two distinct Quaker elements, one bearing a southern stamp and the other being of New England origin. The first of these elements found expression in the building of the "Iowa Yearly Meeting Boarding School" in 1860, close beside the Spring Creek meeting-house, some two and one-half miles northeast of Oska-

loosa.[381]   In contrast, near the Center Grove meeting-house, about two miles to the north of the town,
stood the "Thorndyke Institute", owned and controlled by Henry and Anna Thorndyke, prominent
Friends from New England.[382]

In the fall of 1863, soon after the opening of the
Iowa Yearly Meeting of Friends, the building of the
"Spring Creek Institute", as the "Boarding
School" was now called, caught fire and burned to
the ground.   Finding it difficult to rebuild with the
funds remaining on hand, a large committee was
appointed by the Iowa Yearly Meeting in 1866 to
consider "the Educational wants of the members".[383]   This "consideration" led directly to the
founding of Penn College.   Out of the Spring Creek
school and other interests was formed in 1867 "The
Iowa Union College Association of Friends",[384]
which soon amalgamated with the Thorndyke school;
and the site for a union college where Penn now
stands was chosen in 1869.[385]   In the fall of 1871 the
committee was able to report that ten acres for a
college campus had been procured without cost to
the Yearly Meeting, that the west wing of a new
college building was up and enclosed, and that
"Friends of Philadelphia and other parts of the
East have subscribed $1,000 annually for five years
to assist in filling out the salary of teachers, and
about $1,000 towards the completion of the build-
ing."[386]   On the fifth of November, 1872,[387] amid
much rejoicing, Penn College, named for William
Penn, swung wide its doors for the first time.

Strengthened by the addition of a preparatory academy, Penn College has through a period of forty years steadily pushed ahead into a prominent position among the denominational colleges in the State of Iowa, and among the Quaker schools of higher learning in America. During this period it has trained within its walls over five thousand young men and women, of whom no less than four hundred and seventy-five have received the honors of graduation.[388]   Five presidents have guided its policies;[389] and from among its faculty and student body many have risen into prominence in both the business and the professional world.

With the changing years every effort has been strained to meet the growing demands upon the institution; and without adequate means of support, time and time again its managers have been face to face with financial failure. In 1898 came the first successful attempt to raise a permanent endowment fund, which, through the enticing offer of a $9,000 farm if the Friends would raise an additional $50,000 for their college, was completed at the Yearly Meeting in 1900.[390]   Then came the recent financial struggle to meet the State regulation that all first-grade colleges in Iowa must have a productive endowment of $200,000, or an independent income equal to five per cent of that amount.[391]   To accomplish the task every strategy known to those who had the enterprise at heart was employed, and no stone throughout the realm of Iowa Quakerism was left unturned. As the final day, June 1, 1911, drew near, the interest in the undertaking grew intense; but no authentic information found its way to public ears as to the course of affairs. When the midnight hour of that eventful day arrived, however, every church bell in Oskaloosa pealed forth the glad news and every factory whistle joined the chorus to say that Penn had won the victory. On the following commencement day it was publicly announced that the aggregate of the endowment fund had reached $222,000, and that the future of the college, for a time at least, was safe.[392]

In more ways than one this last financial undertaking will mean much to the Society of Friends in Iowa. Not only does it now assure the church of a permanent training school for future leaders in all lines of church activity; but of more importance is the fact that it opened the purse strings of a people who, through the conservative nature of their training, were untutored in the art of giving. True, the Iowa Quakers have done much in a philanthropic way, as the foregoing pages have shown; but aside from their mission work of recent years in Jamaica and their existing pastoral system, their church connection has cost them little in actual outlay of money. Now they are awakened to a growing consciousness of common interest; and in the third campaign which before long must begin if Penn College is to continue to hold its educational standing, it will no doubt be found that a more liberal spirit prevails.

PART V
RELIGIOUS AND SOCIAL LIFE OF THE QUAKERS

I

RELIGIOUS BELIEFS OF THE QUAKERS

It is difficult to make a concise and satisfactory statement of the religious beliefs of the Quakers. Always mystical and individualistic in their worship, abhorrent of all religious formality, and protestant to the last degree, they have shown little liking for any catalogued statement of their tenets in the form of a creed, fearing that such might easily become a worship of the head rather than of the heart. It is true that in Fox's letter of 1671 to the Governor of Barbadoes one finds something approaching a confession of faith, and in the declarations of the various Quaker sects published from time to time there appear statements closely resembling a religious creed. But, as in the case with the English Constitution, in no document nor in any one place is a complete declaration of the Quaker faith to be found. It is scattered through the writings of the founders of the order; it comes to light here and there in the schisms which have rent the Society; and above all, it manifests itself continuously in the daily manners and customs of the members, thus exemplifying the fact that it is in truth "the product of progressive history". Therefore, to understand Quakerism it will be necessary to examine a few of the sources in which these religious beliefs are expressed.

In his letter to the Governor of Barbadoes, Fox sets forth the elements of the Quaker faith in these words:

Whereas many scandalous lies and slanders have been cast upon us, to render us odious; as that "We deny God, Christ Jesus, and the scriptures of truth," . . . . Yet, for your satisfaction, we now plainly and sincerely declare, That we own and believe in the only wise, Omnipotent, and Everlasting God, the Creator of all things in heaven and earth, and the Preserver of all that he hath made. . . . And we own and believe in Jesus Christ, his beloved and only begotten Son . . . . who was conceived by the Holy Ghost, and born of the Virgin Mary; in whom we have redemption through his blood, even the forgiveness of sins . . . . that he was crucified for us in the flesh, without the gates of Jerusalem; and that he was buried, and rose again the third day . . . . and that he ascended up into heaven, and now sitteth at the right hand of God.

Concerning the scriptures Fox continues: "we believe they were given forth by the holy Spirit of God, who . . . . 'spoke as they were moved by the Holy Ghost.' We believe they are to be read, believed, and fulfilled".[393] This declaration, with the varied interpretations placed upon it, stands to-day as the accepted belief of the Friends on the subjects of the fatherhood of God, the sonship, atonement, resurrection and ascension of Jesus Christ, and the inspiration of the Bible. But for other essential elements of Quakerism one must search elsewhere.

"The one corner-stone of belief upon which the Society of Friends is built", says one writer, "is the conviction that God does indeed communicate with each one of the spirits He has made, in a direct and living inbreathing of some measure of the breath of His own life; that He never leaves Himself without a witness in the heart as well as in the surroundings of man".[394] On this same theme of the "inner light", William Penn wrote:

> That which the people called *Quakers* lay down as a main fundamental in religion is this — *That God, through Christ, hath placed a principle in every man, to inform him of his duty, and to enable him to do it; and that those that live up to this principle are the people of God, and those that live in disobedience to it, are not God's people, whatever name they may bear, or profession they may make of religion.*[395]

"This is that universal evangelical principle", declares Robert Barclay, the noted Quaker apologist, "in and by which this salvation of Christ is exhibited to *all* men, both *Jew* and *Gentile, Scythian* and *Barbarian,* of whatsoever country or kindred he be".[396]

With this teaching of the "inner light" and the direct communion of the individual with God, it is not surprising that from the start the Quakers were led to reject any and all of those religious rites and ceremonies usually thought so necessary by other denominations. For them the ordinances of water baptism, the sacrament of the Lord's Supper, and the like, have no binding force; for to them all such are but symbols of that spiritual communion which forms the very center of their faith. Then, too, this same spiritual turn of their religious thinking led them directly into the teaching of justification and sanctification; for, says Barclay, "as many as resist not this *light,* but receive the same, it becomes in them an holy, pure, and spiritual birth, bringing forth holiness, righteousness, purity, and all those other blessed fruits which are acceptable to God". And again the same writer declares that in those in whom "this pure and holy *birth* is fully brought forth, the body of death and sin comes to be crucified and removed . . . . so as not to obey any suggestions or temptations of the evil one, but to be free from actual sinning and transgression of the *law of God*".[397]

Closely allied with these, the main tenets of the Quaker faith, are a number of precepts, or "testimonies" as they are called by the Friends, which are based on certain scriptural teaching. The two most important of these testimonies are opposition to war and refusal to take oath.[398] While the latter of these has given them little difficulty in Iowa, owing to the general exemption laws in force, their conscientious scruples against bearing arms proved to be a serious matter during the Civil War. When the military draft was issued the Quakers, together with the other noncombatant religionists of Iowa,[399] appealed to the Governor[400] and the General Assembly[401] for relief. The only reply was the obnoxious exemption fee of

$300, or the furnishing of a substitute, in case of draft.[402]

Such in broad outlines are the beliefs of the Quakers in Iowa — aside from the exceptions noted in the case of the Hicksite and Wilbur Friends. In 1912 the Conservative Friends in Iowa united with the other Yearly Meetings with which they correspond in adopting a restatement of their principles in the form of a brief synopsis, which, however, is but a reaffirmation of their ancient doctrines. In like manner the Orthodox Friends of America met in 1912 in their quinquennial conference at Indianapolis, Indiana, where they threshed out their differences on the questions of evangelism and higher criticism. At the close of the spirited discussion the Five Years Meeting united in reaffirming its acceptance of both Fox's letter to the Governor of Barbadoes, and the ''Richmond Declaration'' of 1887,[403] but proposed to leave each Yearly Meeting free to interpret them as it saw fit. In consequence it may be said that the Orthodox body alone among the Iowa Quakers has taken the forward step of attempting to adjust themselves to the changing religious thought of modern times.

17

II

THE QUAKER MEETING

The term "Quaker Meeting", which has long since passed into our language as describing any occasion of a quiet or solemn character, is little understood by the present generation, or even by most of the Friends themselves. There are only a few secluded spots where the real Quaker meeting can now be seen in Iowa, for such meetings belong to a day that is gone.

Fifty years ago, or even less, there might have been seen here and there scattered over Iowa the old-time Quaker meeting-houses, uncrowned by belfry or steeple;[404] but now such houses of worship are all but gone. Those quaint old buildings had an architecture all their own. Of long, low, rectangular form, with plain glass windows and two plain doors (the right one for men and the left for women), they were more suggestive of peace and quiet than are the more ornate and imposing structures which have of late years so generally taken their places. There was the old-time "hopping block" of pioneer days, or the long board platform extending half-way round the house, for the convenience of those who wished to enter direct from their wagons. The meeting-house on the inside was altogether plain. The interior consisted of an open room which was divided by a half partition and sliding shutters into two equal parts, the one for the men and the other for the women. The seats, plain and straight, were set on a level floor. At the front there was a raised platform on which were placed seats in two or more rows, each a step higher than the other, for the use of the ministers and elders. No organ, no pictures, no lamps,[405] and no ornaments of any kind were there to attract the eye or disturb meditation and worship.

As the Friends gathered from far and near they entered the meeting-house with their hats on and took their places in silence, each occupying his accustomed seat as allotted by the committee usually appointed for that purpose.[406] During the service no opening hymns were sung, there were no announcements, no scripture reading, no morning offering;[407] but silence prevailed, and in this silence each one present was expected to listen to the bidding of the "still small voice", unaided by the active contrivances of his own mind and heart. Many times throughout the entire meeting they sat thus in worship without a word being spoken. If, however, some one, either man or woman, felt moved of the Holy Spirit to speak, he slowly arose, removed his hat, and in a peculiarly melodious, half sing-song manner proceeded with his exhortation, which was usually unstudied and with little sequence of thought, but touched with a spiritual freshness and beauty seldom found in the stereotyped discourses of the professional clergy. When the exhortation ended, silence again prevailed, unless another felt moved to continue the exhortation or to introduce a new line of thought. If prayer was offered, the audience arose, the men removing their hats and turning their backs to each other until the petition, usually of a highly figurative character, ended, when all were again seated.

Thus the old-time Quaker meeting for worship proceeded until he who sat at the "head of the meeting" and was known as the "timer", felt that the hour had arrived for the meeting to close. Whereupon he would turn to his neighbor and shake hands — this being the sign for a general greeting — and in this manner the service "broke".

At stated times a business session followed the meeting for worship, in preparation for which the sliding "shutters" were closed so that the men and women were as effectively separated as though they were in two entirely different rooms. A clerk for each body then took charge; and for the handling of matters of mutual concern, "messengers" were appointed to pass back and forth with written or oral messages through a door in the partition. With peculiar phraseology and a minuteness evolved through generations, each item of business, when passed upon by common consent (the Quakers did not vote on matters of business in their meetings), was entered on record in the "Minutes"; and when all was finished, by order of the clerk the meeting "solemnly concluded".

Almost every Quaker custom has had its origin in

some important struggle or "testimony". With their teaching of the "inner light" and the leading of the Holy Spirit, the Quakers were obliged to recognize the ministry of women; for God, so they believed, was no respecter of race or kind and spoke His messages through male and female alike.[408] Again, as early as 1668 the custom of separate meetings for men and women was established and received the approval of Fox, apparently on two substantial grounds,[409] namely, the ability of women to better care for the concerns of their sex in separate meetings and the desire to free the Society from the slanderous charges of immorality early brought against it by its enemies. Strange as it may seem, the custom of separate meetings obtained in the Iowa Yearly Meeting of Orthodox Friends until 1893, when it was formally abandoned.[410]

III

QUAKER MARRIAGES

MARRIAGE has always been regarded by the Quakers as primarily a religious compact. "They say", remarked William Penn, "that marriage is an ordinance of God, and that God only can rightly join man and woman in marriage."[411] Accordingly the Quakers have held that divorce could be granted only on Biblical grounds, namely, fornication or adultery.[412] To safeguard the sacred institution of marriage the Friends have hedged it about with rules and observances which now appear strange or even fanatical to some, but which, nevertheless, have prevented moral laxness and a multitude of divorce cases.

For the moral teaching of its young people the Society of Friends placed the chief responsibility on the parents, requiring of them by frequent reminders that they "exercise a religious care in watching over their children, and endeavor to guard them against improper or unequal connections in marriage". On the other hand, when a young man or woman contemplated this serious step, before entering into a formal engagement they were expected first to consult their parents for advice; while older persons independent of parental care were admonished to consult interested friends with a view to learning their judgment as to the propriety of the union. In any case and above all else the parties concerned were expected to solemnly consider the weightiness of the matter, and to seek divine direction before plighting their troth.

As has been suggested, certain prohibitions were laid down as rules — the observance of which, it should be noted, is rather the exception than the rule among the Friends in Iowa to-day. In the first place, no marriages "between any so near as first cousins, nor the children of half brothers or half sisters" were to be permitted. Furthermore, marriage "between a man and his deceased wife's sister, or between a woman and her deceased husband's brother" was strongly advised against. Then, to prevent unseemly and hasty unions, the Monthly Meetings were usually directed to consider no proposals for re-marriage on the part of any widowed person "sooner than one year after the decease of a former husband or wife."

Perhaps the most serious difficulty of all, and certainly the one of greatest importance to the Society from the standpoint of later losses, arose because of the prohibition placed on the marriage of members with those not within the Quaker fold. Practically all of the early leaders of the Society attacked most vigorously the system of "mixed marriages", as they were called, and on grounds highly defensible in the early day but ill-adapted to the broader spirit of more modern times. By them it was contended that differences in religious connec-

tion or belief almost invariably led sooner or later to
domestic troubles which destroyed the harmony of
the homes concerned and reflected discredit upon the
Society itself. And so, until well towards the close
of the nineteenth century, to "marry out" of meeting almost always brought the stigma of disownment
upon the offending party. Moreover, if parents or
guardians encouraged such a marriage, or even
attended the ceremony, they, too, were disowned.
The only way such persons could regain their standing in the church was to come before the Monthly
Meeting and publicly declare, either verbally or by
written notice, that they were "sorry for their
deviation." This of course rarely occurred.[413]

When "the way seemed clear", the first definite
step to be taken towards a Quaker wedding was for
the man and the woman concerned to inform the
overseers of the Preparative Meeting to which the
woman belonged of the proposed union. The two
parties next appeared at the succeeding Monthly
Meeting, and with evidence at hand that they had the
consent of their parents for their union they informed both the men's and the women's meeting of
their intentions.[414] Thereupon each body of Friends
appointed a committee of two of its members; and
the men were to investigate the man's "clearness of
like engagements with others", while the women
were to do the same for their sister. This done, at
the following Monthly Meeting the committees gave
their reports; and, if satisfactory, the parties concerned were then to go together into both the men's

and women's meeting and there publicly declare their "continued intentions of marriage"— this being commonly called "passing meeting". When each and all of these acts had been recorded in the minutes, the parties would propose a date for their wedding. Then each of the meetings appointed another committee of two of its members to be present and see that "good order be observed".

The eventful day having at last arrived, with parents and friends the man and the woman proceeded to the little meeting-house where the woman usually worshipped; and there in the presence of the assembled community — which was always interested in these nuptial occasions — they took the marriage vow. On entering the door the parties made their way slowly to the front, and in silence quietly took their seats. A time of worship followed, during which anyone so moved might feel at liberty to speak in exhortation or prayer. At the proper time — indicated by the head of the meeting — the man and woman arose, joined hands, and in an audible and solemn manner said, the man first speaking: "In the presence of the Lord, and before this assembly, I take ———— ———— to be my wife; promising, with divine assistance to be unto her a loving and faithful husband, until death shall separate us."[415] The woman having recited the same words, the plain marriage certificate of the Monthly Meeting was produced[416] and signed by the contracting parties and by witnesses. This certificate was then delivered to the clerk of the Monthly Meeting for registry in his records and afterwards returned to the married couple.

After the public ceremony, the relatives and intimate friends repaired to the home of the bride where the joy of the occasion expressed itself in a wedding dinner. Here, however, all due precaution was taken against "immoderate feasting or drinking" or "unseemly, or rude discourses or actions". Some of the overseers were expected to be present, and in case of any noticeable breach they were "to take such [person] aside" and "admonish them to better behaviour". Neither was the making of "an uproar around a house at night where a couple . . . . had consummated marriage"[417] allowed; but more than once, so the records show, the boisterous Quaker youth of Iowa violated this ruling and suffered disownment in consequence.

"Why were these people so strict?" and "How did they meet the common provisions of the law?" are questions which have often been asked concerning the old-time Quaker marriages. In reply to the first of these inquiries it may be said, in brief, that when Quakerism arose as a religious institution in England public and private morals were exceedingly corrupt, and to protect both the members and the Society itself no pains were spared by the founders to preserve moral integrity. The second question, however, opens up a broader field and introduces an interesting phase of legislative history, which, from the Iowa point of view, calls for more detailed discussion.

In 1833 the Territory of Michigan passed a law for the benefit of its Quaker inhabitants, which provided that it "shall be lawful for the society called Friends or Quakers . . . . to solemnize the rites of marriage agreeably to their forms and customs", accepting at the same time the Quaker procedure of having the intention of such a marriage announced "on two different days of public worship" in lieu of the usual civil license.[418] This law was still in force in Iowa when the Quakers first planted their homes in the Black Hawk Purchase. But in 1840 the Iowa Territorial legislature took up the question of marriages, and saw fit to make an addition to these early provisions which required the clerks of meetings at which Quaker marriages were solemnized to file certificates in all such cases with the clerk of the district court, under penalty of fifty dollars fine in case of failure to comply with the law.[419] Jealous of any civil interference, the Iowa Quakers strenuously objected to this innovation. But greater still was their consternation when they found that with the adoption of the *Code of 1851* exemption from the necessity of procuring a civil marriage license had been omitted and the right of "solemnizing marriages" alone had been guaranteed to them.[420]

Protest as they might, the Quakers found no relief until the legislature took up the matter in 1868 and passed an act which freed "the members of the Society of Friends from applying for marriage licenses",[421] and allowed them again to resort to their ancient order of procedure. Then before long there came another revision of the laws of Iowa upon the report of the Code Commission in 1873. In this report all reference to exemption from the necessity of securing a civil marriage license was omitted, just as it had been in the *Code of 1851;* and so the battle for exemption had to be fought over again. The chief interest centered in the Senate, where the Judiciary Committee, to which the subject had been referred, recommended that the exemption clause in question be reinserted. Much parliamentary procedure followed, with the result that Quakers were once more exempted.[422]   Finally, came the revision of 1897, accompanied with a similar attempt to place the legalization of marriage purely on a civil basis; but again the undertaking failed. In the *Code of 1897* may be found the following provision: ''The provisions of this chapter [on marriage], so far as they relate to procuring licenses and to the solemnization of marriages, are not applicable to members of any particular denomination having, as such, any peculiar mode of entering the marriage relation.''[423]

IV

QUAKER MANNERS AND CUSTOMS

THE true explanation of many of those Quaker manners and customs which have always been considered peculiar was expressed by Thomas Clarkson over a hundred years ago in these words:

> The reader should always bear in his mind, if the Quaker should differ from him on any particular subject, that they set themselves apart as a christian community, aiming at christian perfection: that it is their wish to educate their children, not as moralists or as philosophers, but as christians; and that therefore, in determining the propriety of a practice, they will frequently judge of it by an estimate, very different from that of the world.[424]

Without question the chief outward feature which has always distinguished the Quaker from his fellows has been his manner of dress. The broad-brimmed hats or scuttle-shaped bonnets, and the plain grey clothes[425] of peculiar cut, were, at the outset, primarily a protest against the extravagance of the age of Elizabeth and James I, when "the dressing a fine lady was more complicated than rigging a ship of war".[426] Before long the same concern for simplicity in dress found its way to America; and in the records of the New England Yearly Meeting of Friends may be found the following direction to its members:

That all men Friends, both old and young be careful not
to Imatate the vain Fashions of the World in wearing their
hatts set up on three sides (with Ribins broads or Bunched)
nor powder the hair to be seen, nor ware thee Neck cloath
Long hanging down or twisted through the Button holes;
nor bigg superflous, or superfluity of holes, nor bigg Button-
holes, or places wrought in Imatation of holes, nor cross
Pocketts, nor Capes on their Coates. Nor wide Laped
Sleaves, nor gathered Skirts, drawn in Foulds like the vain
practice of the world. Nor unsutable lineings of Gaudy
Coulors, nor the Breeches too Strait, nor bigg Unbecoming
Shubuckles.[427]

This antipathy toward showiness accompanied
the Quaker on his westward migrations. Indeed,
allowing for the natural changes from generation to
generation on grounds of "decency and comfort",
one could see in almost every Iowa Quaker community those who bore in nearly every detail, aside
from silk stockings and knee breeches, the appearance of the Quakers of two hundred years before.
It has been suggested that the maintenance of simplicity here by the Quakers was due, perhaps, more
to the natural limitations attendant upon pioneer
life than to matters of conscience or custom; but this
is far from the truth. To the Quaker mind costume
had a distinct significance and meaning. This was
his badge which was both to distinguish him from
other men and to protect him from the evil influences
of the world; for, thought he, no Quaker wearing this
well-known costume would sully it by appearing in
questionable places or company, nor would evil men
tempt such to do wrong. The wearing of the coat of

peculiar cut, therefore, found its way into the Society's discipline; and the children as well as the grown folks were required to don the garb, being carefully instructed as to its moral value and meaning.

Again, the wearing of the Quaker hat has long been a puzzle to the outside world. Are its broad brim and high crown of really grave concern? Why would not the Quaker remove his hat in the presence of ladies or men of note, or in his own meetings for worship? As with other curious Quaker customs, this, too, had its meaning. To lift or doff the hat was once a sign of servile regard, or at least of personal respect. With his firm belief in the absolute equality of man, the Quaker could not show any such regard either to civil officer, priest, or king. As for religious meetings, there the Quaker continued to wear his hat, seeing no reason why he should remove it even during a sermon, for such came from the lips of a man; but when he addressed God in prayer, then all arose, removed their hats and stood uncovered before the one supreme being.

Another custom which marked the Quakers as peculiar was their use of the pronouns "thou" and "thee" instead of the pronoun "you"— which, it was said, came to be used on account of man's desire to be flattered.[428] In England, "thou" was the form of address of a lord to a servant, of an equal to an equal, and likewise expressed companionship, love, permission, defiance, or scorn; while "ye" or "you" was the language of a servant to a lord and ex-

pressed compliance, honor, submission, or entreaty.[429] The Quakers insisted upon the use of the
former terms in personal address; and they would
not use the latter. Against this custom priests,
and officers, and nobility stormed, and Quakers by
the thousands were thrown into prison for insolence
and contempt; but to maintain their convictions of
human equality they willingly suffered in silence.
Naturally, as the Quakers spread throughout the
world they continued to use both at home and abroad
this simple form of address, which to them is full of
historic meaning.

Following this use of terms of address came
others, and for similar reasons. The term ''Mister''
was rejected on the ground that it was but ''Master''
corrupted, and savored of servility; and instead the
Quakers addressed people by their given name, as
John or Mary — though they had no compunctions
about using an official title such as President or
Governor, since this usage was sanctioned by the
scriptures.[430] Furthermore, the common salutations of ''good morning'' or ''good-bye'' were likewise rejected; for, said the Quakers, ''all times are
good in the providence of God''. In place of such
expressions they simply inquired after each other's
interests with such a query as ''how art thou?'', or
in parting they said ''farewell''.

Peculiar in these respects, the Quakers have been
singular in others. At the time of the rise of the
Society funerals were occasions for pageantry and
worldly show in honor of the dead. Against all this

the Quaker sense of propriety naturally revolted, since to them a funeral seemed an occasion for deepest reflection. As time went on a general order or system for such occasions was adopted and became a fixed part of the Quaker discipline. In Iowa the procedure was very simple. The body of the dead was placed in a plain board coffin and borne from the home to the meeting-house in silence, the attending relatives and friends showing no outward signs of grief by means of crepe or "mourning habits" (clothing). When the coffin was placed before the assembled audience, a period of silence ensued, though this might be broken by anyone at any time with fitting exhortation or prayer. In due time the coffin was then borne to the open grave, where a pause was again observed — this time primarily to call the attention of all to "the uncertainty and short continuance of life, and the wisdom there would be in a preparation for death".[431]

In the beginnings of the order in England, the Quakers, refusing to accept the services of the established church, buried their dead "in their gardens, or orchards, or in the fields and premises of one another".[432] But as time went on they secured their own burying grounds, in which members were interred without expense, the burials being made in regular rows in order of death irrespective of family ties. This system long prevailed, being followed, indeed, during the early years in Iowa. In the early days gravestones were not used — though a careful record was kept of all burials. But it appears that by the middle of the nineteenth century the Indiana Yearly Meeting had provided in its discipline that "if a plain stone [native to the country] should be set to the grave, it should not exceed twelve inches in height or width, and contain only the name, date of the decease, and age".[433] Then came a more liberal provision in the discipline adopted by the Iowa Yearly Meeting in 1865, limiting the size of such gravestones to "not to exceed two feet in height', and allowing "such slight additions as may be desired, simply to define the relation of the deceased";[434] while now there are no restrictions imposed by the Iowa Orthodox Friends.

The manner in which the Society of Friends long held its members to circumspection in temporal affairs and to communal harmony is also interesting. Once each year the following "Query", as the basis of operations, was read in both the Preparative and Monthly Meetings and answered in writing:

Are Friends careful to live within the bounds of their circumstances, and to avoid involving themselves in business beyond their ability to manage; or in hazardous or speculative trade? Are they just in their dealings, and punctual in complying with their contracts and engagements; and in paying their debts seasonably?[435]

Furthermore, it was provided that where there existed any "reasonable grounds for fear in these respects", the overseers were to deal with such persons "seasonably", and proceed as conditions seemed to require. It was due largely to this oversight or supervision for generations that the "Quaker's word was considered as good as his bond" in money matters.

In like manner, every precaution was used by the heads of the church to see that differences or misunderstandings among the membership did not find their way to the courts of law. When such difficulties did arise, the party who felt himself aggrieved was expected to "calmly and kindly, request the other to comply with the demand"; and if refused, he was to take with him one or more of the overseers and in their presence repeat to the offending party his demand. Then, if the difficulty still remained unsettled, the parties concerned were required to choose a number of impartial Friends as arbitrators, and mutually agree by bond or written agreement to abide by their decision. A full and fair hearing was then given to the parties in the presence of each other, whereupon the arbitrators after mutual consultation apart gave their united opinion. If either of the parties refused to abide by this opinion he was to be "complained of" and dealt with in the usual manner of procedure by that body, even to the extent of disownment.[436] In any case, to proceed at law a member was required to first secure the consent of the Monthly Meeting after a thorough investigation of the case; and to do so without such consent, whether he was right or wrong, was in itself a disownable offense.

The attitude of the Quakers relative to music, dancing, the theater, and fiction, is also worth noting.

It is a well known fact that until recent years (and then the change was only among the progressive sect) the Quakers have been a songless people except in their homes. Not that the Friends have ever been insensible to music as an art, but they opposed it because of the excessive amount of time consumed in acquiring proficiency in an art which administered to purely aesthetic pleasure. So far as music in their meetings for worship was concerned, the very thought was incompatible with their idea of waiting upon the Lord in silence for His divine direction.

For far more serious reasons did the Quakers discard dancing, the theater, and fiction. To them, the gaiety of the ball room and the movement of men and women in close bodily contact seemed to be the most conducive means for awakening the human passions and evil desires. To this objection were added the unseemly hours usually kept by dancers, together with the physical exhaustion which followed, the vain attention given to attire, the jealousies and envy aroused in the bidding for personal attention, and the evil excesses which so frequently attended such occasions. These, one and all, they held to be ill calculated to foster and preserve the more sensitive promptings of the soul, or the purity of the mind; and in consequence dancing was early placed under the ban in their discipline. In like manner the Quakers from the time of George Fox to the present have held theater-going to be a diversion warranting disownment. The intrigue and trickery without due punishment so often portrayed, and the unnatural excitement and feeling aroused almost invariably disqualified the habitual attender, so the Quakers conceived, for the more substantial and particularly the religious attitude of mind, and so it could not be countenanced.

While not condemning all fiction, that of a light, worthless, and trashy character was among them scrupulously guarded against. All through the early years in Iowa each of the Monthly Meetings maintained a committee to inspect the books and papers that came into the homes, and to advise against any that might appear to be harmful. To encourage good reading, large numbers of books were sent to these western settlements by interested Friends in the East and in England, so that almost every Monthly Meeting had a library of the standard Quaker works, free for the use of all; and, as indicated by the records, they were widely read and appreciated.[437]

To be sure, most of the manners and customs once peculiar to the Quakers have almost disappeared among the Friends in Iowa, and the rigid application of the policy of disownment for trivial breaches of order has broken down. Still, to a large extent, "plainness in dress and address" is practiced among the Wilburites and Conservatives of this State. Among the Orthodox body, the plain Quaker costume and the "thou" or "thee" are the exceptions rather than the rule, and seldom are either observed among the young; while the matter of amusements, though still discussed,[438] is but little regulated by the church.

V

QUAKER HOME LIFE

FROM the founding of their Society to the present time the Friends have been a people much attached to their homes, not seeking their pleasures in the diversions of the outside world. Home life to them has always stood next to religion.

Sedate and reserved as the Quaker appeared to the world, when met and known in his home he proved to be one of the most congenial of men. Within the domestic circle there was not the slightest show of formality; and the guest who came, whether high or low, was received on a par with the members of the family and given the heartiest of welcomes. Along with the kindnesses or attentions shown there was no attempt at strained entertainment; for the guest was fully expected to indulge himself as he pleased, while the necessary work of the house or of the farm went on as usual. Above all, the guest was told, after the Quaker manner, "to be free", and that to ask for what he wanted was but to show agreeable contentment. Their hospitality was born of the long custom among themselves of frequent and uninvited visiting, especially in this western country.

To the visitor from the world conversation

among the Friends seemed limited, for rarely did they discuss topics of common political or social concern: their chief interest was in church and neighborhood affairs. With them it was not uncommon, while sitting together, for a long period of silence or religious reflection to occur, which oftentimes ended with prayer or religious discussion without the slightest reserve. On the other hand, the Quakers had a wit and humor all their own, which not infrequently displayed itself. Seldom making use of sarcasm or hurtful personal reference, the Quaker joke in anecdote form is thoroughly enjoyable. Much of their humor concerned itself with amusing incidents known to have occurred — such as the story of the eccentric old Quaker who refused to allow his wife to grow red roses in her garden because they reminded him of the devil, while at the same time she might raise as many white roses as she wanted to; or that of the old Quaker preacher who contended that his was the best example of a pure and unadulterated Gospel, because he could neither read nor write.[439]

Noticeable, too, in general was the simple plainness in the furnishings of the Quaker home. The Quakers were trained to this principle, for back in New England the ancestors of the Iowa Friends had been taught through disciplinary requirement to "keep to plainness in household stuff and furniture . . . . avoiding in particular Striped and Flowered Bed or Window hangings of Divers Colours, and Quilts. Counter paines and Table Carpetts

[cloths], of like gaudy Colours & Double Vållants
[drapings] and fringes'', and especially that ''all
Friends that have vessells of Silver do not set them
up in any publick place nor no other flowered painted
vessells, seeming more to bee seen than otherwise''.[440] Nothing was to be kept for mere show,
not even pictures or paintings; and even in Iowa
to-day, among the more conservative members of the
Society, what few pictures there are to be found are
almost invariably of a simple religious character,
set in inexpensive frames.

Lacking in expensive furniture though they were,
one thing almost invariably attracted the visitor's
eye in the Quaker's home, namely, his collection of
books. Among those old-time leather-bound, or
black cloth-covered, volumes one would seldom find
the recognized masterpieces of the world's literature; but, on the other hand, seldom was there
lacking a copy of George Fox's *Journal,* Barclay's
Apology, or the writings of William Penn. A glance
at the family calendar would also be of interest, for,
much to the surprise of one untutored in the Quaker
ways, he would find the common names of the days
and months all missing, and in their places the
simple system of numeration, First Day, Second
Day, Third Day, and so on, or First Month, Second
Month, and so on to the end. On inquiry for the
cause of this strange custom the unembarrassed
reply would be that the common names of the days
and months were of pagan origin, except for the
months of September, October, November, and De-

cember, which were intended in the Latin to stand
for the seventh, eighth, ninth, and tenth months of
the year, but in the change of the calendar these
appellations were made incorrect, and were in consequence rejected by the Quakers.[441]

Of no less interest were meal-times among the
Friends; for with the abundance of simple but
wholesome food and the good cheer that prevailed,
the visitor was always welcome, whoever he might
be. Little given to superfluity of any kind, the question of saying grace at the table was a serious one,
for, thought they, better nothing said than that
which came not from a reverent and honest heart.
In consequence it was their custom when all were
seated to observe a time of meditative silence, and if
any one were moved to vocal utterance, he should
prove obedient to his promptings. Not infrequently
it occurred that for days or even weeks at a time no
grace was said; but when it came, or come as frequently as it might, it was almost invariably sincere
in tone and free from stereotyped expressions.

Thus have the Quakers lived in contentment,
peace, and plenty. Patiently have they toiled and
worshipped. Bravely, too, have they met their
problems, conscious of a mission and a given end and
destiny. Through all the storms of their troubled
course, nothing has seemed permanently to disturb
them: nothing has destroyed their faith. Well have
they served the world, queer though they may have
seemed to be.

APPENDICES

SHOWING THE NUMERICAL STRENGTH OF THE IOWA YEARLY MEETING OF (ORTHODOX) FRIENDS BY 5 YEAR PERIODS

NUMBER OF MEMBERS	INCREASE	DECREASE	Number of Children between 5 and 21 Years	REMARKS
6,000*			2,403	*An estimate. The first report given 1866 sh 7,652 members.
7,639	1,639		2,526	
8,680	1,041		1,124*	*This report is for 1872 and is not complete.
9,077	397		2,243*	*This report is for 1879.
9,431	354			
10,234	803			Period of Evangelism.
11,415	1,181			
11,274		141		
11,022		252		The Yearly Meetings of Oregon, California, Nebraska set off from Iowa during this pe
9,434		1,588		
8,383		1,051		

Table Showing the Results of the Evangelistic Efforts of the Iowa Yearly Meeting of (Orthodox) Friends for the Decades 1883-1893 and 1902-1912

YEAR	Membership of the Yearly Meeting	Number of Series of Meetings Held	Number of Conversions	Number of Sanctifications	Number of Renewals	Total Number Blessed	Additions to the Church	Amount Paid to Evangelists
1883-84	9,597	...	....	...	...	2200	639	(not reported)
1884-85	9,730	123	710	314	286	1310	..?	$1,343.11
1885-86	9,546	...	1228	221	439	1888	...	1,789.81
1886-87	9,742	94	1130	72	386	1588	288	1,785.65
1887-88	10,234	111	430	73	299	802	500	1,568.37
1888-89	10,859	...	3300	365	559	4224	907	3,214.70
1889-90	11,334	...	2570	397	365	3332	900	2,627.23
1890-91	12,118	91	1030	533	221	1784	878	2,830.54
1891-92	12,289	98	1474	425	464	2363	885	2,125.25
1892-93	11,415	109	1337	242	443	2022	686	2,799.64
1902-03	11,022	96	558	248	354	1160	507	1,987.57
1903-04	11,135	85	847	233	390	1470	589	2,036.49
1904-05	11,474	90	727	377	573	1677	776	2,047.55
1905-06	11,506	102	766	326	601	1693	881	2,523.00
1906-07	11,090	85	593	176	342	1111	821	2,561.18
1907-08	9,434	75	669	110	285	1064	669	2,225.00
1908-09	8,929	69	....	...	...	733	...	3,120.55
1909-10	9,035	63	....	...	...	954	495	2,288.67
1910-11	8,578	52	176	77	152	405	475	1,786.16
1911-12	8,383	58	346	97	175	618	458	1,573.91

APPENDIX C

RULES AND REGULATIONS OF THE STAVANGER BOARDING SCHOOL

The following rules and regulations were in force at the Friends' Boarding School at Stavanger, Iowa, during the year 1910–1911:

FIRST

"Students will be expected to show due respect for the officers and teachers of the institution and for each other, giving cheerful compliance to the rules and regulations of the same.

SECOND

"All persons connected with the school are expected to attend meetings for worship at the Friends meeting house nearby, on First and Fifth days of the week, conducting themselves in a manner becoming the occasion.

THIRD

"Visiting will not be expected in or about the building on the 1st day of the week and pupils are not to leave the premises without permission.

.   .   .   .

SIXTH

"It will be expected that the pupils use the

English language in their general intercourse among themselves and others, and in the use of language it is requested that the correct form [thou and thee] in regard to which Friends bear a testimony and is set forth in the Holy Scripture.

SEVENTH

"Students are respectfully requested to dispense with such apparel, jewelry and fashionable customs inconsistent with true simplicity which the committee superintendent and matron shall indicate.

. . . .

NINTH

"Tobacco in any form, chewing gum, musical instruments and firearms are strictly forbidden, and any reading matter found in the possession of the pupils or anything being practiced which the committee or care takers consider objectionable are to be removed."

APPENDIX D

QUAKER QUERIES

The following "Queries" were read annually before each Preparative and Monthly Meeting of Friends, and were answered in writing as prescribed by the *Discipline of Indiana Yearly Meeting, 1854,* pp. 81, 82. Practically the same queries are used among all branches of the Friends in Iowa to-day.

"FIRST QUERY.— Are all the meetings for worship and discipline attended? Do Friends avoid unbecoming behavior therein? And is the hour of meeting observed?

"SECOND.— Are Friends preserved in christian love one toward another? Are tale-bearing and detraction discouraged? And when differences arise, are endeavors used speedily to end them?

"THIRD.— Do Friends endeavor, by example and precept, to educate their children, and those under their care, in the principles of the Christian religion, and in plainness of speech, deportment, and apparel? Do they guard them against reading pernicious books, and from corrupt conversation? And are they encouraged to read the Holy Scriptures diligently?

"FOURTH.— Are Friends clear of importing, vending, distilling, and the unnecessary use of all

19   289

intoxicating liquors? And attending circus-shows and other places of diversion? And do they observe moderation and temperance on all occasions?

"FIFTH.— Are the necessities of the poor, and the circumstances of those who may appear likely to require aid, inspected and relieved? Are they advised and assisted in such employments as they are capable of; and is due care taken to promote the school-education of their children?

"SIXTH.— Do Friends maintain a testimony against priests' and ministers' wages? Against Slavery; oaths; bearing arms, and all military services; trading in goods taken in war; and against lotteries?

"SEVENTH.— Are Friends careful to live within the bounds of their circumstances, and to avoid involving themselves in business beyond their ability to manage; or in hazardous or speculative trade? Are they just in their dealings, and punctual in complying with their contracts and engagements; and in paying their debts seasonably? And where any give reasonable grounds for fear in these respects, is due care extended to them?

"EIGHTH.— Is care taken to deal with offenders seasonably and impartially, and to endeavor to evince to those who will not be reclaimed, the spirit of meekness and love, before judgment is placed upon them?"

APPENDIX E

QUAKER MARRIAGE CERTIFICATE

The following is the accustomed form of the Quaker marriage certificate as prescribed by the Indiana Yearly Meeting of Friends in its *Discipline* for 1854, p. 53:

"*Whereas,* A. B. of ————— in the county of —————, in the state of ————— son of C. and H. B. of —————; and D. E. daughter of F. and G. E. of ————— having declared their intentions of marriage with each other, before a Monthly meeting of the religious society of Friends, held at ————— *(where the parties are under the care of parents or guardians, unless in the case of unreasonable objections, add)* and having consent of parents or guardians concerned, *(as the case may be)* their proposals of marriage were allowed by said meeting. These are to certify whom it may concern, that for the full accomplishment of their said intentions, this ————— day of the ————— month, in the year of our Lord —————, they, the said A. B. and D. E. appeared in a public meeting of the said people, held at ————— aforesaid; and the said A. B. taking the said D. E. by the hand, declared that he took her to be his wife, promising, with divine assistance, to be unto her a loving and faithful husband, until death should separate them: and then the said D. E. did in like manner declare, that she took him the said A. B. to be her husband, promising, with divine assistance, to be unto him a loving and faithful wife, until death should separate them. And moreover, they, the said A. B. and D. E. (she according to the custom of marriage adopting the name of her husband) did, as a further confirmation thereof, then and there, to these presents set their hands.

A. B.

D. B.

"And we, whose names are also hereunto subscribed, being present at the solemnization of the said marriage have, as witnesses thereto, set our hands the day and year above written."

NOTES AND REFERENCES

NOTES AND REFERENCES

PART I

CHAPTER I

[1] In 1698 William Penn, the founder of Pennsylvania, published a little book entitled *Primitive Christianity Revived*. This book has always been acknowledged by the Society of Friends as a clear and candid, though brief, exposition of its beliefs upon the great and cardinal principles of Christianity. It shows clearly that the message of the Quakers was the plain Gospel message of the primitive church.

[2] Some idea of the extent to which the Friends suffered for the sake of their testimonies may be gained by the following facts:

During a period of twenty-five years under Charles II it is said that there were "13,562 Friends . . . . imprisoned in various parts of England, 198 were transported as slaves beyond seas, and 338 died in prison or of wounds received in violent assaults on their meetings."— Quoted from William Beck's *The Friends*, p. 65, in *The American Church History Series*, Vol. XII, p. 204.

During the American Revolution the Quakers were again subjected to the most bitter persecutions because of their refusal to serve in the army or pay war tithes. In one Quarterly Meeting alone in Pennsylvania over $68,000 was levied between 1778 and 1786 in fines against members of the order.— See Sharpless's *A History of Quaker Government in Pennsylvania*, Vol. II, p. 177.

[3] In America the relative numerical strength of the Quakers to other religious denominations is shown by the following statistical table found in *The American Year Book* for 1910, p. 735.

DENOMINATIONS	RANK IN 1909	COMMUNICANTS
Roman Catholic	1	12,354,596
Methodist Episcopal	2	3,159,913
Regular Baptist (South)	3	2,139,080
Regular Baptist (Colored)	4	1,874,261
Methodist Episcopal (South)	5	1,780,778
Presbyterian (Northern)	6	1,311,828
Disciples of Christ	7	1,273,357

DENOMINATIONS	RANK IN 1909	COMMUNICANTS
Regular Baptist (North)	8	1,176,380
Protestant Episcopal	9	912,123
Congregationalist	10	732,500
Lutheran Synodical Conference	11	726,526
African Methodist Episcopal (Zion)	12	545,681
Lutheran General Council	13	452,818
African Methodist Episcopal	14	452,126
Latter-Day Saints	15	350,000
Reformed (German)	16	293,836
United Brethren	17	285,019
Lutheran General Synod	18	284,805
Presbyterian (Southern)	19	269,733
German Evangelical Synod	20	249,137
Colored Methodist Episcopal	21	233,911
Methodist Protestant	22	188,122
United Norwegian Lutheran	23	160,645
Spiritualists	24	150,000
United Presbyterian	25	132,925
Greek Orthodox (Catholic)	26	130,000
Lutheran Synod of Ohio	27	120,031
Reformed Dutch	28	116,174
Evangelical Association	29	106,957
Primitive Baptist	30	102,311
Society of Friends (Orthodox)	31	*100,072

*In 1910.

4 In a little pamphlet of sixteen pages, written by Dr. David Gregg, and entitled *The Quakers as Makers of America*, there is an excellent summary of the contributions which the Quakers have made to society.

5 Fox's *Journal* (Philadelphia), p. 55.

6 Fox's *Journal* (Philadelphia), p. xxiv.

7 Fox's *Journal* (Philadelphia), pp. 56, 57, 58.

8 Fox's *Journal* (Philadelphia), pp. 59, 60.

9 Fox's *Journal* (Philadelphia), p. 60.

10 In October, 1650, George Fox was confined in the house of correction at Derby, where he remained for a period of six months, on a charge of blasphemy. While in confinement there he wrote to the several priests and magistrates who had been responsible for his imprisonment, warning them of the judgments of God which would come upon them, and bidding them to "tremble at the word of the

Lord''. Justice Bennett, one of the magistrates thus addressed, picked up the phrase and called Fox and his followers ''Quakers''. Like most catch-words, the term soon became widely used, usually in derision. The Friends, however, early termed themselves ''Children of Light''; a little later they adopted the name ''Friends of Truth''; and finally they chose the term ''The Religious Society of Friends'', which is generally used as the official title of the Society. The terms ''Quaker'' and ''Friend'', however, are used interchangeably among the members of the order.

11 Green's *A Short History of the English People*, pp. 447, 449.

12 Fox's *Journal* (Philadelphia), pp. xxvi, xxvii.

13 Fox's *Journal* (Philadelphia), pp. 157, 647.

14 For an account of the work of the Friends in Europe see Braithwaite's *The Beginnings of Quakerism*, Ch. XVI.

15 In 1671 George Fox, accompanied by a number of Friends, visited Barbadoes for the purpose of spreading the Gospel. After laboring there several weeks they went to Jamaica, and remained there for about seven weeks before coming to America. In his recent work on *The Quakers in the American Colonies*, p. 26, Rufus M. Jones says, ''The island of Barbadoes was, during the seventeenth century, the great port of entry to the colonies in the western world, and it was during the last half of that century, a veritable 'hive' of Quakerism. Friends wishing to reach any part of the American coast, sailed most frequently for Barbadoes and then reshipped for their definite locality. They generally spent some weeks, or months even, propagating their doctrines in 'the island' and ordinarily paying visits to Jamaica and often to Antiqua, Nevis, and Bermuda.''

CHAPTER II

16 Quoted in Jones's *The Quakers in the American Colonies*, p. 28. See also Ellis's *The Puritan Age in Massachusetts, 1629–1685*, pp. 436, 437.

17 A part of the law passed against the Quakers on October 14, 1656, reads as follows:

''Whereas there is a cursed sect of haereticks lately risen up in the world, which are commonly called Quakers, who take uppon them to be immediately sent of God, and infallibly assisted by the spirit to speake and write blasphemouth opinions, despising government and the order of God in church and commonwealth, speaking evill of dignities, reproaching and reviling magistrates and ministers, seeking to turne the people from the faith and gaine proselites to theire pernicious waies, this Court, taking into serious consideration the premises, and to prevent the like mischiefe as by their meanes is wrought in our native land, doth heereby order, and by the authoritie of this Court be it ordered and enacted, that any commander of a vessel that shall bring into this jurisdiction any knowne Quaker or Quakers, or any other blasphemous haereticks as aforesaid, shall pay the fine of 100 pounds, except it appeare that he wanted true knowledge or information of theire being such; . . . . then to give bonds to carry them to the place whence he brought them.

''Any Quaker coming into this jurisdiction shall be forthwith committed to the house of correction, and at their entrance to be severely whipt, and by the master thereof to be kept constantly to worke, and none suffered to converse or speak with them during the time of their imprisonment, which shall be no longer than necessitie requireth.''— Ellis's *The Puritan Age in Massachusetts, 1629–1685*, p. 439.

18 In the General Court on October 14, 1657, the following provisions were added to the previous acts: that a male Quaker returning after having been once dealt with, should have one ear cut off, and be kept in the house of correction till he could be sent away at his own charges; and for again returning, he should lose the other ear. Every woman Quaker returning, was to be whipped and kept at work in the house of correction till removed at her own charge, and the same punishment was provided for a repetition of the offense. Every Quaker, returning still a third time, should have his tongue bored through with a hot iron, and again to be sent off. The same treatment was also to be visited upon Puritans who turned Quakers as upon strangers.— Ellis's *The Puritan Age in Massachusetts, 1629–1685*, p. 447.

19 For an account of the struggles between the Puritans and the Quakers herein mentioned, see Ellis's *The Puritan Age in Massachusetts, 1629–1685*, Ch. XII; Chandler's *American Criminal Trials*, Vol. I, pp. 33–63; Hallowell's *The Quaker Invasion of Massachusetts;* Jones's *The Quakers in the American Colonies*, Book I, Chs. II, III, IV, V; and Fox's *Journal* (Philadelphia), pp. 346–348.

20 The New England Yearly Meeting was organized about 1671. See *Friends' Library*, Vol. I, p. 119.

21 Fox's *Journal* (Philadelphia), p. 447.

22 Fox's *Journal* (Philadelphia), p. 449.

23 "The heydey of Quakerism in the South is indissolubly connected with the name of John Archdale, Governor-General of Carolina." See Weeks's *Southern Quakers and Slavery*, Ch. IV. The quotation is found on p. 50.

24 Jones's *The Quakers in the American Colonies*, p. 358.

25 Sharpless's *A History of Quaker Government in Pennsylvania*, Vol. I, p. 131.

26 Clarkson's *Memoirs of the Public and Private Life of William Penn*, p. 96.

27 Clarkson's *Memoirs of the Public and Private Life of William Penn*, p. 97.

CHAPTER III

28 Weeks's *Southern Quakers and Slavery*, p. 85.

29 Weeks's *Southern Quakers and Slavery*, pp. 96–125.

30 Quoted in Ramsey's *Annals of Tennessee*, p. 95.

31 Thwaites's *Daniel Boone*, Ch. I.

32 Weeks's *Southern Quakers and Slavery*, p. 252.

33 Weeks's *Southern Quakers and Slavery*, p. 253.

34 The text of the Ordinance of 1787, together with a list of references, may be found in Shambaugh's *Documentary Material Relating to the History of Iowa*, Vol. I, pp. 47–55.

35 For an excellent account of *The Quakers in the Old Northwest* see Harlow Lindley's paper under that title in the *Proceedings of the Mississippi Valley Historical Association for 1911–1912*, pp. 60–72.

36 Sharpless's *A History of Quaker Government in Pennsylvania*, Vol. II, Ch. X.

37 Weeks's *Southern Quakers and Slavery*, p. 307. See note, p. 307, taken from O'Neall's *Annals of Newberry*.

38 For the striking difference between the settlement of the Northwest Territory and that of Kentucky and Tennessee, see Roosevelt's *The Winning of the West* (Prairie Edition, 1903), Vol. V, pp. 5–7.

CHAPTER IV

[39] Joliet and Marquette were the first white men known to have touched Iowa. They landed near the mouth of the Iowa River on June 25, 1673. See Weld's *Joliet and Marquette in Iowa* in *The Iowa Journal of History and Politics*, Vol. I, p. 3.

[40] For a brief but excellent sketch of the Black Hawk War, see Pelzer's *Henry Dodge*, Ch. V.

[41] Newhall's *Sketches of Iowa, or the Emigrant's Guide*, pp. 141, 142.

[42] During the four years while the writer has been engaged in this work he has made numerous visits to Salem and has personally interviewed nearly all of the early settlers who were still living in the vicinity. He also very carefully examined what accounts of the founding of the town there were in the hands of Isaac Pidgeon, Jr., and others, and he feels satisfied as to the conclusions drawn.

[43] "It is somewhat remarkable that the father of the present Aaron Street emigrated from Salem, New Jersey, to Salem, Ohio; from Ohio, father and son came and built up Salem, Indiana; from Salem, Indiana, the subject of this article came and built up Salem, Iowa."— Newhall's *Sketches of Iowa*, p. 142.

[44] The sketch by Henry W. Joy here referred to bears no date, but it is apparent from his introductory statement that it was written towards the close of his life. He died at Salem on November 25, 1883, at the age of seventy-five years.

[45] At the Monthly Meeting held at Salem on February 23, 1839, that meeting received in lieu of certificates of membership a list of 193 persons from the Vermillion Monthly Meeting who had settled in the neighborhood of Salem. See *Minutes of Salem Monthly Meeting of Friends*, 2 mo. 23rd, 1839, pp. 11–14.

[46] *Minutes of Salem Monthly Meeting of Friends*, 10 mo., 8th, 1838, pp. 1, 2.

[47] *Minutes of Salem Monthly Meeting of Friends*, 11 mo., 24th, 1838, p. 5.

[48] *Minutes of Salem Monthly Meeting of Friends*, 12 mo., 29th, 1838, p. 6. The fact that there was three-fourths of a cent in the collections made by Henderson Lewelling is explainable by the likeli-

hood that there were three picayunes in the offering taken. The picayune was a small silver coin valued at six and one-fourth cents, which was in circulation before the introduction of the decimal system into the United States coinage in 1857. This coin was known in New England as a "fourpence", in Pennsylvania and Virginia as the "fip", and in Louisiana as the "picayune".

49 *Minutes of Salem Monthly Meeting of Friends*, 12 mo., 29th, 1838, p. 6.

50 *Minutes of Salem Monthly Meeting of Friends*, 11 mo., 24th, 1838, p. 4.

51 *Minutes of Salem Monthly Meeting of Friends*, 10 mo., 8th, 1838, p. 2; 11 mo., 24th, 1838, p. 4.

52 *Minutes of Salem Monthly Meeting of Friends*, 5 mo., 25th, 1839, pp. 19, 20; 5 mo., 30th, 1840, p. 44.

53 Newhall's *Sketches of Iowa*, pp. 143, 144.

54 *Salem Weekly News*, February 24, 1898.

CHAPTER V

55 Hull's *Historical and Comparative Census of Iowa*, 1880, p. 198.

56 See Garver's *History of the Establishment of Counties in Iowa* in *The Iowa Journal of History and Politics*, Vol. VI, pp. 375–456.

57 Before proceeding at law against a fellow member, all members of the Society of Friends were expected to obtain the advice and consent of their Monthly Meeting. Every possible encouragement was given for the settlement of all disputes outside of the courts, and (quoting from the *Discipline of the Indiana Yearly Meeting*, 1854, p. 48), "if any members of our religious society, disregarding the gospel order prescribed by our Discipline, shall arrest or sue at law other members . . . . [they] do depart from the peaceable principles of which we make profession: and if on being treated with by the Monthly meetings to which they belong, they cannot be prevailed with to withdraw the suit, and pay the costs thereof, they shall be disowned." It is because of this principle that very few members of the Society have followed the profession of law.

58 *Minutes of Salem Monthly Meeting of Friends*, 3 mo., 30th, 1839, p. 16; 4 mo., 27th, 1839, p. 17; 1 mo., 30th, 1841, pp. 56, 57.

59 *Minutes of Salem Monthly Meeting of Friends,* 10 mo., 26th, 1839, pp. 29, 30; 11 mo., 30th, 1839, p. 31; 1 mo., 30th, 1841, p. 57.

60 For a good account of the Mormon influence in Lee County see *Mormonism and Mormon Outrages* in *The History of Lee County* (Chicago: Western Historical Company, 1879), pp. 465–483.

61 A third very important factor in the weakening of Quakerism in this early center was the planting of the Roman Catholic stronghold at Mt. Hamill in the very heart of the Quaker region. In late years these Catholics have bought up nearly all of the available lands in the vicinity, and the Quakers have all but disappeared.

62 William Scearcy, a pioneer settler in both Jefferson and Keokuk counties, writing late in life, says that when he returned in the spring of 1839 from the Illinois side to the site of Pleasant Plain where he had marked out a town and sold lots he found that the Quakers had moved in, ''taken advantage of my absence and 'jumped' my claim, town and all, and as I could not legally hold it, they would not give it up nor pay me anything for what I had done.''— *The History of Keokuk County* (Des Moines: Union Historical Company, 1880), p. 286.

63 *Minutes of Pleasant Plain Monthly Meeting of Friends,* 12 mo., 28th, 1842, p. 1.

64 For the purpose of safeguarding the interests of the Society, it has always been the custom among the Friends for members upon moving into the limits of another Monthly Meeting to present a letter or certificate of good standing in their home Monthly Meeting before being allowed to take part in the business of the meeting in their new home. Such certificates of membership, in a general way, indicate the sections from which the Quakers came to Iowa, but on account of the duplication of the names of Monthly Meetings in different States and the frequent omission of the names of the States in the entries on local records, conclusions on this basis are not always reliable.

65 See *The History of Keokuk County* (Des Moines: Union Historical Company, 1880), pp. 546, 547.

66 *The History of Mahaska County* (Des Moines: Union Historical Company, 1878), pp. 367, 368.

67 For the first settlement of Friends in Warren County, see *The History of Warren County* (Des Moines: Union Historical Company, 1879), p. 287.

68 *Minutes of Salem Monthly Meeting of Friends*, 9 mo., 28th, 1844, p. 222.

69 *Minutes of Salem Quarterly Meeting of Women Friends*, 5 mo., 20th, 1848, p. 1. The first book of minutes for the Salem Quarterly Meeting of [Men] Friends is lost.

70 *Minutes of Salem Monthly Meeting of Friends*, 2 mo., 28th, 1846, p. 279.

71 Quoted in the *Friends' Review* (1848), Vol. I, pp. 675, 676.

CHAPTER VI

72 The movements of the two English Friends, Robert Lindsey and Benjamin Seebohm, among the American Yearly Meetings in 1848 are noted in the *Friends' Review*, Vol. I, p. 377; Vol. II, p. 227.

73 Rachel Kellum, an aged resident of Salem (now deceased), some years ago related to the writer that in the early days her father kept a candle burning at night in his window looking to the eastward, to guide incoming travelers through the darkness to his door. To make the candles burn slowly a thin coating of salt was sprinkled around the wick, and one candle would usually burn through most of the night.

74 Joseph D. Hoag was one of the three commissioners appointed by the General Assembly of Iowa in 1847 ''to locate the permanent Seat of Government of this State, and to select the lands granted by Congress to aid in erecting public buildings.''— *Laws of Iowa*, 1847, p. 85. The quotations in the text are taken from a copy of Robert Lindsey's *Journal*.

75 ''Appointed Meetings'' were such as the name itself indicates. The minister in traveling from place to place among the Friends in the early days would usually have it announced as he came into a community that there would be a meeting for worship either at the meeting-house or at some Friend's home, to which all would be welcomed. At these meetings there usually was preaching by the visiting minister, although many times they were held in silence. Protracted or revival meetings were almost unknown among the Friends before the last half of the nineteenth century. See Lindsey's *Journal*.

76 The Hollanders made their first settlements in Iowa in the summer of 1847. Pella was laid out in September of that year. See Van der Zee's *The Hollanders of Iowa*, Ch. IX.

[77] Among the Friends such salutations as ''good morning'' or ''goodbye'' were seldom used, it being considered that all things in the providence of God were good. In place of these expressions, ''is thee well'', or ''farewell'', were generally, and are still, used.

[78] The manuscript from which the body of this chapter is taken is a copy of that part of Robert Lindsey's *Journal* for 1850 which covers his travels in Iowa. The copy mentioned was made from the original by Elizabeth Lindsey Galleway of Yorkshire, England, the daughter of the late Robert Lindsey, for Professor Rayner W. Kelsey of Haverford College, Haverford, Pennsylvania. Professor Kelsey very kindly loaned the manuscript to the writer. A transcript was made and is now in the possession of The State Historical Society of Iowa.

CHAPTER VII

[79] See census returns of 1910 for the States west of the Mississippi River.

[80] Brinton Darlington, long one of the most prominent members of the Red Cedar Monthly Meeting, was born in Pennsylvania in 1804. He was successful in business, being a partner in a large woolen mill. This mill burned late in 1841, and Darlington moved to Iowa with his family in the spring of 1842.— *Memorials Concerning Deceased Friends, Members of Iowa Yearly Meeting* (Philadelphia, 1872), pp. 15, 16.

See also Tatum's article on the *Early History of the Settlement of Friends at Springdale, Iowa, and their Meetings,* pasted in with the *Minutes of Springdale Monthly Meeting of Friends,* 5 mo., 21st, 1892, p. 217.

[81] On this trip William Evans visited the Friends meetings in the vicinity of Salem, Pleasant Plain, and Richland, as well as the Oakley settlement, but did not go into the more central part of the State.

[82] *Journal of the Life and Religious Services of William Evans* (Philadelphia, 1870), pp. 525, 526.

[83] This concrete meeting-house at Red Cedar was claimed by some to be the first building erected for religious purposes in Cedar County, although there seems to have been an earlier one at Tipton. See Aurner's *A Topical History of Cedar County, Iowa* (Chicago, 1910), p. 127, and note 105 on p. 515.

84 *Minutes of Red Cedar Monthly Meeting of Friends*, 4 mo., 9th, 1853, p. 1.

85 Hull's *Historical and Comparative Census of Iowa*, 1880, pp. 198, 199.

86 *The Friend*, Vol. XXVII, p. 319.

87 Iowa became a State on December 28, 1846. See Shambaugh's *History of the Constitutions of Iowa*, p. 327.

88 In *The Friend* for July 23, 1853, the editor notes ''an account furnished . . . . more than a year ago [by a Friend who had settled in Linn County], descriptive and recommendatory of a settlement that he and some others were then about making far off in the prairies of that State.'' Among the reasons given by the editor for withholding this account are ''the loss experienced by members of our Society who settle remote from the body of Society, and are in some measure freed from the restraint, which, through its meetings and the oversight of the rightly concerned, it exerts over them. We . . . . think Friends everywhere ought to be well persuaded that it is in the ordering of Truth, before they break loose from the neighborhoods and meetings where they have been long living, and where perhaps they may be most likely to prosper in best things.''— *The Friend*, Vol. XXVI, p. 359.

89 At the first and opening meeting of the Red Cedar Monthly Meeting (4 mo., 9th, 1853, p. 2) the following minute was recorded: ''The Friends of Lynn & Jones counties request the privilege of holding a meeting for worship . . . . and a preparative meeting . . . . to be known by the name of Fairview''.

90 *Friends' Review*, Vol. VIII, p. 455.

91 *Minutes of Red Cedar Monthly Meeting of Friends*, 2 mo., 7th, 1855, pp. 107–109.

92 *Minutes of Red Cedar Monthly Meeting of Friends*, 2 mo., 7th, 1855, p. 107.
The committee appointed to visit the Friends in Winneshiek County was made up of Enoch Peasley, Jeremiah A. Grinnell, Asa Staples, Amos Hampton, Brinton Darlington, David Tatum, Elisha Stratton, and James Schooley.

93 See the printed sketch by Laurie Tatum, entitled *Early History of the Settlement of Friends at Springdale, Iowa, and their Meetings*,

pasted into the book of *Minutes of Springdale Monthly Meeting of Friends* for 1892, pp. 217, 218, 228.

94 *Minutes of Red Cedar Monthly Meeting of Friends*, 5 mo., 9th, 1855, p. 121.

95 On this second trip Robert Lindsey was among the Iowa Friends from April 29 to July 19, 1858. The copy of this journal in manuscript form was loaned to the author by the Haverford College Library through the interest of Professor Rayner W. Kelsey. A transcript was made and is now in the possession of The State Historical Society of Iowa.

CHAPTER VIII

96 The writer compiled his data for the Iowa field in 1850 and 1860 chiefly from two booklets published by the authority of the ''Meeting for Sufferings'' of the Indiana Yearly Meeting of Friends, each entitled: *Statement of Indiana Yearly Meeting, and All the Meetings Thereunto Belonging: The Days of Holding them, and Their Location,* one covering the year 1850, and the other the year 1859.

97 With the adoption of the uniform Discipline in 1902 the Orthodox Friends in Iowa abandoned the old Preparative Meeting as a business unit, and it became in most cases merely a meeting for worship.

98 In 1902 all of the American Yearly Meetings of Friends except Ohio, Philadelphia, and Canada, united under a uniform church discipline termed ''The Constitution and Discipline for the American Yearly Meetings of Friends''. Though now banded together in what is called the ''Five Years Meeting'', each Yearly Meeting retains the right ''to adopt additional disciplinary regulations not inconsistent herewith.''— Thomas's *A History of Friends in America* (4th edition), pp. 24, 25.

99 *Minutes of Salem Quarterly Meeting of Women Friends*, 5 mo., 15th, 1852, p. 52. See also p. 67.

100 *Minutes of Red Cedar Quarterly Meeting of Friends*, 5 mo., 8th, 1858, p. 1.

101 *Minutes of Salem Quarterly Meeting of Women Friends*, 11 mo., 19th, 1853, p. 80.

[102] *Minutes of Western Plain Quarterly Meeting of Women Friends*, 6 mo., 5th, 1858, p. 1.

[103] *Minutes of Red Cedar Quarterly Meeting of Friends*, 11 mo., 13th, 1858, p. 20.

[104] *Minutes of Red Cedar Quarterly Meeting of Friends*, 2 mo., 12th, 1859, p. 23; *Minutes of Western Plain Quarterly Meeting of Women Friends*, 3 mo., 5th, 1859, p. 17.

[105] *Minutes of Iowa Yearly Meeting of Friends*, 1863, pp. 1, 2.

[106] *Minutes of Indiana Yearly Meeting of Friends*, 1860, pp. 20, 21.

[107] *Minutes of Red Cedar Quarterly Meeting of Friends*, 2 mo., 9th, 1861, pp. 67–69.

[108] *Minutes of Red Cedar Quarterly Meeting of Friends*, 8 mo., 10th, 1861, p. 76.

[109] *Minutes of Bangor* (Western Plain) *Quarterly Meeting of Women Friends*, 12 mo., 7th, 1861, pp. 62, 63.

[110] *Minutes of Red Cedar Quarterly Meeting of Friends*, 5 mo., 10th, 1862, pp. 89, 90, 91.

[111] *Minutes of Red Cedar Monthly Meeting of Friends*, 5 mo., 10th, 1862, p. 91.

The "Meeting for Sufferings" had its origin in England during the severe persecutions of the Quakers in that country. In order to provide a convenient medium through which the sufferers might reach the ear of the government, in 1675 it was agreed "that certain Friends of this city [London] be nominated to keep a constant meeting about sufferings four times in a year, with the day and time of each meeting here fixed and settled. That at least one Friend of each county be appointed by the Quarterly Meeting thereof, to be in readiness to repair to any of the said meetings at this city, at such times as their urgent occasions or sufferings shall require."— *The Friends' Library*, Vol. I, p. 119.

In later times these "Meetings for Sufferings" became the representative bodies of the Society when the Yearly Meetings were not in session. Among the Iowa Friends to-day this "Meeting" is perpetuated in the "Permanent Board".

[112] *Minutes of Red Cedar Quarterly Meeting of Friends*, 8 mo., 9th, 1862, p. 95.

[113] *Minutes of Indiana Yearly Meeting of Friends*, 1862, p. 5.

CHAPTER IX

114 *Minutes of Red Cedar Quarterly Meeting of Friends*, 2 mo., 14th, 1863, p. 105.

115 At the time of his letter to the writer, December 31, 1912, Charles F. Coffin wrote with trembling hand: ''I am nearing my 90th birthday and am the only living member of the Committees to attend the opening of the Yearly Meeting.''

116 *The Saturday Globe* (Oskaloosa), February 27, 1909.

117 The following named persons came from the several Quarterly Meetings:

''Salem — Joseph D. Hoag, Willet Dorland, Ephraim D. Ratliff, Stephen Hockett, and Thomas Siveter.

''Pleasant Plain — Barclay Johnson, David Morgan, Benjamin Hollingsworth, and Wm. Pearson.

''Red Cedar — Olney Thompson, Enoch Hoag, Israel Negus, Wm. Harris, Laurie Tatum, and Elisha Strattan.

''Bangor — Wm. Hobson, David Hunt, Henry H. Macy, Jacob B. McGrew, Thomas Moore, Ira Cook, Lindley M. Hoag, James Owen, Wm. Farquhar, and Wm. Reese.

''South River — Benjamin Smith, John Tomlinson, Nathan Craven, Jesse Hadley, and Isaac Starbuck''.— *Minutes of Iowa Yearly Meeting of Friends*, 1863, p. 8.

118 Of the representatives officially appointed by other Yearly Meetings to be at the opening of the Iowa Yearly Meeting there were twenty-eight persons present.— *Minutes of Iowa Yearly Meeting of Friends*, 1863, pp. 7, 8.

119 The second national conference of the ''Friends First-Day Scripture Schools'' was held at Spring Creek on the 9th, 10th, 11th, and 12th of September, 1863.

120 *The Saturday Globe* (Oskaloosa), February 27, 1909.

121 A sketch prepared by Dr. J. W. Morgan of Oskaloosa, Iowa, in 1912, at the request of the writer.

122 *Minutes of Iowa Yearly Meeting of Friends*, 1863, p. 9.

123 *Minutes of Iowa Yearly Meeting of Friends*, 1863, pp. 11, 22, 25.

The contention over the site for the yearly meeting-house was presented "to the Friends in attendance by appointment of other Yearly meetings" by two members from each of the Iowa Quarters; and after patiently listening to all the claims and personally visiting the sites in question, John White's lot on the north side of Oskaloosa, was selected "with the understanding that the title shall be unconditional, ... and that the meeting house lot shall be free of cost to the Yearly Meeting as has been proposed to us."

124 *Minutes of Iowa Yearly Meeting of Friends*, 1863, p. 19.

125 *The Saturday Globe* (Oskaloosa), February 27, 1909.

126 *Minutes of Iowa Yearly Meeting of Friends*, 1863, pp. 27, 33.

CHAPTER X

127 In the new thirty thousand dollar yearly meeting-house at Oskaloosa the Iowa Yearly Meeting of (Orthodox) Friends celebrated its fiftieth anniversary on September 5 and 6, 1913. A full account of the proceedings may be found in *The Oskaloosa Herald*, September 5 and 6, 1913.

128 *Iowa Geological Survey*, Vol. II, pp. 37, 38, 340.

129 *Iowa Geological Survey*, Vol. XIX, p. 559.

130 Acknowledgments should here be made of the kindness of Dr. J. W. Morgan of Oskaloosa, Iowa, who made a special trip to this locality with which he was once so familiar, in order that he might correctly write this sketch.

131 *Minutes of Iowa Yearly Meeting of Friends*, 1866, pp. 12, 26.

132 *Minutes of Iowa Yearly Meeting of (Orthodox) Friends*, 1912. See statistical table attached.

133 Between the five-year periods, 1876 to 1880 and 1906 to 1910, the additions in membership by births to the Orthodox Friends in Iowa fell from about 2 1/10 per cent to 1 1/10 per cent of the total membership, respectively. Though this is not the actual rate of birth, it is strongly indicative of what has been suggested. The same fact for the earlier years is even more markedly true, as is shown by the hundreds of biographical sketches of pioneer Quaker families in this State which the writer has collected.

134 It is a noticeable fact that the Orthodox and Conservative Friends usually unite with such denominations as the Methodist, Presbyterian, or Congregational, while the Hicksite and Wilbur Friends generally affiliate with the Unitarian and Universalist bodies.

135 *Minutes of Iowa Yearly Meeting of (Orthodox) Friends*, 1888, p. 9.

136 *Minutes of Iowa Yearly Meeting of (Orthodox) Friends*, 1893, p. 8. The number of members is based on the statistical report of 1892, which gives Newberg 791 members and Salem 164 members.

137 The two Quarterly Meetings originally composing the California Yearly Meeting of Friends were Whittier and Pasadena. See the *Minutes of Iowa Yearly Meeting of (Orthodox) Friends*, 1894, pp. 11, 20, and 1895, p. 7.

138 For a statistical report of the Quarterly Meetings composing the Nebraska Yearly Meeting see *Minutes of Iowa Yearly Meeting of (Orthodox) Friends*, 1907, p. 47.

For the report of the committee which aided in establishing the new Yearly Meeting see the *Minutes of Iowa Yearly Meeting of (Orthodox) Friends*, 1908, pp. 6, 7.

PART II

CHAPTER I

139 *Minutes of Salem Monthly Meeting of Friends*, 1 mo., 30th, 1841, p. 58.

140 *The Discipline of the Society of Friends of Indiana Yearly Meeting*, 1854, p. 87.

141 *Minutes of Pleasant Plain Monthly Meeting of Friends*, 6 mo., 26th, 1844, p. 39.

142 For a sketch of the beginnings of this revival, see *Autobiography of Allen Jay*, pp. 110–112.

143 From a sketch of Center Grove Christian Vigilance Band, prepared by Pliny Fry at the request of the writer.

144 *Minutes of Salem Quarterly Meeting of Friends*, 8 mo., 13th, 1870.

145 *Minutes of Iowa Yearly Meeting of (Orthodox) Friends*, 1883, p. 26.

146 *Minutes of Iowa Yearly Meeting of (Orthodox) Friends*, 1884, p. 8; 1886, p. 24.

147 *Minutes of Iowa Yearly Meeting of (Orthodox) Friends*, 1884, p. 8; 1885, p. 15; 1886, p. 24.

148 *Minutes of Iowa Yearly Meeting of (Orthodox) Friends*, 1887, p. 12.

149 *Minutes of Iowa Yearly Meeting of (Orthodox) Friends*, 1887, pp. 13, 14.

CHAPTER II

150 See Thomas's *A History of the Friends in America*, p. 200.

151 *Minutes of Salem Monthly Meeting of Friends*, 7 mo., 19th, 1845, p. 258.

152 *Minutes of Iowa Yearly Meeting of Friends*, 1875, p. 30.

153 *Minutes of Iowa Yearly Meeting of Friends*, 1871, p. 6.

154 *Minutes of Iowa Yearly Meeting of (Orthodox) Friends*, 1880, p. 13.

155 The members of the committee to which was assigned the important subject of the pastoral system, were the following: John Henry Douglas, Isom P. Wooten, David O. Michener, John Pearson, Josiah Dillon, Erwin G. Tabor, John F. Hanson, David Hunt, Milton J. Hampton, Gilbert L. Farr, Trueman Cooper, Hiram Hammond, Caleb Johnson, A. W. Naylor, Benjamin Trueblood, Cyrus Beede, A. H. Lindley, Elias Jessup, John H. Pickering, C. R. Dixon, William P. Smith, David Thatcher, John C. Hiatt, and Wm. Pettit. See *Minutes of Iowa Yearly Meeting of (Orthodox) Friends*, 1886, p. 6.

156 *Minutes of Iowa Yearly Meeting of (Orthodox) Friends*, 1886, p. 13.

157 *Minutes of Iowa Yearly Meeting of (Orthodox) Friends*, 1886, p. 14; 1887, p. 14; 1889, p. 18; 1900, p. 11; 1912, see statistical table.

158 In the issue of *The American Friend* for tenth month (October), 26, 1911, D. B. Cook of Earlham, Iowa, has an excellent article entitled *The Pastoral System on Trial*.

159 *The American Friend*, Vol. XIX, p. 283.

CHAPTER III

160 Barclay's *An Apology for the True Christian Divinity: Being An Explanation and Vindication of the Principles and Doctrines of the People Called Quakers* (Providence, 1856), p. 271.

161 Stephen's *Quaker Strongholds*, pp. 110, 111.

162 *The Discipline of the Society of Friends of Iowa Yearly Meeting*, Revision of 1865, p. 54.

163 *The Constitution for the Society of Friends in America, with Supplementary Provisions and Rules of Discipline*, adopted by the Iowa Yearly Meeting in 1902, pp. 57–59.

164 In 1910 the Honey Creek Quarterly Meeting proposed to the Iowa Yearly Meeting (Orthodox) the new scheme of a ''Board on Recording Ministers''. The question was placed in the hands of the Permanent Board, which reported favorably in 1912. The Five Years Meeting held at Indianapolis in October, 1912, concurred in the proposed changes, and the matter of final adoption is now pending. See *Minutes of Yearly Meeting of (Orthodox) Friends*, 1910, p. 10.

165 *Minutes of Iowa Yearly Meeting of (Orthodox) Friends*, 1909, p. 52; 1911, p. 13.

166 The average salary received by forty pastors in regular service in the Iowa Yearly Meeting of (Orthodox) Friends was about $465.00. Excluding the three pastorates of Des Moines, Oskaloosa, and Minneapolis (Minnesota), which in 1912 paid $1200, $1425, and $1800 respectively, the average salary of the other thirty-seven pastors was about $382. See *Minutes of Iowa Yearly Meeting of (Orthodox) Friends*, 1912, statistical table.

167 The average pastoral term in the Iowa Yearly Meeting of (Orthodox) Friends is about two years. In the other Yearly Meetings in this country the pastoral term ranges from one year, as in North Carolina, to three or four years, as in Kansas. For a good survey of pastoral conditions among the Friends in America see an account of the work of the ''Commission on the Meeting and its Pastoral Care'' in the *Minutes of the Five Years Meeting*, 1912, pp. 78–113.

CHAPTER IV

168 The years served by each of the General Superintendents of the Iowa Yearly Meeting of Friends are as follows: John Henry Douglas,

1886–1890; Isom P. Wooten, 1890–1895; Zenas L. Martin, 1895–1900; William Jasper Hadley, 1900–1911; Harry R. Keates, 1911–.

169 The writer is indebted to John Henry Douglas for a brief sketch of his life, prepared in May, 1913.

170 John Henry Douglas states that he began preaching in 1853.

171 *Minutes of Iowa Yearly Meeting of (Orthodox) Friends*, 1889, p. 19; 1891, p. 21.

172 Zenas L. Martin was born in Yadkin County, North Carolina, near the old home of Daniel Boone, in 1855. He came to Iowa in 1859 with his parents Daniel H. and Belinda (Reece) Martin, who settled at New Providence, Hardin County. Here he made his home until he entered the services of the American Board of Foreign Missions in 1895. He is now the Superintendent of the Friends missions in Cuba.

173 In connection with his annual report in 1897 Zenas L. Martin made the following recommendation: "I would recommend that, ... all our meetings which have not parsonages consider the matter of building next year, and that there be liberality in the size and convenient arrangement of them. It would be well for good cupboards and closets to be made in all houses, and that stoves be furnished, so that in moving ministers may be saved the expense of handling heavy furniture."— *Minutes of Iowa Yearly Meeting of (Orthodox) Friends*, 1897, pp. 23, 24.

174 *Minutes of Iowa Yearly Meeting of (Orthodox) Friends*, 1900, p. 11.

175 William Jasper Hadley was born in Hendricks County, Indiana, in 1848. He came to Iowa in 1870 and settled in Dallas County. From that time on his career runs as follows: farmer, teacher, Superintendent of Indian Schools, deputy to County Treasurer of Dallas County, 1888–1890, County Superintendent of Schools, preacher and pastor, General Superintendent of the Iowa Yearly Meeting of Friends, 1900–1911, pastor of the Friends Church at Des Moines, 1911–1913.

176 Before accepting the evangelistic superintendency of the Iowa Yearly Meeting of Orthodox Friends, Harry R. Keates had served in a like capacity in the New York Yearly Meeting. Later he had been for three or four years the pastor of the Friends Church at Des Moines, Iowa.— See *Minutes of Iowa Yearly Meeting of (Orthodox) Friends*, 1912, p. 8.

177 In its report, the committee to which was referred the subject of the Evangelistic Board having been granted ''absolute authority to take such action as may seem right in the case'', ''where differences exist likely to cause hurt to a meeting'' (*Minutes of Iowa Yearly Meeting of (Orthodox) Friends*, 1910, p. 17), announced its approval. ''Your committee believes, however, that our Constitution already provides a complete method of dealing with all 'differences' which may arise and that, therefore, the above resolution is in conflict with it.''— *Minutes of Iowa Yearly Meeting of (Orthodox) Friends*, 1912, p. 14.

CHAPTER V

178 A sketch of the Christian Workers' Assembly by E. Howard Brown. Of the forty-eight pastors in the Iowa Yearly Meeting of Orthodox Friends devoting their whole time to the work in 1912, thirty-four were men, fourteen were women; while but seven were college graduates. See *Minutes of the Five Years Meeting*, 1912, p. 92.

179 The first regular board of the Christian Workers' Assembly was made up of A. Rosenberger, Maria Dean, Charles W. Sweet, William L. Pierson, Emma Coffin, and Eli Rees.

180 For information relative to the early history of the ''Assembly'' the writer is indebted to E. Howard Brown, who went through the records of the ''Yearly Meeting of Ministry and Oversight'' to secure the data.

181 *Minutes of Iowa Yearly Meeting of (Orthodox) Friends*, 1911, p. 58.

182 *Minutes of Iowa Yearly Meeting of (Orthodox) Friends*, 1912, p. 61.

CHAPTER VI

183 Politically, the Friends have generally allied themselves, first with the Whig and later with the Republican party. In marked contrast to their usual passive attitude toward politics stands the campaign of 1896 when the Orthodox Friends in Iowa became so wrought up that ''but little evangelistic work could be done in our meetings until late in the season'', because, says the General Superintendent, of the ''deceptive absorption of a political campaign''.— *Minutes of Iowa Yearly Meeting of (Orthodox) Friends*, 1897, p. 24.

184 The following table is of interest as a comparison between the number of communicants of the various religious denominations in Iowa, and the number of inmates in the State penitentiaries in 1906 declaring their affiliations or preferences for the same denominations:

NAME OF DENOMINATION	NUMBER OF COMMUNICANTS	IOWA STATE PENITENTIARIES FT. MADISON MALES	ANAMOSA MALES	FEMALES	TOTALS	RELATIVE PERCENTAGE OF INMATES BASED ON WHOLE NUMBER OF COMMUNICANTS
Baptists	44,096	31	4	..	35	.00079
Christian	57,425	34	3	4	41	.00071
Methodist	164,329	63	11	1	75	.00045
Roman Catholic	207,607	43	36	1	80	.00038
United Brethren	11,236	3	..	1	4	.00035
Friends	10,088	2	..	..	2	.00019
Presbyterian	60,081	7	1	..	8	.00013
Lutheran	117,668	7	7	1	15	.00012
Congregational	37,061	2	..	..	2	.00005

The above table was compiled from the *Special Reports of the Bureau of the Census, Religious Bodies*, 1906, Pt. I, pp. 190, 191, 192, 193, 194; and *Report of the Board of Control of State Institutions of Iowa*, 1906, p. 383.

185 A brief sketch of the young people's forward movement both in England and in America may be found in an article by Horace Mather Lippincott and John S. Hoyland, entitled *The Movement*, published in *An Account of the Young Friends' Conference at the Whittier Fellowship Guest House*, pp. 21–28.

PART III

CHAPTER I

186 The "Germantown Protest", issued by the Germantown Monthly Meeting of Friends, Pennsylvania, in 1688 is usually cited as the first formal document issued against the institution of slavery in America.

187 In an article entitled *The Society of Friends and Abolition*, published in *The Friend*, Vol. XVI (1842–1843), pp. 374, 375, a clear and full statement is made of the reasons why the Friends held aloof from the early abolition movement.

188 See *Reminiscences of Levi Coffin, the Reputed President of the Underground Railroad* (Cincinnati: Western Tract Society), Ch. VII.

189 Quoted in Hodgson's *The Society of Friends in the Nineteenth Century*, Vol. II, p. 25.

190 Osborn's *A Testimony Concerning the Separation Which Occurred in Indiana Yearly Meeting of Friends, in the Winter of 1842 and '43; together with sundry remarks and observations, particularly on the subjects of War, Slavery, and Colonization* (Centerville, 1849), p. 44.

191 An excellent account of the events leading up to the ' anti-slavery separation in the Indiana Yearly Meeting may be found in *The Friend*, Vol. XVII (1843–1844), pp. 85, 86, 93, 94.

192 *The Address, from the Meeting for Sufferings, of Indiana Yearly Meeting of Friends, held at White Water, on the 6th and 7th of the Third month, 1843*, cites this date.

193 Seebohm's *Memoirs of William Foster* (London, 1865), Vol. II, pp. 198, 199.

194 See *Western Work* (Oskaloosa), May, 1908, pp. 2, 3.

195 *Minutes of Salem Monthly Meeting of Friends*, 3 mo., 25th, 1843, pp. 149, 150.

196 *Minutes of Salem Monthly Meeting of Friends*, 9 mo., 30th, 1843, pp. 167, 168.

197 Osborn's *A Testimony Concerning the Separation Which Occurred in Indiana Yearly Meeting of Friends, in the Winter of 1842 and '43*, pp. 17, 18.

198 For the materials concerning what transpired among the Anti-Slavery Friends at Salem on this occasion the writer has depended largely on quotations found in Edgerton's *A History of the Separation in Indiana Yearly Meeting on the Anti-Slavery Question* (Cincinnati, 1856), pp. 337–343; and in Hodgson's *The History of Friends in the Nineteenth Century*, Vol. II, pp. 39, 40.

199 *Minutes of Salem Monthly Meeting of Friends*, 10 mo., 31st, 1845, p. 268.

200 *Minutes of Salem Monthly Meeting of Friends*, 12 mo., 17th, 1862, p. 292.

For a full and careful account of this anti-slavery separation see Edgerton's *A History of the Separation in Indiana Yearly Meeting of Friends on the Anti-Slavery Question.*

CHAPTER II

201 The materials on the Hicksite separation are voluminous, including official addresses or declarations by each body on the subject; sectarian papers; personal journals; treatises; etc. In *A History of the Friends in America*, p. 122, A. C. and R. H. Thomas cite the following as the fairest representations on either side: ''Hicksite, Elias Hicks, 'Journal,' New York, 1832; 'The Berean,' Wilmington, Del., 1825; 'The Friend or Advocate of Truth,' Philadelphia, 1828–1830, 3 Vols.; The Journal of John Comly; 'The Quaker,' Philadelphia, 1827, 1828, 4 Vols.; Orthodox, 'The Friend,' Philadelphia, 1827–1832, Vols. 2–4; 'Miscellaneous Repository,' Mt. Pleasant, O., 1827–1832, Vols. 1–4; Journal of Thomas Shillitoe, London, 1839, Vol. 2.''

202 For an account of the founding of the Prairie Grove settlement, see *Friends' Intelligencer* (Philadelphia, 1858), Vol. XIV, pp. 293–295.

203 The writer is indebted to L. O. Mosher of West Liberty for the information concerning the early settlement of Friends about West Liberty.

204 The Monthly Meeting at West Liberty was established about 1859 or 1860; the records for these first years being lost, the exact date is now obscured. *Minutes of Illinois Yearly Meeting of the Society of (Hicksite) Friends*, 1912, p. 42.

205 In 1906 the seven Yearly Meetings of Hicksite Friends in America reported a total membership of 18,560 persons, while in 1890 they reported 21,992, thus showing a loss of 3,432 in sixteen years.— *Special Reports of the Bureau of the Census — Religious Bodies*, 1906, Part II, pp. 300–303.

206 The following table shows something of the decline in numbers of the Prairie Grove Quarterly Meeting, composed as it is of the

Monthly Meetings of Prairie Grove in Henry County, Wapsinonoc in Muscatine County, and Marietta near Marshalltown in Marshall County:

YEAR	ADULTS	MINORS	TOTAL	NUMBER OF NON-RESIDENTS
1893	288	115	403	168
1903	193	52*	245	80
1904	193	49	242	81
1905	196	47	243	94
1906	197	42	239	89
1907	198	35	233	94
1908	193	27	220	93
1909	187	20	207	93
1910	188	18	206	100
1911	180	17	197	103
1912	174	17†	191	99

*A decline of nearly 55% of the young people.
†This 10 year period shows a decline of over 67% of minors.

[207] Out of a total membership of 885 persons in 1912 the Illinois Yearly Meeting of (Hicksite) Friends had 441 non-resident members; and of the 191 persons belonging to the Prairie Grove Quarterly Meeting in that year, 99 were non-resident. The Yearly Meeting has a most effective method, however, of dealing with this situation through a committee on ''Isolated Members'', and by publishing each year as an appendix to its *Minutes* the names and addresses of all its non-resident members by Monthly Meetings.

[208] See the sketches by Luke Woodard on the subject of Hicksism in the *Evangelical Friend* (Cleveland), November 23, December 7, 14, 21, and 28, 1911.

[209] *Minutes and Accompanying Documents of Illinois Yearly Meeting of the Society of (Hicksite) Friends,* 1908, p. 24.

CHAPTER III

[210] John Wilbur was born at Hopkinton, Rhode Island, in 1774, of a prominent Quaker family, and was carefully educated in the teachings of the Society. He was early acknowledged a minister but was disowned by the Orthodox body owing to his controversy with Gurney. Later he was recognized as a minister by his followers and retained that position until his death in 1856.

[211] Joseph John Gurney, likewise of Quaker ancestry, was born near Norwich, England, in 1788. He was educated at Oxford, became

a finished scholar, an extensive writer, and a reformer intimate with Buston and Wilberforce. In 1847 he met a violent death while riding horseback.

212 See Gurney's *Essays on the Evidences, Doctrines and Practical Operation, of Christianity* (Philadelphia, 1884).

213 A clear idea of John Wilbur's tenets may be obtained from the *Letters of John Wilbur to George Crosfield, published by the ''Meeting of Sufferings of New England Yearly Meeting of (Wilbur) Friends''* (Providence, 1895).

214 D. C. Mott's article on *The Quakers in Iowa* in *Annals of Iowa,* Third Series, Vol. IV, pp. 266, 267.

215 D. C. Mott's article on *The Quakers in Iowa* in *Annals of Iowa,* Third Series, Vol. IV, pp. 266, 267.

216 Hodgson's *The Society of Friends in the Nineteenth Century,* Vol. II, p. 227.

217 Quoted in Hodgson's *The Society of Friends in the Nineteenth Century,* Vol. II, p. 228.

218 *Minutes of Red Cedar Monthly Meeting of Friends,* 8 mo., 9th, 1854, pp. 81, 82.

219 *Minutes of Red Cedar Monthly Meeting of Friends,* 8 mo., 9th, 1854, p. 82.

220 An aged Friend now living at West Branch, Iowa, who was in attendance at the Red Cedar Monthly Meeting at the time of the difficulties there related this incident to the writer, stating that the words made such an impression on her youthful mind that she had never forgotten them.

221 *Minutes of Red Cedar Monthly Meeting of Friends,* 9 mo., 7th, 1854, p. 84; 10 mo., 12th, 1854, pp. 87, 88.

222 See *Minutes of Iowa Yearly Meeting of (Conservative) Friends,* 1866, pp. 2, 3; 1887, p. 5; *Minutes of Ohio Yearly Meeting of (Wilbur) Friends,* 1912, p. 4.

223 *Catalogue of Friends Boarding School,* 1909–10, pp. 1–4.

CHAPTER IV

224 The Conservative Friends, unlike the other Quaker sects in Iowa, do not record detailed statistics of their membership, and in

consequence it is difficult to determine just how many members of that body there are in this State.

225 For the materials dealing with the separation in the Bear Creek Quarterly Meeting the writer is indebted to Darius B. Cook of Earlham, Iowa, who compiled the data from official records in the hands of the Conservative Friends. Mr. Cook intends to publish the full results of his researches.

226 *Minutes of Iowa Yearly Meeting of Friends*, 1872, p. 6.

227 *Minutes of Iowa Yearly Meeting of Friends*, 1877, pp. 2, 4. See also the Cook Manuscript.

CHAPTER V

228 *Minutes of Salem Monthly Meeting of Friends*, 8 mo., 2nd, 1879, pp. 275, 276.

229 *Minutes of Salem Quarterly Meeting of Friends*, 8 mo., 9th, 1879, p. 131; 11 mo., 8th, 1879, p. 136.

230 *Minutes of Springdale Monthly Meeting of Friends*, 5 mo., 21st, 1881, p. 258.

231 The facts concerning the Conservative separation at West Branch were carefully related to the writer by Jesse Negus, one of its chief leaders, and by other responsible persons of the community who were concerned in the movement.

232 *Minutes of Springdale Monthly Meeting of Friends*, 4 mo., 21st, 1883, p. 309.

233 *Minutes of Iowa Yearly Meeting of (Conservative) Friends*, 1884, p. 1.

CHAPTER VI

234 See Flom's *A History of Norwegian Immigration to the United States*, Chapter XXI. See also *The Iowa Journal of History and Politics*, Vol. IV, pp. 233, 244.

235 The Scandinavian immigrants have been a valuable addition to the population of Iowa. The younger men in coming to the State usually hire out for a year or so until they become acquainted with the soil; then they rent land wherever possible; and before long, by reason of their industry, they become land-owners.

²³⁶ The writer is indebted to Mr. Carney Meltvedt of LeGrand, Iowa, for many of the facts contained in this chapter, particularly those concerning the first Friends at Stavanger.

²³⁷ Stavanger in Norway, is one of the most important commercial centers on the southwest coast of the peninsula. A strong meeting of Friends has long been located in the city.

²³⁸ *Minutes of Bangor Quarterly Meeting of Women Friends*, 11 mo., 5th, 1864, p. 100.

²³⁹ Of the fifty Norwegians coming to LeGrand in 1869 as above described, but thirty-six were Friends. Among them were the following men with their families: Knut Botnen, Lars Botnen, Jon Rinden, Mons Vinye, Gulik Medhus, and Torno Thompson, all of whom are now (1913) deceased except Mons Vinye.

²⁴⁰ For the account of Lindley Murray Hoag's visit to Norway in 1853 and its results see an article entitled *A Remarkable Chapter in the History of Friends*, written by John Marcussen, which is reprinted from the *American Friend* in the *Friend's Intelligencer*, Vol. LXIV, 1907, pp. 548, 549, 563–565.

²⁴¹ *Minutes of Iowa Yearly Meeting of Friends*, 1871, p. 4.

²⁴² *Minutes of Iowa Yearly Meeting of (Conservative) Friends*, 1885, p. 5.

²⁴³ *Minutes of Iowa Yearly Meeting of (Conservative) Friends*, 1888, pp. 10, 11.

²⁴⁴ *Stavanger Mirror* (a paper published monthly for a time at LeGrand in the interests of Stavanger Boarding School), Seventh Month, 1903, p. 3.

²⁴⁵ *Minutes of Iowa Yearly Meeting of (Conservative) Friends*, 1890, p. 5; 1892, p. 8; 1893, pp. 9, 10.

²⁴⁶ See the ''Rules and Regulations'' of the Stavanger Boarding School for 1910–1911, as printed in the *Appendix* above, pp. 287, 288.

²⁴⁷ *Minutes of Iowa Yearly Meeting of (Conservative) Friends*, 1912, pp. 10, 11.

²⁴⁸ In her excellent work on *Amana: The Community of True Inspiration*, pp. 99–102, Bertha M. H. Shambaugh mentions the struggle which the people of this unique settlement have had to maintain their social integrity.

249 The general status of the Conservative Friends in Iowa is seen by the following table, compiled from the minutes of their Yearly Meeting:

YEAR	NUMBER OF FAMILIES	NUMBER OF PARTS OF FAMILIES	CHILDREN BETWEEN 5 AND 21 YEARS	NUMBER OF MINISTERS
1880	72	47	(not given)	8
1890	91	124	121	11
1900	86	121	113	7
1910	76	105	100	9
1912	71	125	107	6

250 *Minutes of Iowa Yearly Meeting of (Conservative) Friends,* 1891, p. 4.

251 Proverbs, 29: 18.

PART IV

CHAPTER I

252 *A View of the Present State of the African Slave Trade,* published by the direction of a meeting representing the Religious Society of Friends in Pennsylvania, New Jersey, and other States (Philadelphia, 1824), p. 3.

253 See *Reminiscences of Rachel Kellum* in *Western Work,* April, 1908, pp. 4, 5.

254 For a discussion of the Missouri-Iowa boundary dispute see Pelzer's *Augustus Caesar Dodge,* Ch. VI; and Parish's *Robert Lucas,* Ch. XXII.

255 The Lewelling house, still in a good state of preservation, is an excellent sample of the first stone houses erected in early Iowa. The walls of solid stone are nearly two feet thick. Great stone chimneys at either end of the house made possible a large open fire place in each room. A stone extension to the rear provided a spacious dining room and kitchen combined, with plenty of pantries. In the center of the floor of this large room a trap door, always covered with a rag carpet and the dining table, led into an extensive opening separate from the cellar. It was here that the fugitive slaves were kept, and though the house was searched many times by the Missourians, this opening was never found nor the slaves secured.

256 Of the nine slaves in question, but four were taken back to Missouri, two women and two children. In 1850 Ruel Daggs brought suit against Elihu Frazier, Thomas Clarkson Frazier, John Comer, Paul Way, John Pickering, William Johnson, and other citizens of Henry County in the District Court of the United States at Burlington for $10,000 damages. The case was there tried and dismissed on demurrer (see 6 Federal Cases, No. 3538). For his account of the affair in general the writer has depended on the testimony taken at the trial, found in the Fugitive Slave Case, Daggs *vs.* Frazier, et als, as reported by George Frazee.

257 In her reminiscences (*Western Work*, April, 1908, pp. 4, 5) Rachel Kellum states that word reached Salem concerning the approach of the Missourians, and a messenger was at once despatched on horse to notify the county sheriff at Mt. Pleasant, about ten miles away. When the sheriff arrived at Salem he found most of the Missourians at the hotel with their dinner cooked and on the table. He entered at once and ''gave them just fifteen minutes'', says Rachel Kellum, ''to leave town.'' ''They swore that they would have their dinners. He said that one blast of his bugle would bring on the company of well trained men, and if they came at his command, they would come to shoot, and shoot to kill. 'Now, gentlemen, you have your choice, to clear the town in fifteen minutes or take the consequences.' They went . . . . grabbing what dinner they could carry.''

Another old settler, who was a boy living in Salem at the time, states that upon the approach of the Missourians Jonathan A. Frazier rode in haste to the Congregational settlement at Denmark and made known the attack. The Congregationalists immediately responded in arms and when the Missourians saw them coming up the dusty road they at once took to horse and fled.

258 See Lloyd's *John Brown Among the Pedee Quakers* in *Annals of Iowa*, Vol. IV, pp. 669, 670.

259 The men brought by Brown to Springdale on this occasion were his own son, Owen Brown, Aaron D. Stevens, John Kagi, John E. Cook, Richard Realf, Charles W. Moffitt, Luke J. Parsons, Charles H. Tidd, William Leeman, and Richard Richardson, a colored man. See Lloyd's *John Brown Among the Pedee Quakers* in *Annals of Iowa*, Vol. IV, p. 712.

260 In his excellent work on *John Brown Among the Quakers* (Third Edition), pp. 22, 23, Irving B. Richman makes the following statement, to which the present writer takes exception: "To be sure, John Brown and his followers were not men of peace; they, one and all of them, had fought hard and often in the Kansas war; but much was pardoned to them by the Quakers because of the holiness of their object". To grant the truth of this statement would be to concede that through leniency the Springdale Friends were willing to compromise their principles of non-resistance, something of which the strong men who then were in control of the Springdale Monthly Meeting were incapable.

261 See the answers made by Richard Realf in his examination before Senator Mason's committee, as given in Richman's *John Brown Among the Quakers* (Third Edition), pp. 56–59.

262 Lloyd's *John Brown Among the Pedee Quakers* in *Annals of Iowa*, Vol. IV, pp. 714, 715.

263 Lloyd's *John Brown Among the Pedee Quakers* in *Annals of Iowa*, Vol. IV, pp. 715–719.

264 Quoted in Richman's *John Brown Among the Quakers* (Third Edition), p. 49.

265 Brown's attack on Harper's Ferry occurred on Sunday night, October 16, 1859; the Government troops retook the place on the morning of the 18th. See Villard's *John Brown: A Biography Fifty Years After*, Ch. XII.

266 For an excellent description of Barclay Coppoc's escape and flight see Teakle's *The Rendition of Barclay Coppoc* in *The Iowa Journal of History and Politics*, Vol. X, pp. 519–522.

267 See Teakle's *The Rendition of Barclay Coppoc* in *The Iowa Journal of History and Politics*, Vol. X, pp. 522–566.

268 Aurner's *A Topical History of Cedar County, Iowa*, p. 424.

269 The men appointed on this committee were Joel Bean, Henry Rowntree, Israel Negus, Laurie Tatum, James Schooley, Samuel Macy, Amos W. Hampton, James Staples, Benjamin Miles, Thomas Barrington, and Samuel Jepson.

270 *Minutes of Red Cedar Monthly Meeting of Friends*, 11 mo., 9th, 1859, p. 70.

271 *Minutes of Red Cedar Monthly Meeting of Friends*, 12 mo., 7th, 1859, pp. 77, 78.

272 *Minutes of Red Cedar Monthly Meeting of Friends*, 5 mo., 6th, 1857, p. 220.

273 Showing signs of tuberculosis, Barclay Coppoc went to Kansas in 1857 for his health, and while there is said to have taken part in some of John Brown's expeditions in that State.

274 *Minutes of Red Cedar Monthly Meeting of Friends*, 6 mo., 10th, 1857, p. 225.

275 *Minutes of Red Cedar Monthly Meeting of Friends*, 1 mo., 11th, 1860, p. 83.

276 Lincoln's Emancipation Proclamation was given to the press on September 23, 1862, and was intended by him to go into effect on January 1, 1863.

277 *Minutes of Iowa Yearly Meeting of Friends*, 1863, p. 13.

278 *Minutes of Iowa Yearly Meeting of Friends*, 1864, p. 13.

279 *Minutes of Iowa Yearly Meeting of Friends*, 1865, p. 35; 1866, pp. 17, 18.

280 Quoted in *Minutes of Iowa Yearly Meeting of Friends*, 1871, p. 11.

281 *Minutes of Iowa Yearly Meeting of Friends*, 1884, p. 24.

282 R. D. Bowles opened the school in September, 1889, with a crowded enrollment, but he broke down in health in January, 1890. The school was closed and he, with his wife, went to Springdale where he died on July 8th.

283 *Minutes of Iowa Yearly Meeting of Friends*, 1898, p. 69.

284 *Minutes of Iowa Yearly Meeting of Friends*, 1901, p. 47.

CHAPTER II

285 Fox's *Journal* (Philadelphia), p. 449.

286 For an account of the early contact of the Friends with the Indians see Sharpless's *A History of Quaker Government in Pennsylvania*, Vol. I, Ch. VI; also Rufus M. Jones's *The Quakers in the American Colonies*, index.

287 Laurie Tatum's book, *Our Red Brothers*, gives many sketches of his own work and that of other Friends among the Indians.

288 *Minutes of Salem Monthly Meeting of Friends*, 11 mo., 12th, 1851, p. 56; 12 mo., 17th, 1851, pp. 61, 62; 2 mo., 18th, 1852, pp. 72, 73; 3 mo., 17th, 1852, pp. 77, 78.

289 In 1846 the Kansa or Kansas Indians were assigned the reservation at Council Grove, where they remained until they were removed to Indian Territory in 1873. See *Bureau of American Ethnology, Bulletin 30*, Part 1, p. 654. See also *Minutes of Salem Monthly Meeting of Friends*, 4 mo., 14th, 1852, pp. 81, 82.

290 *Minutes of Salem Monthly Meeting of Friends*, 12 mo., 15th, 1857, pp. 131, 132.

291 For one view of the dealings of the United States Government with the American Indians see Helen H. Jackson's *A Century of Dishonor* (Boston, 1903).

292 Copy of the *Minutes of the Representative Meeting of Iowa Yearly Meeting* made by Laurie Tatum, the clerk, for Enoch Hoag. Enoch Hoag collected a large quantity of materials, intending to write a history of the work of the Friends among the Indians under President Grant, but he died before getting the work under way. The writer is indebted to his son, Edward F. Hoag, for free access to these materials upon which he has largely drawn for the contents of this chapter.

293 *Congressional Globe*, 3rd Session, 40th Congress, pp. 17–21, 39–43. See also a copy of the *Minutes of the Representative Meeting of Iowa Yearly Meeting*, made by Laurie Tatum.

294 See ''Introductory'' to Laurie Tatum's *Our Red Brothers*, pp. xvii, xviii. See also *The Friend*, Vol. XLII, 1868–1869, pp. 255, 256.

295 *House Executive Documents*, 2d Session, 41st Congress, No. 1, Part 3, pp. 471–478.

296 Richardson's *Messages and Papers of the Presidents*, Vol. VII, pp. 38, 39.

297 Tatum's *Our Red Brothers*, pp. 24–26.

298 *Memorial Concerning Deceased Friends, Members of Iowa Yearly Meeting* (Philadelphia, 1872), p. 22. Brinton Darlington died in the Indian country on the first day of May, 1872.

299 *The Friend*, Vol. XLIII, 1869–1870, pp. 69, 70, 76, 77. See also *House Executive Documents*, 2nd Session, 41st Congress, No. 1, Part 3, pp. 829, 830.

300 *Minutes of Iowa Yearly Meeting of Friends*, 1873, pp. 5, 6; 1874, p. 15.

301 *House Executive Documents*, 2d Session, 41st Congress, No. 1, Part 3, p. 476.

302 The new Osage Reservation was ''bounded on the north by the south line of Kansas, east by the ninety-sixth degree of west longitude, and south and west by the Arkansas River, and contained approximately 1,760,000 acres.''— *Report of the Commissioner of Indian Affairs*, 1872, p. 40.

303 *Minutes of Iowa Yearly Meeting of Friends*, 1874, pp. 15, 16; 1875, p. 18.

304 *Minutes of Associated Committee of Friends on Indian Affairs*, 1878, pp. 23, 24, 31, 32.

CHAPTER III

305 Quoted in the *Friends' Review*, Vol. IV, 1850, p. 174. See also Coffin's *Philanthropy of Josiah White* in *Western Work*, Vol. XVIII, July, 1909, pp. 4, 5.

306 Quoted in the *Friends' Review*, Vol. IV, 1850, p. 175.

307 *Minutes of Indiana Yearly Meeting of Friends*, 1854, pp. 35, 36.

308 *Minutes of Iowa Yearly Meeting of Friends*, 1864, pp. 4–6, 21.

309 *Minutes of Iowa Yearly Meeting of Friends*, 1866, pp. 22, 23.

310 *Minutes of Iowa Yearly Meeting of Friends*, 1867, p. 21.

311 *Minutes of Iowa Yearly Meeting of Friends*, 1868, p. 7.

312 *The Iowa Instructor*, Vol. I, p. 377.

313 *Iowa Senate Journal*, 1868, p. 55.

314 *Iowa House Journal*, 1868, p. 121.

315 *Laws of Iowa*, 1868, Ch. 59, pp. 71–77.

316 *Report of the Iowa Reform School* in *Iowa Documents*, 1870, Vol. II, pp. 3, 4.

³¹⁷ *Report of the Iowa Reform School* in *Iowa Documents*, 1870, Vol. II, pp. 12–14.

³¹⁸ *Report of the Joint Committee to Visit the State Reform School* in *Iowa Documents*, Vol. II, p. 3.

³¹⁹ *Report of the Iowa Reform School* in *Iowa Documents*, 1870, Vol. II, pp. 23, 24.

³²⁰ *Report of the Iowa Reform School* in *Iowa Documents*, 1872, Vol. II, pp. 5, 19, 21.

³²¹ *Laws of Iowa* (General and Public), 1872, Chapter 77, p. 79.

³²² *Report of the Iowa Reform School* in *Iowa Documents*, 1874, Vol. II, p. 25.

³²³ *Report of the Iowa Reform School* in *Iowa Documents*, 1876, Vol. III, pp. 46, 48, 49.

³²⁴ *Minutes of Iowa Yearly Meeting of (Orthodox) Friends*, 1878, p. 15.

³²⁵ *Report of the Joint Committee to Visit the Girls' Department of the State Reform School* in *Iowa Documents*, 1880, Vol. IV, p. 3.

³²⁶ *Report of the Joint Committee to Visit the Girls' Department of the State Reform School* in *Iowa Documents*, 1882, Vol. IV, p. 3.

³²⁷ The trustees at this time were Clarkson T. Penrose of West Branch, Benjamin C. Andrews of Pleasant Plain, and Henry Dorland of Salem, Iowa.

³²⁸ *Minutes of Iowa Yearly Meeting of (Orthodox) Friends*, 1880, pp. 10, 11.

³²⁹ *Minutes of Iowa Yearly Meeting of (Orthodox) Friends*, 1882, p. 17; 1883, p. 13; 1884, p. 18. It should also be noted that in the spring of 1884 the trustees leased the remaining 960 acres of the farm for five years to Charles and Mathew Lowder, the profits to be divided equally.

³³⁰ *Minutes of Iowa Yearly Meeting of (Orthodox) Friends*, 1886, pp. 30, 31.

³³¹ *Minutes of Iowa Yearly Meeting of (Orthodox) Friends*, 1887, p. 6.

³³² *Minutes of Iowa Yearly Meeting of (Orthodox) Friends*, 1889, p. 8.

333 *Minutes of Iowa Yearly Meeting of (Orthodox) Friends*, 1904, p. 28.

334 *Minutes of Iowa Yearly Meeting of (Orthodox) Friends*, 1904, pp. 29, 30.

335 Quoted from a copy of Judge Bank's decision in the District Court of the State of Iowa, at Fort Madison, July 30th, 1908.

336 *Minutes of Iowa Yearly Meeting of (Orthodox) Friends*, 1907, p. 40; 1912, p. 34.

337 Personal letter from James B. Bruff to the writer, July 28, 1913.

CHAPTER IV

338 Pumphrey's *Missionary Work in Connection with the Society of Friends* (Philadelphia, 1880), p. 13.

339 *Minutes of Iowa Yearly Meeting of (Orthodox) Friends*, 1879, p. 21.

340 *Minutes of Iowa Yearly Meeting of (Orthodox) Friends*, 1880, p. 17.

341 *Minutes of Iowa Yearly Meeting of (Orthodox) Friends*, 1881, p. 9.

342 Bowles's *Jamaica and Friends' Missions*, pp. 49–51.

343 *Minutes of Iowa Yearly Meeting of (Orthodox) Friends*, 1883, p. 24.

344 Bowles's *Jamaica and Friends' Missions*, pp. 56, 57.

345 *Minutes of Iowa Yearly Meeting of (Orthodox) Friends*, 1884, pp. 30, 32.

346 *Minutes of Iowa Yearly Meeting of (Orthodox) Friends*, 1887, p. 32.

347 *Minutes of Iowa Yearly Meeting of (Orthodox) Friends*, 1906, p. 26.

348 In 1889 the "Happy Grove Estate", consisting of about 150 acres, was purchased by the Yearly Meeting for $2,100. See Bowles's *Jamaica and Friends' Missions*, p. 116. In 1903 the Haining estate of 866 acres and 60 head of cattle was also purchased for about $8,000. See *Minutes of Iowa Yearly Meeting of (Orthodox) Friends*, 1903, p. 58.

[349] Relative to the immorality on the island of Jamaica Jesse George, an Iowa Missionary, says of the Hordley and Amity Hall districts: "I should think 95 percent of the adult population were living together indiscriminately, regardless of the marriage tie."— Bowles's *Jamaica and Friends' Missions*, p. 82. Gilbert L. Farr also observes "that more than sixty per cent. of births are out of wedlock." This was one of the most difficult problems which the Christian missionaries in Jamaica had to meet. See Farr's *Friends' Mission in Jamaica*, p. 1.

[350] *Minutes of Iowa Yearly Meeting of (Orthodox) Friends*, 1903, p. 54.

[351] *Western Work*, Vol. XIII, August, 1909, p. 21.

[352] Letter of Alsina Andrews to Josepha Hambleton, July 5, 1909.

[353] *Minutes of the Jamaica Mission Council*, July 5, 1909.

[354] Farr's *Friends' Mission in Jamaica*, pp. 23, 24.

[355] With the rise in the interest of the Iowa Friends in foreign missions came a corresponding decline in the work of home missions until at the present time there is almost no real organized home mission work being done among the Orthodox or other bodies of Friends in Iowa.

[356] The various American Yearly Meetings of Orthodox Friends now maintain missions in Japan, East and West China, India, Palestine, Africa, Jamaica, Cuba, Mexico, Guatemala, and Alaska. See *Minutes of the Five Years Meeting of the Friends in America*, 1912, p. 42.

[357] Pumphrey's *Missionary Work in Connection with the Society of Friends* (Philadelphia, 1880), p. 44.

[358] *Minutes of Iowa Yearly Meeting of (Orthodox) Friends*, 1894, p. 38.

[359] *Minutes of Iowa Yearly Meeting of (Orthodox) Friends*, 1911, p. 69.

[360] The "Foreign Mission Committee" now consists of "three members of the American Friends' Board of Foreign Missions appointed by the Yearly Meeting for five years, seven members appointed by the Yearly Meeting for one year to be nominated as follows: five by the Yearly Meeting Nominating Committee, one by the W. F. M. S.,

one by the C. E. Union''.— *Minutes of Iowa Yearly Meeting of (Orthodox) Friends*, 1912, p. 18.

CHAPTER V

361 *Encyclopedia Britannica* (Werner Edition, 1902), Vol. XX, p. 150.

362 *Minutes of Salem Monthly Meeting of Friends*, 8 mo., 31st, 1839, p. 26.

363 *Minutes of Salem Monthly Meeting of Friends*, 7 mo., 31st, 1841, p. 71.

364 *Discipline of the Society of Friends of Indiana Yearly Meeting*, 1854, pp. 85, 86.

365 *Annual Catalogue of Salem Seminary*, 1851.

366 *Sixty-Sixth Anniversary of the Organization of the Friends Church of Salem, Iowa*, p. 5.

367 Whittier College was named in honor of the Quaker poet, John Greenleaf Whittier, who subscribed fifty dollars to the ''Whittier College Association''.

368 *Salem Weekly News*, May 5, 1904.

369 *Sixty-Sixth Anniversary of the Organization of the Friends Church of Salem, Iowa*, p. 5.

370 *Minutes of Red Cedar Monthly Meeting of Friends*, 10 mo., 5th, 1859, pp. 63, 64.

371 Aurner's *A Topical History of Cedar County*, pp. 159–165.

372 *Minutes of Springdale (Red Cedar) Monthly Meeting of Friends*, 4 mo., 3rd, 1867, p. 166.

373 Dr. J. W. Morgan's account of Ackworth Institute, prepared at the request of the writer. See also *Western Work*, Vol. III, May, 1899, p. 2.

374 *Minutes of Iowa Yearly Meeting of (Orthodox) Friends*, 1881, p. 14.

375 *Minutes of Iowa Yearly Meeting of Friends*, 1869, pp. 15, 16. The available material on the history of these three schools is ex-

332 THE QUAKERS OF IOWA

ceedingly scarce, being confined to a few brief references in the *Minutes* of the Yearly Meeting.

376 *Western Work*, Vol. III, May, 1899, p. 5.

377 *Western Work*, Vol. III, May, 1899, p. 3.

378 *Western Work*, Vol. III, May, 1899, p. 3.

379 *Western Work*, Vol. III, April, 1899, p. 5.

380 *Minutes of Iowa Yearly Meeting of (Orthodox) Friends*, 1900, pp. 13, 14.

381 Dr. J. W. Morgan, one of the first teachers, states that the "Iowa Yearly Meeting Boarding School" was founded by interested Friends of the Pleasant Plain and Bangor Quarterly Meetings, and was opened in the presence of a joint committee of the two Quarters on the 27th of November, 1860.

382 The "Thorndyke Institute" was of high grade for its time, having as early as 1865 a library containing some two thousand volumes.

383 *Minutes of Iowa Yearly Meeting of Friends*, 1866, p. 35.

384 *Minutes of Iowa Yearly Meeting of Friends*, 1867, p. 4.

385 *Western Work*, Vol. II, June, 1898, p. 10.

386 *Minutes of Iowa Yearly Meeting of Friends*, 1871, pp. 16, 17.

387 *Minutes of Iowa Yearly Meeting of Friends*, 1873, p. 10.

388 *Western Work*, Vol. XVII, April, 1911, p. 7. To the number of graduates here recorded the writer has added those for the years 1911–1912 and 1912–1913.

389 The following, in the order named, have been the presidents of Penn College: John W. Woody, also the first president of Whittier College, Salem, Iowa; William B. Morgan; Benjamin F. Trueblood; Absolom Rosenberger; and David M. Edwards, who is the present incumbent.

390 *Minutes of Iowa Yearly Meeting of (Orthodox) Friends*, 1898, p. 25; 1900, p. 14.

391 *Iowa Educational Directory*, 1907–1908, p. 86.

392 *Western Work*, Vol. XVII, June, 1911, p. 1.

PART V

CHAPTER I

393 Fox's *Journal* (Philadelphia), pp. 443, 444.

394 Stephen's *Quaker Strongholds* (Philadelphia, 1891), p. 20.

395 Penn's *Primitive Christianity Revived* (edited by James M. Brown, Philadelphia, 1877), p. 9.

396 Barclay's *An Apology for the True Christian Divinity: being an explanation and vindication of the Principles and Doctrines of the people called Quakers* (Providence, 1856), p. 195.

397 Barclay's *Apology*, pp. 196, 241.

398 The scriptural passages cited against war are numerous, among them being the following: Matthew V: 43, 44; Luke X: 27; Romans XII: 19, 20, 21. Likewise on the question of oaths, the following Bible references are pointed out: Matthew V: 33, 34, 35, 36, 37; James V: 12.

399 At the extra session of the General Assembly of Iowa in 1862 the Mennonites, the Amana Inspirationists, and the German Baptists likewise petitioned for relief from military service. See *Senate Journal*, 1862 (extra session).

400 Governor Samuel J. Kirkwood in his message to the General Assembly on September 3, 1862, very strongly recommended that those ''who cannot conscientiously render military duty, be exempted therefrom in case of draft, upon the payment of a fixed sum of money to be paid to the State.''— Shambaugh's *Messages and Proclamations of the Governors of Iowa*, Vol. II, pp. 316, 317.

401 Petitions to the General Assembly for relief from the military draft at this time came from Friends in the following Iowa counties: Dallas, Madison, Guthrie, Adair, Muscatine, Jefferson, Warren, Clarke, Jasper, Mahaska, Poweshiek, and Keokuk. See *Senate Journal*, 1862 (extra session), p. 11. The bill looking towards this relief was killed in the House after a most story career. See *House Journal*, 1862 (extra session), pp. 41, 42, 43, 44, 67, 70.

402 Certain members of the Salem Monthly Meeting who were unable to pay the exemption money fell under the draft, and the

Monthly Meeting borrowed the amount and assumed the obligation. See *Minutes of Salem Monthly Meeting of Friends*, 1864, p. 14.

[403] For the "Richmond Declaration of Faith" see *The Constitution for the Society of Friends in America adopted by Iowa Yearly Meeting in 1902*, pp. 12–46.

CHAPTER II

[404] With the most fiery bitterness Fox attacked the formality of the "steeple-house" and the bells that called men to church.

[405] Not until of late years, with the holding of evangelistic meetings at night and of regular night services under the pastoral system, have the Friends had need of lamps in their churches, it being their earlier practice to have regular meetings only in the morning, with an occasional "appointed meeting" in the afternoon.

[406] In like manner there was a committee appointed to grant to outsiders "the right to sit", if way seemed clear, in business meetings; such meetings being otherwise closed to all non-members.

[407] The church expenses among the Iowa Quakers were early met by proportioning and collecting the same outside of the meeting. At the present time morning offerings are taken in most of the Orthodox congregations.

[408] Gurney's *Observations on the Distinguishing Views and Practices of the Society of Friends* (New York, 1856), Ch. VIII.

[409] *The Friends' Library*, edited by William and Thomas Evans (Philadelphia, 1837), Vol. I, pp. 117, 118.

[410] *Minutes of Iowa Yearly Meeting of (Orthodox) Friends*, 1893, p. 35.

[411] Penn's *The Rise and Progress of the People Called Quakers* (Philadelphia, 1865), p. 29.

[412] Matthew V: 32.

[413] A detailed statement of the Quaker regulations on the subject of marriage may be found in *The Discipline of the Society of Friends of Indiana Yearly Meeting*, 1854, pp. 48–57.

[414] In case the man were not a member of the Monthly Meeting thus concerned, he was expected to have ready at this time a statement from his own Monthly Meeting certifying to his membership.

415 *The Discipline of the Society of Friends of Iowa Yearly Meeting*, 1865, pp. 76, 77.

416 For a copy of a Quaker marriage certificate see *Appendix* above, pp. 291, 292.

417 *Minutes of Salem Monthly Meeting of Friends*, 9 mo., 24th, 1842, p. 130.

418 *Laws of the Territory of Michigan*, Vol. III, p. 1191.

419 *Laws of the Territory of Iowa*, 1839–1840, Ch. 25, pp. 40, 41.

420 *Code of Iowa*, 1851, Ch. 85, Sec. 1477, p. 222.

421 *Weekly Iowa State Register*, Vol. XIII, No. 8, Wednesday, April 8, 1868.

422 *Senate Journal*, 1873, pp. 111, 121, 122, 158, 160. See also *Code of Iowa*, 1873, Sec. 2198.

423 *Code of Iowa*, 1897, Sec. 3148.

424 Clarkson's *A Portraiture of Quakerism Taken from a view of the Education and Discipline, Social Manners, Civil and Political Economy, Religious Principles and Character, of the Society of Friends* (New York, 1806), Vol. I, p. 64.

425 The Quaker drab was made of the plain white wool, undyed; while the Quaker grey, of which the men's clothes were almost always made, was composed of the white wool mixed with some black wool, undyed.

426 Rowntree's *Quakerism, Past and Present* (Philadelphia, 1860), p. 141, quoted from *Pictorial History*, Book VIII, p. 632.

427 Taken from notes by Clarence M. Case on the *Minutes of New England Yearly Meeting*, Vol. I, 1683–1789.

428 Clarkson's *A Portraiture of Quakerism*, Vol. I, p. 280.

429 *Webster's International Dictionary*, see the word "thou".

430 Matthew XXII: 21; Romans XIII: 7; I Peter II: 17.

431 *The Discipline of the Society of Friends of Indiana Yearly Meeting*, 1854, p. 30.

432 Clarkson's *A Portraiture of Quakerism*, Vol. II, p. 27.

433 *The Discipline of the Society of Friends of Indiana Yearly Meeting*, 1854, p. 31.

434 *The Discipline of the Society of Friends of Iowa Yearly Meeting*, 1865, p. 80.

435 *The Discipline of the Society of Friends of Indiana Yearly Meeting*, 1854, p. 82.

436 *The Discipline of the Society of Friends of Indiana Yearly Meeting*, 1854, pp. 27–30. Also *The Discipline of the Society of Friends of Iowa Yearly Meeting*, 1865, pp. 86–89.

437 As early as 1839 the Salem Monthly Meeting received from the Cherry Grove Monthly Meeting, Indiana, eighty-eight volumes, including eighteen titles. Such gifts continued from time to time to such an extent that the Salem meeting divided its library in 1842 with the meetings at Cedar Creek and Pleasant Plain.

438 See the *Report of Committee to Consider Question of Amusements* in the *Minutes of Iowa Yearly Meeting of (Orthodox) Friends*, 1912, pp. 71–73.

439 Many interesting anecdotes of this character may be found in *Biographical Sketches and Anecdotes of Members of the Religious Society of Friends* (Philadelphia, 1870).

440 Taken from notes by Clarence M. Case on the *Minutes of New England Yearly Meeting*, Vol. I, 1683–1789.

441 Clarkson's *A Portraiture of Quakerism*, Vol. I, pp. 291–293.

INDEX

INDEX

Abolition, attitude of Friends toward, 133, 134

Abolitionists, 133; attitude of Quakers toward, 135

Academies, 241; establishment and maintenance of, by Quakers, 243-247; reasons for decline of, 247

Ackworth Academy, history of, 245, 246

Ackworth Quarterly Meeting, 99; propositions introduced by, 106

Adair County, 333

Address, terms of, used by Quakers, 271, 272

Adrian (Michigan), 56

Africa, missionary work in, 239, 330

African Methodist Episcopal Church, membership of, 296

Alabama, 151

Alaska, missions in, 330

Allegheny Mountains, 34, 98

Allen, John, 141, 143

Allen, Lizzie, 239

Allen, Tristram, 71

Amana Inspirationists, 333

America, spread of Quaker faith to, 22, 23; landing of first Quakers in, 24, 25; first Yearly Meeting of Friends in, 28; labors of Fox in, 28; stronghold of Quakerism in, 30; simplicity of dress among Quakers in, 269; membership of churches in, 295, 296

Amity Hall (Jamaica), 237, 238, 239

Amusements, attitude of Quakers toward, 275-277

Andrews, Alsina M., 238

Andrews, Benjamin O., 328

Anglo-Saxons, 67

Annotto Bay (Jamaica), 239

Antiqua, 297

Anti-Slavery Friends, history of, 133-145; organization of Yearly Meeting of, 136; labors of English deputation among, 137-144; resistance of, to summons of London Yearly Meeting, 143, 144; purchase of burying ground of, 145

Anti-Slavery Society, American, 134

Appointed Meetings, character of, 303

Arapaho Indians, 208

Arbitration of disputes, 275

Archdale, John, 299

Arkansas, 151

Arkansas River, 327

Ascension, 254

Asia, missionary work in, 239

Atchison (Kansas), negro school at, 200

Atlantic (Iowa), 229, 230

Atlantic Coast, 31, 86, 241

Atonement, 254

Austin, Ann, landing of, at Boston, 25; deportation of, 26

Baltimore Yearly Meeting of Friends, 56, 81, 147, 206

Baltimore Yearly Meeting of Hicksite Friends, 149

Bangor, 75, 234, 308

Bangor Monthly Meeting, 164

Bangor Quarterly Meeting, 77, 79, 99, 332

Baptism, attitude of Quakers toward, 255, 256

Baptist Church, membership of, 295; number of members of, in penitentiary, 315

Baptist missionaries, 234

Baraboo (Wisconsin), 83

Barbadoes, movement of Quakers to, 23; reference to, 25; letter of Fox

Methodists, mission established by, 204
Mexico, missions in, 330
Mexico (Missouri), negro school at, 200
Miami (Ohio), 35
Michener, David O., 311
Michigan, 56, 71
Michigan, Territory of, 267
Middle Quarter (Jamaica), 239
Middle River settlement, 61
Migration of Quakers, 31-37
Miles, Benjamin, work of, among Indians, 212, 213; school conducted by, 224-226; reference to, 324
Miles, Elizabeth B., work of, among Indians, 212; school conducted by, 224-226
Miles, Isaac N., 226
Miles, Laban J., 213, 214
Ministers, method of choosing, 112, 113; change in economic condition of, 114, 115; character of, 115; number of, among Quakers, 120; salaries of, 120; fund for care of aged, 122; method of training of, 124-126; course of reading for, 126 (see also Pastors)
Ministers, Board on Recording, duties of, 113; reference to, 126, 312
Ministry, change of policy toward, 104, 105; fundamental principles of, 109; change in system of, 110, 111; problems confronting, 111, 112; problem of payment of, 113, 114; reasons for lack of efficiency of, 116, 117; recommendation of Martin relative to, 120; efforts of Keates to improve, 123 (see also Pastoral System)
Minneapolis, 83, 312
Minneapolis and St. Louis Railway, 175
Minneapolis Quarterly Meeting, 99
Minnesota, 101, 151
Mission Board, 237
Missionary Association, organization of, 232; work of, 233; reference to, 234, 235
Missionary Board, Home and Foreign, 233

Missions, 121, 150, 182, 199, 330; work of Quakers in, 128; labors of Quakers in, in Jamaica, 232-239
Mississippi River, 37, 38, 39, 43, 49, 56, 65, 66, 70, 73, 75, 79, 85, 137, 205, 304; first Quaker meeting west of, 44; first Quarterly Meeting west of, 54, 55; settlement of region west of, 67
Missouri, slave-catchers from, 51, 144; reference to, 138, 151; escape of slaves from, 187-191; work of Iowa Quakers among negroes in, 199-201; negro schools in, 200
Missouri River, 61
Missourians, attempt of, to recapture slaves, 189-191; presence of, at Salem, 323
Mister, rejection of term, 272
Mitchellville, reform school located at, 223
Moffitt, Charles W., 323
Monroe County (Ohio), 155
Montana, 151
Montgomery, Thomas, resignation of, 172, 173
Monthly Meeting, first, in Iowa, 44; establishment of, 52; character of, 74; duty of, in choice of ministers, 112; reference to, 264, 275
Monthly Meetings, number of, 150; committees of, on welfare of negroes, 198; schools maintained by, 240, 241; queries read in, 274, 289, 290; libraries maintained by, 277; reference to, 302
Moore, Thomas, 308
Moorman family, 52
Morant Bay (Jamaica), 237, 238
Morgan, David, 205, 308
Morgan, J. W., statement by, 82; school founded by, 245; reference to, 308, 332; acknowledgment to, 309
Morgan, William B., 332
Morgan County (Ohio), 155
Mormons, objections of Quakers to, 51; reference to, 175, 193
Mosher, L. O., acknowledgment to, 317

Ohio River, 35, 49
Ohio Valley, 37
Ohio Yearly Meeting, 56, 147, 155, 199, 206, 306; Wilburite separation in, 154
Ohio Yearly Meeting of Wilbur Friends, 158
Oklahoma, 151
Oleson, Anna, removal of, to Marshall County, 176
Oleson, Soren, removal of, to Marshall County, 176
Olson, Anna, 179
Olson, Omund, 175
Orange Bay (Jamaica), 239
Ordinance of 1787, 33, 34, 37, 187
Oregon, 101, 151; emigration to, 205
Oregon Yearly Meeting, establishment of, 92
Orthodox Friends, 88, 274, 277, 306; decline among, 88, 89; reasons for decline among, 89-92; obliteration of ancient characteristics among, 95; effect of evangelism on, 96; ministry among, 109-117; method of choosing ministers among, 113; modern activities of, 128, 129; comparison of Hicksite Friends and, 149-153; number of meetings of, 150; withdrawal of Norwegian Friends from, 179; possible reunion of Conservatives and, 183; Indian superintendency given to, 207; work of, among Indians, 208-214; missionary activities of, 232-239; progressive character of, 257; membership of, in America, 296; birth-rate among, 309; uniting of, with other churches, 310; average salary and term of pastors among, 312
Osage Agency, 210, 224; conduct of, by Iowa Quakers, 210-214
Osage Agency Manual Labor Boarding School, report on, 212, 213
Osage Indians, 208; beginning of work of Gibson among, 209, 210; work of Iowa Quakers among, 211-214
Osage Reservation, 327

Osborn, Elwood, complaint against, 138; retraction of, 138, 139
Osborn family, 43
Oskaloosa, 7, 8, 76, 78, 82, 98, 125, 165, 168, 171, 236, 247, 248, 250, 309, 312; coal mine near, 86; organization of Conservative Yearly Meeting at, 170
Oskaloosa Quarterly Meeting, 99
Overseers, duties of, 274, 275
Owen, D. D., coal discovered by, 86
Owen, James, 205, 308

Pacific Coast, 31, 86, 241
Painter, John H., coming of, to Iowa, 68; meetings held at home of, 69; Brown at home of, 193; Brown's plans known by, 193
Palestine, visits of Quakers to, 23; missions in, 330
Parents, moral teaching of children by, 262
Parker's Mill, 60
Parsons, Luke J., 323
Parsons (Kansas), negro school at, 201
Parvin, John A., bill introduced by, 218; reference to, 219, 221
Pasadena Quarterly Meeting (California), 310
Pastoral care, committees on, 103, 104, 106
Pastoral system, importance of, 103; origin of, 103-105; adoption of, 105-107; operation of, 107, 108; problems connected with, 108; reference to, 150 (see also Ministry)
Pastors, increase in number of, 107, 108; support of, 107, 108; duties of, 111, 114, 115; effect of constant changing of, 116; average salary of, 312; average term of, 312; sex of, 314 (see also Ministers)
Pearce family, 34
Pearson, John, 311
Pearson, William, 308
Peasley, Enoch, 305
Pella, 62, 303
Penitentiaries, inmates of, 315

dress used by, 271, 272; first names used by, 272; attitude of, toward funerals, 272, 273; attitude of, toward gravestones, 273, 274; circumspection in temporal affairs among, 274, 275; settlement of disputes among, 275; attitude of, toward amusements and fiction, 275-277; home life among, 278-281; calendars of, 280, 281; queries asked of, 289, 290; marriage certificate of, 291, 292; origin of term, 297; other names borne by, 297; law against, in Massachusetts, 297, 298; politics of, 314; number of, in penitentiary, 315

Quarterly Meetings, establishment of, 72, 75, 83; character of, 74, 75; number of, 88; duty of, in choice of ministers, 112; committees of, on welfare of negroes, 198; schools maintained by, 241

Quebec, 178

Queries, 289, 290

Randolph County (Indiana), 41
Ratliff, Ephraim B., 172, 182, 308
Reader, Rachel, 52
Realf, Richard, 323
Red Cedar, 154, 158, 304, 308
Red Cedar Monthly Meeting, establishment of, 69; growth of, 69; reference to, 71, 155, 244, 304, 305, 319; attempt of, to discipline Gregg, 155-158; Wilburite separation in, 157, 158; Gregg disowned by, 158
Red Cedar Preparative Meeting, 158
Red Cedar Quarterly Meeting, establishment of, 72, 75; proposal of, relative to Yearly Meeting, 75, 76; reference to, 77, 79, 83
Reece family, 34
Rees, Eli, 314
Reese, William, 308
Reform school, use of White's Institute as, 218-223; location of, at Eldora, 222; location of, at Mt. Pleasant, 223; location of, at Mitchellville, 223

Reformation, 20
Reformed Dutch Church, membership of, 296
Reformed German Church, membership of, 296
Religious beliefs, statement of, 152, 153, 253-257, 295
Renewals, number of, 286
Representative Meeting, subject of Indians taken up by, 205, 206
Republican party, 314
Resurrection, 254
Revival, appearance of spirit of, 97, 98
Revival meetings, recommendation relative to, 121; holding of, among Quakers, 164, 165; number of, held, 286; reference to, 303
Revolutionary War, 34, 295
Rhode Island, spread of Quakerism in, 27
Richards, Jonathan, 210
Richardson, Richard, 323
Richland, 49, 55, 62, 304; founding of, 52
Richmond (Indiana), speech of Clay at, 135; reference to, 137
Richmond Declaration, 257
Rinden, Jon, 321
Robinson, Ann, 233
Robinson, William, banishment and execution of, 27
Rocky Mountains, 119
Rocky Run, founding of, 52; reference to, 62
Rogers, Ansel, 71
Roldol Valley (Norway), emigration from, 178
Rosenberger, Absolom, 314, 332
Roundheads, 17
Rowntree, Henry, 324
Ruebottom, Thomas, 44
Rushville (Illinois), 38, 39

St. Albans (Maine), 118
St. Joseph (Missouri), negro school at, 200
St. Maria (Jamaica), 239
Salaries, recommendation relative to, 120

Slavery, protest of Quakers against, 18, 133; emigration of Quakers on account of, 35-37; opposition of Quakers to, 133-145, 187; first formal document against, 315

Slaves, escape of, from Missouri, 188-191; attempt of Missourians to recapture, 189-191; bringing of, to Springdale by Brown, 194; fugitive, 322, 323

Smith, Benjamin, 308

Smith, Evan, 158

Smith, William P., 311

Snow, G. C., 210

Sonship, 254

South, migration of Quakers to, 32; emigration of Quakers from, 35-37; work of Quakers among negroes in, 199-201; heydey of Quakerism in, 299

South Carolina, settlement of Quakers in, 32; emigration of Quakers from, 35, 36; reference to, 38

South River, 308

South River Quarterly Meeting, 77

Southland College, 201

Spanish, 67

Spiritualists, number of, 296

Spring Bank Quarterly Meeting (Nebraska), 92

Spring Creek, 53, 76, 78, 247, 308; English Quakers at, 62; description of, 80; first Yearly Meeting at, 80-84; decline and disappearance of, 86, 87

Spring Creek Boarding School, 82

Spring Creek Institute, 248

Spring Creek Preparative Meeting, 62

Spring Creek Quarterly Meeting, establishment of, 83

Spring River, 55

Springdale, 69, 70, 208, 323, 325; separation at, 172, 173; John Brown and his men at, 191-197; schools at, 244, 245

Springdale Monthly Meeting, 173, 245, 324; statement by, concerning Brown, 195, 196

Springdale Preparative Meeting, 197

Springdale Quarterly Meeting, 99

Springdale Quarterly Meeting of Conservative Friends, establishment of, 174

Springdale Seminary, history of, 244, 245

Springfield (Missouri), negro school at, 200

Springville, 152, 154, 158

Springwater Preparative Meeting, establishment of, 71, 72

Spurrier, R., 46

Squatters, rush of, into Iowa, 48

Stacey, George, address read by, 139, 140; reference to, 141, 143

Stafford, Thomas, 53, 62; coming of, to Iowa, 86

Stanfield family, 34

Stanford Seminary, 246

Stanley, Jeremiah, 158

Stanley, Sada M., 238

Stanley, Thomas, visit of, among Indians, 203, 204; work of, among Indians, 204, 205

Stanton family, 43

Staples, Asa, 305

Staples, James, 324

Starbuck, Isaac, 308

State, White's Institute under control of, 218-223

Stavanger, 175; beginnings of, 176; meeting established at, 177; meeting-house erected at, 177; arrival of newcomers at, 177; union of Friends at, with Conservatives, 178, 179; boarding school at, 179, 180; unique character of, 180

Stavanger (Norway), emigration from, 178; reference to, 321

Stavanger Boarding School, rules and regulations of, 287, 288

Stephenson, Marmaduke, banishment and execution of, 27

Stevens, Aaron D., 323

Stockholders' Association, 246

Story County, Quakers in, 53

Stratton, Elisha, 305, 308

Street, Aaron, coming of, to Iowa, 39, 40; meeting of Pidgeon and, 40; part of, in laying out of Salem, 41; reference to, 45, 46, 190, 300

www.ingramcontent.com/pod-product-compliance
Lightning Source LLC
Chambersburg PA
CBHW070716280326
41926CB00087B/2238